How to Talk About Hot Topics on Campus

Robert J. Nash
DeMethra LaSha Bradley
Arthur W. Chickering

How to Talk About Hot Topics on Campus

From Polarization to Moral Conversation

JOSSEY-BASS
A Wiley Imprint
www.josseybass.com

Published by Jossey-Bass
A Wiley Imprint
989 Market Street, San Francisco, CA 94103-1741—www.josseybass.com

Readers should be aware that Internet Web sites offered as citations and/or sources for further information may have changed or disappeared between the time this was written and when it is read.

Limit of Liability/Disclaimer of Warranty: While the publisher and author have used their best efforts in preparing this book, they make no representations or warranties with respect to the accuracy or completeness of the contents of this book and specifically disclaim any implied warranties of merchantability or fitness for a particular purpose. No warranty may be created or extended by sales representatives or written sales materials. The advice and strategies contained herein may not be suitable for your situation. You should consult with a professional where appropriate. Neither the publisher nor author shall be liable for any loss of profit or any other commercial damages, including but not limited to special, incidental, consequential, or other damages.

Jossey-Bass books and products are available through most bookstores. To contact Jossey-Bass directly call our Customer Care Department within the U.S. at 800-956-7739, outside the U.S. at 317-572-3986, or fax 317-572-4002.

Jossey-Bass also publishes its books in a variety of electronic formats. Some content that appears in print may not be available in electronic books.

Library of Congress Cataloging-in-Publication Data

Nash, Robert J.
    How to talk about hot topics on campus : from polarization to moral conversation / Robert J. Nash, DeMethra LaSha Bradley, Arthur W. Chickering.
        p. cm.
    Includes bibliographical references and index.
    ISBN-13: 978-0-7879-9436-5 (cloth)
  1.   Academic freedom—United States. 2.   Freedom of speech—United States.   I. Bradley, DeMethra LaSha. II. Chickering, Arthur W., date.
III. Title.
    LC72.2.N37 2008
    378.1'213—dc22
                                 2007038035

Printed in the United States of America
FIRST EDITION
HB Printing 10 9 8 7 6 5 4 3 2 1

The Jossey-Bass
Higher and Adult Education Series

Contents

Preface

Our book, *How to Talk About Hot Topics on Campus: From Polarization to Moral Conversation*, focuses on justifying, creating, setting up, and facilitating a campuswide process that we call *moral conversation* (Nash, 1996, 1997). This process encompasses both classrooms and out-of-classroom settings throughout the campus. It includes faculty, student affairs staff, administrators, and students in all campus venues. Moral conversation has the potential to teach all constituencies how to talk with, and about, controversial types of "otherness" in higher education today.

We have listened well to the Ford Foundation's request for grant proposals on a topic it called Difficult Dialogues: Promoting Pluralism and Academic Freedom on Campus (see Appendix B). The sixteen college presidents who signed the "Letter from Higher Education Leaders and Susan V. Berresford to College and University Presidents," introducing the request for proposals, were troubled by three concerns:

1. There is a need for a recommitment on the part of campus leaders to sustain "informed political and civil discourse" during a time in our nation's history when "the tone of academic debate has become increasingly polarized, and, in some cases, we see attempts to silence individuals, faculty and students alike, with controversial views."

2. Threats to academic freedom proliferate on our nation's campuses with "the recent rise in anti-Semitic incidents . . . [and a] troubling increase in anti-Muslim and anti-Arab incidents." The key is to promote "open and honest dialogue . . . [in an] atmosphere of mutual respect, in which diversity is examined and seen in the context of a broader set of common values."

3. "Promoting new scholarship and teaching about cultural differences and religious pluralism, while supporting academic freedom, requires a significant commitment at every level of the academic community. . . . It is no longer adequate for student affairs staff to bear, largely alone, the responsibility for sponsoring and overseeing difficult dialogues." Rather, all constituencies on college campuses, including students, will need to know how to engage one another "in constructive dialogue around different religious, political, racial/ethnic, and cultural issues."

We are heeding the call of those presidents.

We are also responding to the *Wingspread Declaration on Religion and Public Life: Engaging Higher Education* (see Appendix B; also, see Chapter Five). This declaration was generated by twenty scholars from public and private colleges and universities—representing diverse disciplines, geographical regions, and faith perspectives, with support from the Society for Values in Higher Education (www.svhe.org) and the Wingspread Foundation. It calls for (1) improving religious literacy, (2) creating standards and ground rules for civic discourse on matters of religion and public life, and (3) responding to students' search for purpose and spiritual meaning.

But neither of these important initiatives, nor others mentioned in recent *Chronicle of Higher Education* articles, talk about *how* to construct and foster a process for carrying out "difficult [pluralistic] dialogues" on college campuses. In fact, there are very few precedents anywhere in the literature on higher education for doing this. What research there is on the topic of effective communication exists mainly in self-help books as well as in the business management sciences.

There has also been a recent effort by some writers to introduce the principles of intercultural and interfaith dialogue on college campuses. Intercultural dialogue has a clearly defined social justice purpose. It targets particular types of audiences in order to raise consciousness about white privilege and white oppression in predominantly white, secular societies. High-level intercultural group leaders have specific goals in mind: among them are raising awareness of injustice and inequality due to imbalances of power, producing tangible social changes, and eliminating racial and ethnic stereotypes that all too often lead to oppression and victimization (see Zuniga, Nagda, Chesler, and Cytron-Walker, 2007).

Interfaith dialogue shares many of these same purposes, but its chief emphasis is to bring about attitudinal change regarding religious difference. It does this by getting people of different faith traditions to work together on concrete tasks and actions. These include exploring the differences and similarities in various religious narratives, increasing insight and empathy for other spiritual beliefs and practices, acknowledging collective religious wrongdoing, and stopping those violent cycles between and among religious groups that prevent cooperative activities (see Smoch, 2002). In contrast to intercultural and intergroup dialogue approaches, we will develop throughout this book a theory and practice of moral conversation that differs in many respects from these approaches, even though there are significant commonalities among all three.

We are inspired by the words of William Isaacs (1999, p. 14): "Too many of us have lost touch with the fire of conversation. When we talk together, it is rarely with depth. For the most part, we see our conversations as either opportunities to trade information or arenas in which to win points." Isaacs goes on to say that it is only through dialogue that people are able to find the "creative intensity . . . that . . . lies dormant within and between us. It is an intensity that could revitalize our institutions, our relationships, and ourselves. It can rekindle our fire."

Our book will attempt to explain and apply one proven, very successful approach to promoting and facilitating pluralistic dialogue on hot topics throughout the college campus. We call this process *moral conversation*. We three authors have experienced moral conversations in various campus venues: the classroom and the seminar room, a variety of cocurricular settings, and several levels of administration. Each of us describes our respective take on this process. We ground our understandings in a knowledge base that is both current and relevant to our expertise and practice. We keep our language direct and clear at all times, and, when appropriate, we speak from both our personal and professional experiences. We attempt always to be practical in our advice without being patronizing. We provide frameworks and ground rules for moral conversation.

In the pages to come, after a brief introduction explaining our objectives in each chapter, we will include either a chapter-specific case scenario or a brief review of a series of real-world "hot" issues and conflicts relating to the specific topic under discussion. We will end each chapter with a summary of salient points regarding how the central ideas of moral conversation relate to the particular case scenarios and real-world issues we have discussed in the chapter. For those readers who might appreciate a step-by-step application of how they can actually use the moral conversation when discussing a controversial, hot topic on a college campus, we will present this practical framework in Appendix A. Also, for practitioners who would like to know more about open cross-campus conversation and dialogue, we also include Appendix B, "Additional Text References and Internet Resources." This list identifies additional texts and Web sites not directly referenced in the book.

Chapters One and Two are written conjointly by the three of us. Chapter Three is written by a veteran classroom professor, Robert J. Nash. Chapter Four is written by a student affairs administrator, DeMethra LaSha Bradley. Chapter Five is written by a nationally known leader and scholar in higher education, Arthur W. Chickering. Chapter Six is written conjointly.

We have decided on separate authorship of each of the middle three chapters in order to maintain the integrity of our individual voices on the need for moral conversations throughout the college campus on a number of hot-button topics. Speaking as separate voices, we are able to draw on our own personal and professional experiences in our respective fields of scholarly expertise and professional experience. Separate authorship of these three chapters also allows us to speak with a more personal "I" voice in addition to the more traditional academic "they said" voice. In contrast, writing as conjoined voices in the first two chapters, as well as in the last, we are able to speak as *one* voice on the basic principles and practices of moral conversation that we share in common.

Acknowledgments

With profound gratitude to all my past and present students throughout my forty-year teaching career, without whom there would be no moral conversation . . . or book about it. To Madelyn, my *sine qua non*, who laid the groundwork for moral conversation through her training in mediation and simply by being who she is. To David Brightman, our editor at Jossey-Bass, for encouraging us to write this book and for helping us to refine it for publication.

—Robert J. Nash

Allie Mae Polite, for being the spirit that guides me to continue to work hard and stay the course. Debrah P. Bradley, Danielle C. Bradley, and Devon M. Bradley for their unwavering family support. Candice E. Brooks, Colette Reid, Dawna I. Ballard, Sabrina T. Kwist, Garrett Naiman, Stacey Miller, Harriet Williams, Akirah Bradley, the Center for Student Ethics & Standards staff, various members of the UVM Division of Student and Campus Life, and the UVM Higher Education and Student Affairs Administration program community for your kind words of encouragement and support of my scholarly endeavors.

—DeMethra LaSha Bradley

Jo Chickering, my wife and patient companion for fifty-seven years, has been my main mentor and exemplar when it comes to discussing hot topics without getting burned. She has an unparalleled and boundless capacity to empathize with persons of whatever age, race, national origin, or socioeconomic status. In five minutes they are communicating on a deeply personal basis of mutual respect and understanding. She exemplifies and lives by the basic orientation and ground rules we try to articulate in this book. I am deeply indebted to her for whatever modest capacity I have developed.

—Art Chickering

The Authors

Robert J. Nash has been a professor in the College of Education and Social Services, University of Vermont (UVM), Burlington, for thirty-nine years. He specializes in philosophy of education, applied ethics, higher education and student affairs administration, and religion, spirituality, and education. He has published more than one hundred articles, book chapters, monographs, and essay book reviews in many of the leading journals of education at all levels. He is a member of the editorial board for the *Journal of Religion & Education*, and one of its frequent contributors. Since 1996, he has published eight books, several of them national award winners. He has also made a series of major presentations at national conferences and at universities on the topics of ethics, character education, religious pluralism, scholarly personal narrative scholarship, and moral conversation. In 2003, he was named an Official University Scholar in the Social Sciences and the Humanities at UVM, only the third faculty member in the history of the College of Education and Social Services to be so honored.

DeMethra LaSha Bradley serves as an assistant director in the Center for Student Ethics and Standards at the University of Vermont (UVM). She is currently pursuing a doctorate of education degree in the Educational Leadership and Policy Studies program at UVM. In 2005, DeMethra received a master of education degree from UVM's Higher Education and Student Affairs

Administration program. She is an undergraduate alumna of the University of California, Santa Barbara. DeMethra has coauthored book chapters in *Searching for Spirituality in Higher Education* and *The American University in a Postsecular Age: Religion and the Academy*. She has also made various presentations at national conferences and universities across the United States. Throughout ten years of service within higher education, she has served in professional and paraprofessional roles in judicial affairs, residential life, Greek life, leadership programs, museum administration, and admissions. Her research interests include social class identity, moral conversation as a tool for dialogue, and religious and spiritual differences on college campuses.

Art Chickering is currently Special Assistant to the President of Goddard College, where he started his career in higher education in 1959. Since then he has occupied a variety of teaching and administrative roles in diverse institutions. Beginning with his early research at Goddard and in the Project on Student Development in Small Colleges back in the 1960s, he has written widely on teaching and learning, college impacts on student development, institutional change, and, most recently, authenticity and spirituality in higher education. Despite the slow pace of change in higher education, he still believes that colleges and universities can help make the world a better place for all its beleaguered inhabitants.

How to Talk About
Hot Topics on Campus

Part I

Laying the Theoretical Groundwork for Moral Conversation

1

Igniting the Fire of Moral Conversation

In this chapter, we provide a rationale for the idea of moral conversation. We discuss its basic premises, and we point out its strengths and weaknesses in a general sense. More specifically, we give several examples of particular hot topics that we believe ought to receive a campuswide airing according to the principles of moral conversation. Finally, we summarize our basic philosophical assumptions regarding the theory and practice of moral conversation, and we identify a number of internal contradictions for those educators who wish to engage in moral conversation in order to "ignite the fire of conversation."

What does it mean to ignite the fire of conversation? How can all constituencies on college campuses experience the fire of robust and respectful conversation on the controversial topics that we will discuss in this book? Think of the various meanings of the word *fire*. Its Greek root, *pyra*, means "glowing embers." Fire entails both heat and light resulting from combustion. Although fire can be destructive and painful, it can also suggest brilliance, strength, and excitement, as in "setting the world on fire" with striking achievements. "Playing with fire" implies a willingness to do something risky. Being "on fire" conveys the state of being full of ardor and excitement. And "striking a fire" is to ignite something—as in sparking the imagination or the creative intellect.

3

Conversing about highly controversial topics can be threatening to people. The ordeal of talking openly about difficult topics in full public view, across a wide range of constituencies on a college campus, can be anxiety producing and, at times, very painful. Feelings can be hurt. Conversations about politics, religion, social class, and cultural difference can fray nerves and even destroy once amiable relationships. Anger, frustration, and self-righteous aggression can result. In this sense, the fire of conversation can burn terribly. It can destroy. But in the best sense, the fire of conversation can produce excitement. It can encourage risk taking and push us to our creative limits. It can ignite the passionate imagination that resides in each and every one of us.

A CULTURE OF CONVERSATION, NOT A CULTURE OF CONTESTATION

The fire of conversation that we are talking about is different in tone and intent from such terms as *discussion* and *dialogue*, although conversation shares some things in common with each of them. The Latin root of discussion (*discutere*) is revealing. It means to strike asunder, scatter, shake, beat, and quash. A *discussion* involves talking about an issue in a deliberative fashion so as to air a variety of conflicting opinions. The major objective of discussion is to settle an issue or to decide on a course of action. Often a discussion implies an *argument*, a putting forth of one point of view in order to refute another point of view. Sometimes an argument becomes a *debate* wherein debaters engage in public contests with opposing groups in order to win points for a particular belief or proposition. Arguments and debates have been known to devolve into angry and heated *disputes*, whereby disputants openly clash with those whose opinions are different.

Dialogue is closer to the meaning of conversation we are talking about here. Dialogue implies an open and frank talking together in order to seek mutual understanding and harmony. The intention of most dialogue is exploration of an idea or problem with the objective of finding solutions. For example, diplomats of nations or blocs often set up dialogues with one another in order to exchange proposals that will lead to mutual understanding and agreement. Dialogue, in this case, is close to *discourse*, which is a long and formal treatment of some subject with the aim of imparting ideas and information in one-way communication. In discourse, there is little or no effort made to achieve a sense of mutual reciprocity or vulnerability.

Unfortunately, too many discussions of controversial topics in the American university tend to foster a *culture of contestation*, not a *culture of conversation*. All of us on college campuses are conditioned to think of communication as debate, not dialogue; as a win-lose contest; as a battle to be fought to the death, and may the best scholar win. In this more traditional case of academic discourse, the fire of contestation can leave people scorched and wounds raw. It is the academic game we have all learned to play so well, and we carry its lessons over to discussions on every conceivable topic, including, foremost, the ones mentioned in the sections to follow.

We are advocating for a different campus culture, a culture of *moral conversation*. Such a culture has the potential to ignite fires of conversation that, in theory, can transform people's lives. Although they may not always change people's minds, they do have the potential of opening their hearts. Although they may not always result in quick and tangible policy changes, they often do result in an empathic airing of mutual differences that could later pave the way to more collaborative and consensual decision making. Recall William Butler Yeats's famous aphorism: "Education is not the filling of a pail but the lighting of a fire." How does this work? It starts, we submit, with understanding the theory and practice of moral conversation.

MORAL CONVERSATION

In our opinion, a college campus is a lot of things, but it should not simulate a rancorous legislative session in a state house. Neither ought it replicate a television station for predictable attack ads, blindly partisan debates, or dueling talking heads frothing at the mouth—the usual components of a heated political campaign coming down to the wire. Yes, we like what John Stuart Mill said in his essay *On Liberty* ([1859] 1982) about the importance of healthy disagreement in a democracy: in a democratic society, all opinions must be heard because some of them may be true; and those that aren't true must be vigorously contested. In either case, free people only stand to gain. Mill, in 1859, was actually articulating the rationale for a type of academic freedom in the university that would later be introduced by the American Association of University Professors in the twentieth century.

But make no mistake: we appreciate that Mill was, first and foremost, a gentleman and a reconciler. He encouraged healthy disagreement, to be sure, but a disagreement grounded in exquisite respect for the right of all human beings to be persuaded and convinced by rational argument. Mill took a strong stand against the name-calling, silencing, and tyrannizing of minority voices in those societies where a majority rules. Mill was, if nothing else, a champion of the individual voice in the ideological wilderness. Moreover, Mill's essay *On Liberty* is itself a model of the kind of intellectual restraint he called for in a secular, liberal democracy. Always polite and considerate, the essay strikes a nice balance between strong intellectual conviction and a genuine empathy for those who might reside outside the majority view. It is our hope that moral conversation can come close to the ideals of democratic dialogue described in Mill's masterpiece.

But we are also realistic. As a result of our mixed experiences leading difficult talks on college campuses throughout the United States, we know from firsthand involvement that we must never underestimate the difficulties in promoting campuswide conversation on hot topics. Each of us, through the years, has failed often enough to stimulate moral conversation to understand the folly of being overly optimistic whenever it comes to advocating for something innovative in the campus academic culture.

However, we have also had our moments of success, owing to the tireless and enthusiastic assistance of others in helping us bring to campuses new ways of conversing about tough topics.

We are convinced that the American university can become a true culture of cross-campus conversation, along the lines of what Diana Eck (1993) describes as "a truth-seeking encounter. . . . [W]e do not enter into dialogue with the dreamy hope that we will all agree, for the truth is we probably will not. We do not enter into dialogue to produce an agreement, but to produce real relationship, even friendship, which is premised upon mutual understanding, not upon agreement. . . . [A] culture of dialogue creates a context of ongoing relatedness and trust in which self-criticism and mutual criticism are acceptable and valuable parts of the exchange" (pp. 197, 225).

So, what does the term *moral conversation* mean to us? Let us start immediately to correct a few of the obvious caricatures of conversation in higher education. We are not talking about the famous college "bull session" that is often nothing more than a heated series of one-way monologues, prominent for their outrageous opinions and biases. Neither are we talking about a social chit-chat session featuring a polite exchange of aimless chatter and "friendly noises." In contrast to bull sessions and chit-chat sessions, both of which do serve important purposes for young adults at a certain stage in their intellectual and moral development, we mean something far more substantial when we refer to conversation.

Listen to Martin E. Marty (1997): "If argument is impelled by the answers, conversation is moved and marked by the questions. Conversation does not have to be seen as soft, tolerant, muffled and mumbling, wishy-washy, or nice. But it differs from argument in that it is more open to the use of stories to advance understanding" (p. 155). And here is David Tracy (1987): "A conversation is not a confrontation. It is not a debate. It is not an exam. It is questioning itself. It is a willingness to follow the question wherever it may go" (p. 231). Tracy goes further: "Conversation is a game with some hard rules: say only what you mean; say it as accurately as you can; listen to and respect what the other says, however different or other[;] . . . be willing to endure necessary conflict, and to change your mind if the evidence suggests it. . . . Be attentive, be intelligent, be responsible, be loving, and, if necessary, change" (p. 231).

The Greek and Latin etymologies of the word *moral* have to do with ethics, conventions, and customs that emphasize the fundamental worth and dignity of each and every person. The Latin etymology of the word *conversation* is to live with, to keep company with, to turn around, to shift perspective. Thus a moral conversation is literally a manner of living whereby people keep company with each other and talk together in good faith, in order to exchange sometimes agreeable, sometimes opposing, ideas. Above all, however, moral conversation is a mutual sharing of all those wonderful stories that give meaning to people's lives. In most cases, these stories are rich in religious, political, social class, ethnic, and cultural content. Moral conversation obligates each of the participants to listen actively and respectfully to the stories of others, both to understand and affirm them as well as to discover whatever "narrative overlap" might exist among them.

Moral conversation, therefore, starts with the premise that each of the college constituencies must learn how to talk respectfully and openly with one another if they are to avoid going to war with one another. Thus moral conversation begins with an assumption that there is nothing inherently erroneous or immoral about any initial presumption of a particular truth. What *is* erroneous is the attitude that one individual or group possesses *all* the truth, and that those who disagree do so because they are in error or because there is something wrong with them. Barbara Herrnstein Smith (1997) puts it this way: "If a particular claim to an absolute truth is that which is manifestly obvious, self-evidently right, and intuitively and universally preunderstood, then how is it that its absolute truth and rightness elude the skeptic?" (p. 83). How, indeed! How often has the skeptic or the sincere questioner on college campuses been ridiculed, dismissed, or ignored as someone who is drastically deficient in matters of intellect, faith, politics, and character?

Moral conversation begins with an awareness of the wisdom in Michael Oakeshott's words: "Taste the mystery without the necessity of at once seeking a solution" (1950, p. 424). And David Bromwich's paradoxical words are also to the point: "The good of conversation is not truth, or right, or anything else that may come out at the end of it, but the activity itself in its constant relation to life" (1992, pp. 131–132). Both Oakeshott and Bromwich reinforce our assumption that moral conversation begins and ends in a fondness for mystery. It implies a commitment to cooperative story construction. Moral conversation is aimed at the tireless support of the other person's flourishing. It features an ethic of *do no harm* and *do much good*. It is rooted in an awareness that virtue and vice are social constructs that people must create and act on collectively, but always starting from a base of compassion. Most of all, though, moral conversation is grounded in a love of robust, honest, and respectful interchange for its own sake, absent all the usual off-putting, dialogue-stopping, ideological prerequisites.

Jonathan Sacks expresses our essential need to learn how to engage in difficult conversations. He says, "Bad things happen when the pace of change exceeds our ability to change, and events move faster than our understanding. It is then that we feel the loss of control over our lives. Anxiety creates fear, fear leads to anger, anger breeds violence, and violence—when combined with weapons of mass destruction—becomes a deadly reality. The greatest single antidote to violence is conversation, speaking our fears, listening to the fears of others, and in that sharing of vulnerabilities discovering a genesis of hope" (2003, p. 2). Even though it is far from a panacea, moral conversation is our proposed antidote to intellectual, emotional, and even physical violence on college campuses. It is a way, albeit flawed and still evolving, to share vulnerabilities, to make connections, and to enlarge and deepen worldviews and perspectives. In our experience, it does indeed help people discover a genesis of hope.

Throughout our book, you will have ample opportunity to see how the theory and practice of moral conversation can lead to genuinely pluralistic, cross-campus dialogues on highly volatile topics. It is our contention that moral conversation is an excellent way to engage in dialogues about controversial topics because it forces participants to come face-to-face with the ubiquity of pluralism in all aspects of their lives. This is a fact of life in the world of the university and in the world at large. This is a condition that all of us in the twenty-first century must accept as a global reality, as the risks and benefits of pluralism grow increasingly apparent both in higher education and throughout the world.

It is necessary for us to acknowledge at this point that in no way do we intend to slight or ignore the vital importance of all types of pluralism that have found a place in the academy today. Issues of race, ethnicity, gender, sexual orientation, and many others rightfully deserve the attention they have received on campuses throughout the United States. Often these differences are lumped together under the categories of diversity, cultural pluralism, or multiculturalism. As authors, however, we have decided, after much deliberation, to concentrate much of our attention on three types of pluralism—religion, social class, and politics—that have received considerably less time and space in the public square of higher education in this country. At times, we will certainly note the interplay of cultural pluralism with the three types of pluralism we are examining in our book, but our emphasis, because of space and focus limitations, will tend to be on differences of religion, social class, and politics. What follows is a selective list of controversial issues focused on these three topics.

A SELECTIVE LIST OF HOT TOPICS ON COLLEGE CAMPUSES

A recent issue of the journal *Foreign Policy* listed what the editors thought were the "world's most dangerous ideas" (cited in "Dangerous Ideas," 2004, p. B2). The editors claimed that these ideas were particularly volatile because "if embraced, they would pose the greatest threat to the welfare of humanity." Here, in brief, are six of those ideas, some of which we will be discussing in the chapters ahead:

1. The "war on evil, based on the idea of evil as a unified entity," embodied in a particular group, nation, religion, or politics

2. "Undermining free will, based on the idea of science's gradual erosion of the concept of self" and, along with it, consciousness, mind, and individual responsibility

3. "Spreading democracy, based on the idea that Western-style democracy is a cure-all for the world's problems"

4. "Transhumanism," based on the idea that it is "bio-technology that will change the nature of the human species" during the next several decades, and there is nothing we can do about it

5. "Religious intolerance," based on the idea that religious differences will intensify during the twenty-first century, resulting in violence on a global level

6. "Hating America," based on the idea that internal and external critics have steadily increased the decibel level of their denunciations of American foreign and domestic policies, thus creating enemies everywhere, both in this country and abroad

It is our strong belief that each of these "world's most dangerous ideas" deserves to be taken out of the closet and discussed openly in honest, robust, and respectful conversation on every college campus in the United States. Why? The obvious academic reason is that any liberal education worth its salt ought to provide numerous opportunities for students everywhere to critically investigate a wide range of contrasting ideas, no matter how dangerous or controversial they might at first seem. All of us in higher education—students, faculty, student affairs professionals, staff, and administrators alike—need to do this in order to enlarge and enrich our understandings of differing points of view. In a rapidly expanding, unavoidably interdependent world, we need to explore more deeply our taken-for-granted assumptions on a variety of political, economic, religious, and cultural issues. What better place to do this than on a college campus protected by the principles of academic freedom and unbiased scholarly inquiry?

Moreover, all of us *together* must find ways to solve those persistent problems that arise out of contrasting, sometimes dramatically colliding, worldviews between and among individuals, groups, states, and nations. As a history of even the recent twenty-first century will confirm, we will need to learn new ways to engage with one another in conversations about the most volatile topics, or else we will inevitably end up doing physical violence to one another. Ignorance or apathy regarding what makes the "other" tick often leads to terrible acts of cruelty among peoples and nations.

How so? Misunderstandings and stereotypes tend to run wild. It is not long before we begin to caricature our opponents as "evil" by attacking their moralities, nationalities, religions, politics, and philosophies. They are evil because "they just do not think or act like us." The final stage in this downward spiral, as hate begets hate, is to wage war with the "enemy." We bomb their buildings, maim and kill their civilians, and, if necessary, plot to assassinate their leaders. We do all this in the name of "God's chosen people," "freedom fighters," "bearers of democracy," or "liberators."

Closer to home in the American university, what follows is a short list of some hot topics related directly or indirectly to the list of the "world's most dangerous ideas" that we have enumerated. These issues, covered almost weekly in such publications as the *Chronicle of Higher Education*, have appeared front and center on college campuses throughout the United States during the last few years. The list is far from exhaustive. Each issue is ripe with the potential to become an incendiary, potentially divisive force in the academy, as well as in the world at large. Some of these issues already have split college campuses. However, in spite of the academy's benign neglect of many of them (understandable given the risks of confronting them openly in the face of competing interest groups in higher education), each of these topics, as well as a score of others, refuses to go away. We will be referring to many of these hot topics in the chapters to come, because the issues touch either directly or indirectly on matters of religion, social class, and politics, among others.

We believe that unless university administrators, staff, faculty, student affairs professionals, and students learn how to engage with one another in productive and civil campuswide conversation about just these types of controversies, we risk losing those precious learning opportunities that are always present in such key teachable moments. These are the moments, as disturbing, even terrifying, as they might seem initially, that often result in truly transformative learnings for all the diverse college groups involved. One advantage of learning how to talk *locally* with one another on college campuses about the divisive issues we cite here is to prepare all of us to talk *globally* with those who are different from us about the "world's most dangerous ideas." What follows are several controversial questions related to religion, politics, and social class that need to be openly talked about on college campuses. We frame our observations in the form of questions, not declarative statements, because it is only in the spirit of open-ended questioning that we have been able to ignite moral conversations on some of these topics on college campuses throughout the United States.

Religion

Secularism

At what point should a secularist point of view accommodate, or give way to, a religious and spiritual emphasis both inside and outside the college classroom? Should a college education be as much a religious as a secular enterprise? Should we make room in a liberal education for the big metaphysical questions? In this regard, survey after survey of first-year college students (upwards of 70 percent) shows that religion and spirituality guide students' lives, even though many of these students remain conflicted and confused about their beliefs. On another note, is there a place for the scientific study of religion? For example, should neuroscientists on secular campuses who might be interested in such research be encouraged to explore whether or not there is something one might call a "God gene"?

More specifically, should biblical creationism and intelligent design receive equal treatment with evolution in the curricula of the sciences and social sciences? How, if at all, should the academy accommodate the religious concerns of evangelical Christians, orthodox Jews, and conservative Muslims, both inside and outside the college classroom? Is it possible to do this and still avoid what happened at the U.S. Air Force Academy, where fundamentalist-evangelical Christian officials were found to be openly proselytizing cadets to accept Jesus Christ as their Lord and Savior?

Moreover, ought observant female Muslim students be allowed to wear their burqas, hijabs, or head scarves without being branded by secular feminists as "oppressed" or "brainwashed" by Islamic men? In Turkey, the law prohibits any public expression of religious faith on college campuses, and, therefore, the head scarf is banned, under the threat of expulsion. In reaction, many Muslim women in that country have gone to inventive extremes to act in defiance of what they consider to be a direct attack on their freedom to practice religion. These women have become highly adept at disguising their veils and head scarves whenever they enter "religion-free zones," such as cafeterias, classrooms, residence halls, and libraries. Will we one day face a similar scenario in the United States given the Islamophobia so rampant throughout the land?

God and Morality

Can a person be good without God? Is religious belief a precondition of, or a hindrance to, moral and ethical behavior? What role, if any, do evolution and sociobiology play in the formation of moral conscience? What moral status, if any, do animals and the natural environment possess? Is it possible to accommodate the variety of moral stances on such inflammatory issues as stem cell research, cloning, and abortion in the American university without stigmatizing any of the respective position holders? At what point does an embryo become a human being vested with rights, legal or sacred or both? From a moral perspective, are we "one nation under God" or "one nation crammed with many mansions of belief," including even the nonbelief known as atheism? Do politicians (and college presidents) need God (that is, need to be theists) in order to be elected to office in the United States, or in order to do good for their various constituencies?

Politics

Political Correctness

How can higher education avoid treating some students unfairly because of what outspoken social justice activists might consider their incorrect politics? Recently, a Republican lawmaker in Pennsylvania has begun to study whether higher education in his state is deliberately discriminating against certain students because of their conservative political views. The conservative activist David Horowitz has gotten into the act by asking the lawmaker to help him construct an "academic bill of rights" that will make campuses in Pennsylvania more intellectually and politically diverse. A major opponent of the bill, the American Association of University Professors (AAUP), rejects the assumption that the professorate needs watchdogs from outside to protect the rights of conservative students. They resent the infringement of their academic freedom.

This raises the question of whether a controversial, left-leaning professor at the University of Colorado, Ward Churchill (2005), has the academic right to publicly compare the victims of the 9/11 terrorist attacks on the Twin Towers to "little Eichmanns." Here is what he said: "They [those who worked in the Twin Towers] formed a technocratic corps at the very heart of America's global financial empire—the 'mighty engine of profit' to which the military dimension of U.S. policy has always been enslaved—and they did so both willingly and knowingly. . . . If there was a better, more effective, or, in fact, any other way of visiting some penalty befitting their participation upon the little Eichmanns inhabiting the sterile sanctuary of the twin towers, I'd really be interested in hearing about it."

A related, no less controversial, example involves the rights of students to bring Michael Moore, the anti–Bush administration filmmaker, to a politically conservative college in Utah. This caused quite an uproar among conservative students and alumni, resulting in a precipitous drop in alumni fundraising, a threat to block traffic on the day of Moore's scheduled appearance, bomb threats, and even anonymous death threats to the president of the college (Gravois, 2004). Another example concerns the right of some conservative scholars to advocate for nuclear proliferation as a way to make the world safer for democracy, while other scholars argue just the opposite.

Or, closer to home at our own state university here in Vermont, what ought to be the limits to which dissenters may go in order to inhibit the free speech rights of such recent speakers on our campus as the political conservative Dinesh D'Souza and the utilitarian ethicist Peter Singer? While on our campus, D'Souza went on the attack against a number of so-called left-wing topics, such as gay marriage, abortion, environmental issues, feminism, and multiculturalism. Singer advocated the ethical case for animal rights, vegetarianism, and aborting a genetically damaged fetus, all the while inveighing against the prima facie Judeo-Christian granting of special moral privileges to human beings only. Upon arriving on campus, both speakers, because of their respective ideologies, were met with pickets, insults, and angry personal vilification by their opponents.

Are issues like these open or closed to academic inquiry because they are too ideological? Is there room in the academy, for example, for professors and students alike to challenge the wisdom of trying to plant our particular version of democracy in the very different cultural and historical contexts of Iraq and Afghanistan? Or is such critical inquiry considered, prima facie, to be un-American and unpatriotic?

One more example should suffice. As we write, the U.S. Senate is only one vote away from passing an amendment to the U.S. Constitution that would make it a crime to desecrate the American flag. The American Civil Liberties Union (ACLU) is arguing that although no one likes to see our flag abused, it is nevertheless a worse crime to abuse the principles for which it stands: "liberty, justice, and freedom—freedom of conscience, freedom of speech and expression." These are the values declared and protected by our Constitution, "the very values that are threatened by this proposed amendment." Is this a blatant attempt, as the ACLU argues, to restrict our rights—our freedom of speech and expression? To what extent is there real academic freedom on college campuses, not just in the lecture halls and seminar rooms but in the faculty senate, offices of student life, residence halls, student newspapers, campus ministries, and even centers for judicial affairs?

Identity Politics

To what extent should academic subject matter be taught from the perspective of identity politics? Should group identity, whether of race, gender, sexual orientation, social class, or religion, continue to be the dominant, defining framework in the humanities and social sciences? Is it possible ever to get outside one's identity in order to study subject matter with any kind of nonpolitical objectivity? Or is this question itself proof positive of the existence of elitist, white, male, middle-class bias and intellectual privilege in the academy?

Or does it instead offer the opportunity to do some serious scholarly investigation regarding whether any subject matter might, in fact, be context independent, despite the protestations of postmodern scholars to the contrary? In other words, are such questions as these open or closed on their face? Is keeping the issue of the influence of gender identity closed, rather than open, to intellectual scrutiny, for example, likely to prevent the praiseworthy work of the three female chemists who have successfully challenged the hegemony of male-dominated chemistry departments in higher education? The outcome of their activism has been a court order to stop gender bias and provide for more gender equity in hiring practices, not just in chemistry departments but in all the scientific disciplines.

Social Class

Is the historical ideal of upward mobility for every single person in the United States a myth or a reality? Is social class still a powerful sorting force in American life? Is it ever really possible to have a genuine policy of equal access to higher education, given the reality of significant social class divisions that continue to exist in the United States? Is the notion of equal access simply another example of well-meaning, but unachievable, liberal rhetoric? To what extent is the concept of privilege in the United States influenced as much by social class background as by the impact of skin color, gender, sexual orientation, and religious and political affiliation?

Are social class differences still influential in how people vote, what religious groups they belong to, what schools they attend (kindergarten through college), what health care they receive, what jobs they hold, what recreational experiences they enjoy, how long they live, how they groom themselves and what they wear, where they live, who they marry and how they raise their children, and what products they consume? (See Correspondents of the *New York Times*, 2005.)

One issue that continues to plague higher education is this: Are race-exclusive admissions policies hurting or helping some students? Is affirmative action still a viable admissions policy in the academy? Do such policies unwittingly discriminate against poor, working-class students, whatever their color or ethnicity? For example, the recent lacrosse team scandal at Duke University raised as many social class questions as it did issues of race, gender inequity, and sexual violence on college campuses. (All charges in the case were ultimately dropped, the district attorney was fired, and the students were completely exonerated.) Duke is a predominantly middle- to upper-middle-class institution, wherein most sorority and fraternity members come from well-off social groups. The Duke culture is decidedly privileged. It is highly unlikely that a blue-collar, working-class student, of whatever color or ethnicity, would be playing on the Duke University lacrosse team, let alone even be a student there. Lacrosse is a middle- to upper-middle-class sport, and most urban public high schools across the country have no varsity lacrosse teams.

UNDERLYING ASSUMPTIONS WE MAKE ABOUT MORAL CONVERSATION

What follows are several pivotal assumptions that we make whenever we engage in moral conversation with our various campus constituencies.

• *The best way to talk about controversial topics is to converse, not pontificate, about them*.

We have a choice regarding how we converse with others. We can *open* conversational spaces or we can *close* them. We can spend most or all of our time pontificating and lecturing at others, or we can spend our time connecting with them. We can teach or we can preach. In the words of William Butler Yeats we can "fill buckets" or we can "ignite a fire" under them. The best way to draw out participants is to engage in honest give-and-take conversation with them. A genuine conversation that ignites fires relies less on pontification and oratory and more on interchange that is open ended, inquiry based, and civil. Moreover, the outcome is never predetermined, but always up for grabs. Critical thinking, the imparting of information, even group consensus—though certainly desirable achievements in many instances—are not the ultimate proof of whether moral conversation has been effective.

Where religion, social class, politics, and a host of other, traditionally underrepresented topics on college campuses are concerned, the point is to avoid narrowing campus conversations to one-way declarations of our unassailable beliefs to others. It is to realize that no matter how different our views, what we all have in common is the fact that our beliefs are at once true and false, whole and partial, strong and weak, each in their own ways. Thus, we need to turn down the volume of self-righteousness and dogmatic certainty in our moral conversations by turning up our empathy rheostats. We need to practice the golden rule of moral conversation: listen to others as we would be listened to. We need to question and challenge others as we would be questioned and challenged. And, most of all, we must pontificate to others only under the condition that we want others to pontificate to us. One of the authors, Robert, sometimes tells his students that the best way to convince others that we have something important to offer them is by using our ears, not our mouths—by listening, not preaching, to them.

• *No matter how "outrageous" a point of view might at first appear, we must always grant it the right to be heard and understood.*

Mark R. Schwehn (1993) proposes that four virtues in particular—humility, faith, self-denial, and charity—are necessary for respecting, rather than changing, the views of others.

The first quality is *humility*. This means that we must work hard to attribute the best motive to others, whenever they take the risk to express their thoughts in public. In the name of humility, then, we need to listen carefully to these publicly expressed beliefs and inquiries. We do this because tolerance and compassion begin with an assumption that we are not the only ones who possess wisdom and insight into truth. We, too, tend to stereotype and dismiss. We, too, hold fast to half-truths. We, too, are liable to understate and overstate, or worse, to misstate.

The second quality is *faith*. This means trusting that what we hear from another person is worthwhile in some way, if only and especially to the speaker. In fact, we need to go one step further. We must have confidence that what others have to offer about their particular understanding of a hot topic might even be valuable to us in some way. In the words of Schwehn (1993), we need to "believe what we are questioning, and at the same time question what we are believing" (p. 49). In any campuswide conversation about the hot topics, we maintain that success is measured by how well each of us is able to make the other person look good. To the extent that we try to make ourselves look good, and the other person look bad, then *we* look bad.

The third quality is *self-denial*. This suggests that, at some advanced point in any conversation about the hot topics, each of us will need to reexamine at least a few of the assumptions (and misassumptions) about these topics that we cherish. This includes, of course, our pet unchecked biases and uninformed stereotypes. Moreover, we will need to learn how to surrender ourselves to the possibility that what might be true to others could, at least in theory, be true to us as well. Self-denial is the inclination to acknowledge that we are willing and able to search for the truth in what we oppose, and the error in what we espouse, at least initially. It means avoiding the opposites of self-denial—arrogance, unwavering certainty, and self-righteousness.

Finally, the fourth quality is *charity*. This is about attributing the best motive and looking for the good in others, especially including in what others are willing to fight and maybe even die for. Charity is about exercising generosity, graciousness, and even, in some instances, affection. This, of course, does not mean ignoring or excusing errors in judgment, faulty reasoning, or one-sided zealotry. Rather it means that any critique or correction must always come from a spirit of kindness and love, motivated always by a commitment to help and not to harm.

Charity is the willingness to build open, safe spaces on college campuses. We can do this by showing all of our constituencies that it is as important to *give* as it is to *take* from conversations about controversial ideas. It is also important to listen respectfully to the views of others, even when they might be in conflict with our own. Open, safe spaces are all about mutual perspective sharing and listening to understand rather than merely to critique or to denounce. With this goal in mind, the focus in campus conversations about difficult topics shifts from issuing edicts of right and wrong to asking genuinely open-ended, clarifying questions that reflect an honest interest in the meaning-making of others.

 • *The golden rule of moral conversation is a willingness to find the truth in what we oppose and the error in what we espouse . . . at least initially.*

Every single person deserves a presumptive respect for any views expressed. The core responsibility of all participants in moral conversation is to find the truth in what they oppose and the error in what they espouse—before they go on the critical offensive. This means that we need to display empathy and understanding for others at all times. Moral conversation begins with the resolution to see others as possible allies instead of enemies. It attempts to find common ground and overlapping middles in discussions rather than establishing irreconcilable dichotomies. It progresses from there to mutually constructive encounters. Unfortunately, the traditional model of communication in the academy, particularly in its scholarly publications, has been more adversarial and polemical than reconciling. In contrast, we stress the need to listen to and to read one another with generosity, trying always to attribute the best, not the worst, motives. This works best when people speak, not simply in the voice of an omniscient third person, but from the heart of what they personally believe—from their subjective I.

However, in the interest of intellectual integrity, we also need to listen to one another critically and, whenever appropriate, be willing to change or to modify our own previous positions on controversial topics, given the persuasive force of what we hear. Ethically, we need to commit ourselves to the principle of nonmaleficence (do no harm): at all times, we must refrain from going on the attack only for attack's sake. We must engage in spoken and written language always on the supposition that a genuine attempt to understand another's views is the prerequisite for active engagement with those views.

The ideal end of moral conversation is to reach a point where there are only conversation starters rather than conversation stoppers. At the very least, moral conversationalists must be able to have their say, and when it's time, leave the conversation with their dignity and integrity fully intact

• *What can "kill" moral conversation from the start is to approach a controversial issue with an either-or, all-or-nothing attitude.*

Either-or thinking oversimplifies complexity and dichotomizes diversity. Worse, when it dominates conversations about any of the controversial topics we've described, it frequently polarizes opposing narratives. Cognitive-behavioral therapists call this either-or thinking, and it is a common characteristic among people who tend to see the world in black or white rather than in shades of gray. These people tend to engage in clear-cut, right or wrong thinking because they experience the world as a series of false dilemmas that are easily and quickly resolvable. They avoid complexity in their world views by attempting to cut through the confusion as if all the controversial issues can be resolved by a simple yes or no. This way, ambiguous intellectual dilemmas are manageable rather than overpowering.

John Stuart Mill, during the nineteenth century, believed that the temptation to become a member of the "moral police" squad was "one of the most universal of all human propensities." Nothing has changed today. There will always be True Believers on college campuses who are positive that they alone know the truth, and they are equally convinced beyond any doubt that their truth will set all the rest of us free if only we will accept their certainties. Such stringent, all-or-nothing views, in our opinion, endanger the future of a pluralistic democracy. Sincere and thoughtful people on all sides—not the extremists or the fanatics—will always have serious, deeply held differences of opinion over such important topics as politics, social class, religion, race, and ethnic diversity. We are advocating, in the words of Tivnan, that each of us try always to "imagine the world from the other side of the barricade" (1995, p. 250).

In our conversational spaces, we encourage our students to take nothing at face value. There will always be alternative interpretations of what is said when people engage in conversations about politics, religion, and social class. Narratives of meaning on each of these topics, as well as on a variety of other controversial issues, are tied closely to the unique experiences of each person. But the words that people use to describe those experiences are limited in number. In conversations about the hot topics, it is inevitable that the same words will take on different meanings for different people with different narratives and worldviews. Think, for example, of these words: God, church, spirituality, democracy, liberal, conservative, upper class, poverty, social justice, and wealth. All of these words, and a host of others that we use in difficult campus conversations, are indeterminate. They carry many meanings, not one clear meaning, and they always insert a degree of inexactness, uncertainty, and vagueness into our conversations. In moral conversations about the hot topics, nothing is ever settled once and for all—but settling on one answer is not the point.

Conversations about pluralism are, by definition, open-ended. Because of that, we encourage students and others to be open-minded, but not so open-minded that nothing is ever challenged. In fact, we urge them to ask clarifying questions whenever the hot issues are being discussed. We urge people to question one another, to ask for more detail or depth of description. Our goal is to get as many people as possible engaged in cross-campus conversation. This helps keep the conversation as a whole fair and reciprocal, and it does not shy away from complexity and ambiguity.

F. Scott Fitzgerald once said that the test of a first-rate intelligence is the ability to hold two or more opposing ideas in the mind at the same time and still retain the ability to function somewhat normally. We would go one step further. The test of a superior intelligence is to know that, on most political, social class, and religious issues, there are rarely clear and unequivocal opposites. There are only differences of degree and transitions. Looking for what Richard Rorty (1989) calls "shared premises" or "narrative overlaps" is often a better way to proceed in moral conversation about the most difficult and controversial topics. We can only add to Rorty's suggestion that discovering shared premises is impossible without a commitment to what we are calling moral conversation.

In a democracy, it is not by stricture or fiat that complicated social problems get addressed and resolved. It is through hard work, responsiveness, energy, constructing a case in behalf of a perspective, and reaching out to build bridges to others who do not share that perspective. It is also through generosity, humility, and, above all, realizing that in a pluralistic world, visions of truth and reality are infinitely variable and interpretable and sometimes hopelessly incompatible.

   • *On matters of truth about religion, social class, and politics, as in all the other controversial topics, we do not live in reality itself. We live in subjective stories that captivate us about these realities.*

   It is self-evidently true, of course, that there is a material, "factual" world out there that all of us must consciously negotiate every day. There are red lights to stop our automobiles, street markers to keep us from getting lost, groceries to buy, faulty plumbing to fix, meals to prepare, houses to maintain, and so forth. There is also a naturalistic world out there that scientists have verified as factual. This world consists of the laws of gravity, quantum mechanics, combustion, natural selection, planetary motion, general relativity, and chemical composition. Yet it is also the case, as cognitive scientists and brain researchers have documented, that "believing is seeing." We are not cameras and tape recorders. About 85 percent of our perceptions of that "factual" world are determined by our mental models, our cognitive screens, built out of our prior experiences and anchored in our preexisting assumptions and values. Each of us experiences and reacts to that world in our own ways.

   It does not follow that because there is a material world "out there" that therefore our *truths* are also "out there." Rather, they are our own creations. Truths about religion, social class, and politics are very far from being objectively verifiable—like life-threatening illnesses, crab grass, and black holes in the universe. These truths are not available to everyone in the same, unmediated way. They are largely a product of the way we were raised to think and feel about these topics, embedded as each of us is in our unique containers of contingent meanings.

The problem with trying to locate objective truths in our thinking about religion, social class, and politics is that if they even exist we cannot avoid distorting them with our unique perspectives and value filters. Scientists are able to make empirical truth claims that are based exclusively on a value-free observing, weighing, measuring, testing, replicating, and counting of data. But this is only one version of truth, the naturalistic version. There are several other versions of truth whenever the phenomena are as ambiguous and complex as religion, politics, and social class. The reality is that on these hot topics there is simply no objective, value-free, impartial truth that exists outside of our unique individual and group narratives. Thus, in moral conversation about the hot topics it is crucial to understand that people will often disagree because their truth narratives will be different. (See Appendix E for a more complete analysis of the difference between what one of the authors, Robert, calls *naturalistic* versus *narrativistic* truth criteria and their implications for moral conversation.)

The upshot for moral conversations about the difficult, explosive topics on college campuses, then, is not to give in to the temptations of skepticism or cynicism. Rather, it is to approach these interchanges with curiosity, modesty, humility, compassion, caution, and, when fitting, a sense of humor. It is to realize that nobody ever makes judgments outside a particular truth narrative. When all is said and done, every one of our worldview narratives will remain forever contestable, depending on our unique aesthetic and philosophical perspectives. Thus we need to learn how to engage in difficult conversations with an attitude about pluralism that says, "Let a thousand, even a million, alternative stories bloom. Maybe some of them will correct the deficiencies in my own story, even while confirming its richness."

Joseph Natoli (1997, p. 19) suggests several good questions that we might ask ourselves in our moral conversations about difficult and controversial topics. In our own words, his questions take this form:

- What is the particular story that I am hearing the other tell about religion, politics, and social class?

- What are the key words that the speaker is using in order to make sense of these topics, and what do these words mean to the speaker?

- What is the best way for me to communicate effectively with people whose worldviews are so dissimilar from my own?

- What psychological variables are affecting the ways I'm hearing what others are saying, especially when I am feeling threatened or confused?

- Is there any way for me to connect with the worldviews and narratives of others when they are so different from mine?

- What exactly is unsettling about what I'm hearing?

In summary, then, we encourage all campus participants in the moral conversation to "find the story" of the other. We believe that whenever we locate the story of the other, we are most likely to find the person who lies behind the persona. Identify those stories that carry intellectual and emotional meaning for someone, and we have gone a long way to making an intimate connection with the other on the deepest level imaginable. Why? Because we are our stories. They define us. They enrich and deepen our meanings. They are the fuel for our fire. They make a passionate claim on our hearts and heads. We live in our stories in such an indelible way that their impact on our lives may very well be mostly unconscious.

This is why moral conversation, as we practice it, is all about evoking (calling forth), understanding (standing with and among), and affirming (supporting, offering assurance, saying yes instead of no) those defining narratives of meaning that touch all of us. Before we can move on more robustly in the moral conversation to constructively challenge specific interpretations and help others to reveal nuances of meaning in these stories, it is crucial, first, to get the stories out on the floor in an environment free of intimidation.

INTERNAL CONTRADICTIONS

We are not romantic idealists who are in complete denial when it comes to the downside of moral conversation. We know full well that our conception of moral conversation is not without its internal contradictions. Thus, we make every effort in our teaching, consulting, and administering to openly acknowledge these contradictions. Getting these out on the floor early (and often, whenever necessary) is a precondition for open, agenda-free interchange on the hot topics. What follows are two of the most glaring internal contradictions. We will speak of additional internal problems in the final chapter.

First, moral conversation is premised on a particular philosophical-political set of assumptions. This is a worldview that celebrates pluralism on postmodern liberal terms. It urges that we allow an indeterminate number of narratives, languages, perspectives, and points of view to flourish on equal standing in the cross-campus conversation. What bothers Stephen Carter (1993), a constitutional law professor and devout Christian, about this postmodern assumption is that it posits an apparent moral equivalence among the multiple takes on what constitutes truth. Also, it (wittingly or unwittingly) excludes strong personal beliefs and commitments from the mix, particularly those we do not share in common. It asks religious believers, for example, to act as if they were nonbelievers or, at the very least, religious nonpartisans. It requires that they bracket their deepest, self-defining faith convictions—remove from the public conversation the most distinguishing aspect of themselves—in order to inhabit a religiously neutral piece of the conversational space that a liberal democracy requires. Unfortunately, Carter believes, this forced denial of the religious self ends up reinforcing the antiliberal stereotype that when it comes to political matters, liberals want religious faith to remain intensely private and miles removed from the public political process.

Although we hope for exactly the opposite outcome in cross-campus religio-spiritual dialogues, Carter's point is still well taken. We do not seek a denial of any aspect of the self in higher education. In fact, we are hoping that all aspects of the multiple selves that each of us possesses will get a hearing. Still, if we are being honest, we are talking about a moral conversation that celebrates pluralism on *postmodern liberal terms*. For postmodern liberals, truth is always plural. Moreover, it is contextual, conditional, and contingent. In short, truth, for postmodern liberals, is situational, not absolute.

However, for most strong religious believers, to take but one example, truth does have an irreproachable foundation. Although it may be accurate to say that interpretation, context, and preference always bias one's view of truth, this, for them, does not mean that everything is therefore up for grabs. There are morally correct positions to take, positions that rest on objective moorings such as the authority of prophets and messiahs, sacred scriptures, church traditions, time-tested rituals, and official magisterial teachings. These positions exist beyond the subjective reach of preference and perspective. A concept of moral conversation predicated on the assumption that multiple narratives need to circulate freely and that the most we can ever expect is to distill a small nugget of common truth from them misses the point completely. For these individuals, there needs to be a way to talk about difficult issues and topics that ultimately produces a conception of absolute truth on which we can all agree and act. Proponents of moral conversation must understand that to say truth is infinitely contestable and interpretable is to take sides ipso facto against all those who think just the opposite.

We empathize with those who have problems with the putative dominance of a liberal-postmodern worldview in cross-campus moral conversations. But we also know that, in principle, none of us can ever prove, once and for all, that our own favorite truth narratives will be the answer to everyone's problems. However, at a minimum, we can show the utmost respect for other narratives. We can go out of our way to understand them. We can practice empathy and restraint whenever we are tempted to ridicule them. Furthermore, when necessary, we can challenge them in a humble and nonviolent manner. On occasion, some of us might even embrace them. Moral conversation, when working well, can help fellow travelers inch a bit closer to some kind of mutually beneficial coexistence in the face of what can often be a fiercely contested terrain of worldview difference. It does this, not so that people can finally get to the bottom of things (because, on principle, who can determine what is finally the "bottom"), but so that they might find out what, if anything, they have in common.

Second, there is another way that moral conversation is politically biased, and this time the critique comes from the activist left. One of the authors, Robert, remembers a black student activist once saying to him that she found it impossible to relate to his notion of moral conversation because it was too white and too middle class. For her, the "civility movement" is "hung up" on a politics of politeness; thus it completely misses the need to attack at their source the basic social problems that plague America. Moral conversation, in her view, implies a kindness and empathy among opponents trying to deepen understanding of each other's perspective that is unrealistic in the face of tangible oppression and cruelty. Moral conversation is another example of the naiveté implicit in white privilege, she said, because often the only way that black Americans and other oppressed minorities can get heard is when they raise their voices in anger.

There are times, she said, that the enemy does indeed need to be demonized, that evils like racism, sexism, and homophobia must be named for what they are, and that truth needs to speak harshly to corporate greed and vested interests. Voices need to be strident (for example, the Vietnam antiwar movement), and sometimes violent dissent (for example, an urban riot against racism) is often the only way out of dismal social arrangements. Holstein and Ellingson (1999) argue, "Civility is not the language of urgency. It is not the language of people struggling to put food on the table or to stop the violence in their communities. It is instead the language of relative privilege, available to people who can afford to wait until some common areas emerge from ongoing conversations" (p. 14). To the activist left, moral conversation is nothing more than a tool of those entrenched in power, and this is the group that sets the terms of civil dialogue. The rules of civil discourse privilege the well educated, such as professors, students, and college administrators, while penalizing those who do not care to speak empathically to their persecutors.

As proponents of moral conversation, we are highly sensitive to the charge that our conversational process runs the risk of "cooling out" and "coopting" dissent and righteous indignation. For one, talking and interacting with one another does not ensure that action to correct injustices will occur. It does not automatically follow that conversation will inevitably lead to significant structural changes in hierarchies of institutional oppression and victimization. Even though we are in basic agreement with the black activist's critique of moral conversation, at least as we are thinking about the process here, participants in moral conversation are more concerned with procedure than policy. Their goals are small. Their main agenda is to provide a dynamic educational setting whereby students with different narratives of meaning can come together to talk, to listen, to learn, to question, and, sometimes, to find common ground. Moral conversation can be transformative in the broadest sense of that term. When conversation about the hot topics goes well, it can change the usual forms of adversarial exchange in the academy—expressing self-righteousness, contempt, and distrust—to new forms of cooperation—seeking common ground, sharing mutual, intellectual energy, and exhibiting compassion and understanding.

In the chapters to follow, we will explore in greater depth the hot-button social issues of religion, social class, and politics on college campuses. We will also suggest several ways to talk about these issues across a wide variety of college audiences and venues. Our goal is to ignite the fire of conversation about difficult topics so that every participant in the moral conversation leaves the experience both affirmed and informed.

2

Promoting a Spirit of Pluralism
on College Campuses

In this chapter, we examine the concept of pluralism. We make key distinctions among such terms as *tolerance, diversity, multiculturalism,* and *pluralism,* and we argue that pluralism is a far more fitting background framework for moral conversation than the other three frequently used terms. We go on to make concrete suggestions for how to ask pluralistic questions in moral conversation. We also discuss a principle that we call the paradox of pluralism, and we show how it presents difficulties, as well as opportunities, for moral conversation leaders.

Recall one of the "world's most dangerous ideas" that we mentioned in the previous chapter: the "war on evil." Imagine the cacophony of perspectives on this dangerous idea on a typical secular college campus in the United States. There are those in our federal administrations and houses of Congress who believe that this country has a moral responsibility to wage a war on evil, based on their assumption that evil exists as a unified entity. The ongoing war on terrorism has been grounded in the supposition that there is an identifiable, clear-cut "axis of evil," a label that has been applied to such nations as Iran and North Korea, as well as to such past enemies as the former Saddam Hussein regime in Iraq and the Taliban regime in Afghanistan. If an open forum were to be held on every college campus in the United States on the issue of whether or not there is such an entity as a unified, embodied evil, we predict that the conversation would be emotionally charged and, in most cases, hopelessly divided.

From one side, questions such as the following would flood the dialogue: What do you mean by "evil"? What do you mean by waging a "war" against it? Is it possible for evil to be categorized as a unified entity, or is it far more complex than that? In what ways does a notion of evil depend on the worldview of the beholder? Isn't the concept intricately tied up with an endless array of self-interested nationalistic, religious, and political perspectives? Who, in the end, has the right to impose a label of "evil" on any other group of people or belief system? Who, or what, according to such privileged judgments, might be exempt from such a label, and on what grounds?

From the other side, people would also ask a wide array of questions: Isn't an understanding of evil pretty much self-evident? Isn't it intuitively obvious that evil is an objective phenomenon? Haven't the world's three major monotheistic religions—Judaism, Christianity, and Islam—taken a proactive stand on what con-stitutes evil? Didn't the General Assembly of the United Nations adopt and proclaim the Universal Declaration of Human Rights, and doesn't this spell out clearly what actions against the rights of others are to be considered good and what are to be taken as evil? Isn't any dithering at all on the meaning of the term "evil" bound to have a deleterious effect on global peace, because such intel-lectual hairsplitting threatens to turn nations into wishy-washy moral relativists? If one nation is harming another, isn't this a good definition of evil? Aren't there times when going to war is justified, perhaps even morally obligatory?

Take another one of the "world's most dangerous ideas"—that "Western-style democracy is a cure-all for the world's problems." Or still another—that "religious intolerance" will ultimately lead to global violence. Each of these ideas will inspire its advocates, and its critics, to take strong, often dogmatic positions either for or against. It is an easy prediction to make that the decibel level of the cross-campus dialogue will rise to deafening heights. People will take sides. Either-or thinking will rule the day. The temptation to resort to acrimonious name-calling will be almost insurmountable. Self-righteous claims of truth, tinged with an undeniable air of certitude, will threaten all attempts to create genuine, open-ended dialogues. Self-designated vigilantes on whatever side will work hard to ridicule and silence those who might be audacious enough to question the apparent self-evidence of their truths.

In the case of Western-style democracy, the following questions are bound to arise in any open campus discussion: Who says that democracy is the ideal government? Who has the right to impose a one-size-fits-all political arrangement on any country? Isn't there a diversity of approaches to democracy, and if there is, why is a Western-style approach necessarily the best one? On the other side, these types of questions will emerge: Doesn't democracy represent the most forward-thinking, humane, just, and liberty-enhancing way of life for all peoples, especially when it is working well? If so, why not sing the praises of something that is intrinsically beneficial? Even better, why not actively convince other nations that it is in their best interest, as well as our own, to adopt democracy as the best way to organize their political systems?

And, in the second case, no subject matter is more likely to stir up heated controversy on a college campus today than religion. Religious identity is, for some people, their primary identity. Challenge their religious views, and you question their very reasons for being. Sides will polarize very early on the following types of questions: Shouldn't we avoid open discussion of religious issues on college campuses as much as possible, because emotions get unleashed too quickly? If it is true that religion is more about feeling and less about thinking, how then is a rational conversation about religious differences possible? Isn't religious belief really all about certitude and exclusivity, and, if it is, how can such conversations ever be truly inclusive, or at the very least tolerant, of other points of view? Aren't animosity, exclusivity, and intolerance always the inevitable outcomes of any campuswide discussions of religion? Aren't religion and spirituality private matters, best left to the church, temple, synagogue, or campus ministry? Isn't there a "wall of separation" between church and state, according to the Constitution?

On the contrary, says another group of participants in the conversation. Is it inevitable that strong expressions of religious belief will necessarily lead to intolerance? Who has the right to exclude religious voices from the public square of higher education? Why should participants in the campuswide conversation have to deny their religious identities whenever they engage in dialogue across campus on some of the most explosive social and political issues facing us today? After all, we don't ask people who possess a number of other, more politically correct identities to silence themselves on these matters. Shouldn't we be looking for ways to encourage religious believers to come out of their theistic closets, precisely for the reason that it is open disclosure and open-minded conversation, not closeted silence, that will defeat religious intolerance by others? How better to know people on a heart-to-heart level than to encourage them to talk about those religious beliefs that move them most deeply, along with those spiritual practices that give their lives the richest meaning?

THE PROMISE AND PERIL OF PLURALISM

It should be more than obvious that conversations about good and evil, democracy, and religion, to mention only the three topics just covered, will elicit a variety of perspectives across the continuum of extremes on college campuses. Some positions will be potentially reconcilable, some divisive. Some will be complementary, some competing. Some will be heartfelt, some "headfelt." Some will be extreme, some moderate. Some will evoke wrath, some calm. Some will put people on the defensive, some on the offensive. Some will turn strangers into friends; some, friends into strangers. Some will cry out for accommodation, some for isolation.

But what all conversations about such difficult topics as evil, democracy, and religion will have in common is that differences of perspective on the large questions will be so diverse that there will rarely, if ever, be any all-encompassing solution to the conflicts that will surface. We live in a pluralist society, where, in the words of Martin E. Marty (2005), it is inevitable that "strangers will face strangers," "tolerance will give way to intolerance," and, at some point, "strangers will collide." But Marty does go on to say that "stranger hospitality" is more than achievable—if, and only if, we make a "sedulous effort not to laugh at, not to cry over, not to denounce, but to understand" (p. 12).

What do we mean by the term *pluralism*, and how does it relate to the topics of religion, politics, and social class? Furthermore, how does it relate to our notion of moral conversation? First, let us dispel some of the cultural stereotypes of pluralism, a term that in some activist circles has a bad name. Pluralism is not about aimless chaos or anarchy—a "live and let live" approach to life and "let the chips fall where they may." Nor is it relativistic. In fact, pluralism is not without its inspiring ideals and purposes. It has nothing whatever to do with moral equivalence, or a wild, ungrounded hedonism that proclaims "anything goes, as long as it makes me happy." Instead, in our conception, pluralism is a philosophy that encompasses the moral principles of individual liberty, social justice, compassion, hospitality to strangers, an abiding respect for alternative narratives of meaning, and a commitment to fostering close relationships both within and without traditional communities of belonging.

Where does the term *pluralism* come from? As early as 1915, Horace Kallen first used the word to argue against the image of democracy as a "melting pot." Kallen was critical of any ideal that melted away significant identity differences of individuals and groups. In fact, he felt that such a metaphor was antidemocratic. Instead, he coined the term *cultural pluralism*, which refers less to a kind of nationalistic homogeneity and more to what he called an image of the United States as a symphony orchestra.

He opted for achieving a "harmony among difference" instead of working toward an ersatz political and cultural unity that would obliterate difference. Thus, instead of melting cultural dissonance into a bland national sameness, Kallen preferred the political metaphor of a classical music symphony. This is a musical construction that combines a diversity of ranges and harmonies, yet retains a common, readily identifiable, thematic motif (see Kallen, 1956).

In general, we support Kallen's understanding of pluralism, but we choose to postmodernize it somewhat to bring it into the twenty-first century. We prefer the metaphor of the jazz ensemble instead of the symphony orchestra, in keeping with the spirit of such contemporary pluralists as Ninian Smart (2000), Sharon D. Welch (1999), and Diana Eck (2001). Here is Welch on jazz as the most fitting metaphor for pluralism: "Jazz emerges from the interplay of structure and improvisation, collectivity and individuality, tradition and innovation. . . . Jazz is not completely free form, though. . . . [F]rom a set chord progression and melody, the players innovate and improvise, modifying the chords, melodies, and rhythm."

Welch believes that like a jazz ensemble, a robust, pluralist society is fueled by the ability to improvise, and this requires "individual effort, creativity, technique, and group synergy" (p. 16). The spark for a spirited pluralist society, as in a jazz ensemble, comes from everyone's willingness to play off one another despite individual "failures, limits, and mistakes" (p. 17), which are inevitable whenever participants in a pluralistic conversation are willing to push the limit. In the end, a truly pluralistic society, like a jazz group, requires a willingness to admit that our "strengths also carry with them their own, unique flaws and weaknesses" (p. 25). We also add to Kallen, Smart, Eck, and Welch a strong, postmodern focus on the narrative construction of meaning, as well as an emphasis on moral conversation. For us, talking about the hot topics on a typically diverse college campus during these first decades of the twenty-first century will require some postmodern fine-tuning. More on this later.

Most important, however, we prefer to use the term *relationalism* rather than *relativism* to describe our take on pluralistic values. Relationalism puts the emphasis on such unitive values as generosity, empathy, compassion, hospitality, affection, understanding, and connection. Without these values, how is it possible, we wonder, for the endless variety of campus constituents to have productive conversations with one another about such topics as the embodiment of evil, the primacy of democracy, and the proper role of religion in the public square—to mention three of the most "most dangerous ideas" that we discussed at the beginning of this chapter? Absent a strong commitment to relationalism, conversation about difficult topics on college campuses will become just another exercise in dogmatic coercion, accompanied by the usual self-righteous denunciations of those who might think differently from the Chosen Few—those who alone possess the Truth about peace, truth, justice, and the American Way.

Isaiah Berlin (1969, p. 167) captures our sentiments exactly:

> One belief, more than any other, is responsible for the slaughter of individuals on the altars of the great historical ideals—social justice, or progress, or the happiness of future generations, or the sacred mission or emancipation of a nation or race or class, or even liberty itself, which demands the sacrifice of individuals for the freedom and equality of society. This is the belief that somewhere, in the past or in the future, in divine revelation or in the mind of an individual thinker, in the pronouncements of history or science, or in the simple heart of an uncorrupted good human being, there is a *final solution.*

As authors, we do not know of a single universalizing principle that one set of elites, no matter how praiseworthy, ought to be able to ordain for all people. Final solutions represent, at best, the prejudices and biases of particular individuals and groups—nothing more, nothing less. If there is such a thing as universal "core values," then it will be the responsibility of each of us, both as individuals and as groups, to construct them together, and these will always be up for grabs, always in process, and always flawed, as we engage one another in the cooperative construction of stories. In the moral conversation, we make it a point to urge participants to beware of those who deliver their absolutes as "bottom lines." We ask, who, on principle, has the right to assume that one set of bottom lines is "more bottom" than other bottom lines? For us, as for a number of postmodern philosophers, it is only perspective, interpretation, and taste that go all the way down, and the "down," like it or not, is bottomless (for example, see Fish, 1999; Rorty, 1991). There will always be one more line to draw . . . and then another one . . . and another . . . ad infinitum.

What exactly are we saying about pluralism, then? In a nutshell, we hold that *pluralism* is a morally thicker term than *tolerance* and *diversity*. *Tolerance* calls simply for noninterference regarding different points of view and beliefs. *Diversity* is a demographic fact, nationally and in our colleges and universities. It is a morally neutral term, describing a state of difference, and it does not enjoin us even to respect, let alone celebrate, these differences, in spite of what many higher educators think today. In contrast, *multiculturalism* is morally thick in its meanings. It is an honest, no-holds-barred look at a multiplicity of cultural identities. It also points out the existence of oppression and exclusion that has taken place in this country—including institutionalized racism, sexism, homophobia, classism, and a number of other isms and phobias.

Pluralism, in contrast, is a more normative perspective. It raises the conversational bar throughout college campuses in that its primary objective is to put faculty, staff, and students in mutually respectful, yet lively and candid, conversation about difference and otherness. For us, pluralism is best thought of as a value orientation. It is both a worldview and a process. It is a way of engaging the presence of differences and otherness that does not set up winners and losers before the cross-campus conversation even begins, as some approaches to multiculturalism tend to do. Nobody is silenced. Nobody is shamed. Nobody defers to a particular form of political, moral, or religious rectitude. Nobody enters the moral conversation as a priori victimized, privileged, good, or evil. According to the comparative religions scholar Diana Eck (1993), "pluralism aims to build bridges of exchange and dialogue . . . and this must include constant communication—meeting, exchange, traffic, criticism, reflection, reparation, and renewal" (pp. 197–198).

Pluralism, therefore, is about unbounded discourse wherein all points of view, even those that might be considered the most retrograde as well as the most progressive, are included in cross-campus conversations. Pluralism, as we conceive and practice it, does far more than the standard academic work of critique, challenge, and debate. It goes on to look for commonalities and agreements, as well as differences, between and among diverse individuals and groups. It means that at times, the principle of *e pluribus unum* ("out of many, one") might have to give way to the principle of *e pluribus plures* ("out of many, many"), and vice versa. In the pages ahead, we will examine several of the relevant angles of moral conversation, both its dangers and opportunities, in producing and strengthening a constructive pluralism on college campuses, particularly on the volatile issues of religion, social class, and politics.

THE PARADOX OF PLURALISM IS ALSO ITS POTENTIAL PERIL

Daniel Callahan (2000) describes the paradox of pluralism with keen insight: "How are we as a community, dedicated to pluralism, to find room for the different values and moral perspectives of different people and different groups? How, that is, are we to respect *particularism?* . . . How can we as a community, made up of diverse individuals and groups, find a way to transcend those differences in order to reach consensus on some matters of common human welfare? How, that is, are we to respect *universalism?*" (p. 37).

Richard Rorty (1999, pp. 275–276) summarizes our own post-modern position on the paradox of pluralism with admirable succinctness:

> We have learned quite a lot, in the course of the past two centuries, about how races and religions can live in comity with one another. If we forget these lessons, we can reasonably be called irrational. . . . Insofar as "postmodern" philosophical thinking is identified with a mindless and stupid cultural relativism—with the idea that any fool thing that calls itself culture is worthy of respect—then I have no use for such thinking. But I do not see that what I have called "philosophical pluralism" entails any such stupidity. The reason to try persuasion rather than force, to do our best to come to terms in conversation with people whose convictions are archaic and ingenerate, is simply that using force, or mockery, or insult, is likely to decrease human happiness.

It is our position that all constituents in a university ought to be encouraged to wrestle with the possibility of multiple truths in the company of their peers, and to deal with the prospect of multiplicity in a way that is both self- and other-respecting. No matter what one's perspective might be on the "most dangerous ideas" we mentioned earlier, if one's mind is closed a priori to another point of view, there is a major risk that the cross-campus conversation on all the difficult topics will be doomed before it ever gets started. We believe that in academia, at least in theory, everything ought to begin and end with conversation, and that the outcome is always up for grabs. Thus the mission of higher education is to open up minds rather than shut them down. How then do we get students, faculty, and student affairs professionals in a university to wrestle with the enigmas of contrasting truth claims in the company of their peers, if some participants believe that the very principle of pluralism is the enemy to be vanquished?

Pluralism in a democracy will always create difficulties, because in the interest of consistency and fairness, even those who would seek to destroy the notion of pluralism, and democracy along with it, have an "inviolable" right to exist. Even though absolute belief of any kind in a democracy, as on a college campus, sometimes promotes more darkness than light, we, as authors, will strenuously resist any effort to suppress or curtail its expression. We also hold, however, that cultural absolutists reach the limits of this expression whenever they seek to suppress or curtail the rights of others to speak their own truths, no matter how heretical or out of step with the majority. Prudence will always be necessary whenever we begin to define these limits, of course. However, until these boundaries are reached, educators must remain committed to the paradoxical principle that the very best way to help all parties on college campuses deal intelligently with dissent and compromise is to expose conversationalists to as much intense, divergent belief as possible. This includes those *intolerant* belief systems that, on principle, forbid compromise and dissent.

For example, in a very controversial free-speech twist, in response to an ongoing lawsuit filed by two conservative student leaders earlier this year, the Georgia Institute of Technology (Georgia Tech) decided to change portions of a speech policy for students living in on-campus housing that lawyers have alleged is vague and unconstitutional. U.S. District Judge J. Owen Forrester ordered Georgia Tech to abide by an agreement to change the code. Tech took out wording that prohibits students from any attempt to "injure, harm" or "malign" a person because of "race, religious belief, color, sexual/affectional orientation, national origin, disability, age or gender." At Georgia Tech, therefore, in on-campus housing venues, all speech is now legally protected—even harmful, intolerant speech—in the name of tolerance.

The speech code issue was just one of a list of complaints brought by Tech students Ruth Malhotra, a conservative Christian, and Orit Sklar, the president of Hillel, a Jewish organization, who argued that Tech's policies aimed at protecting students from intolerance end up, instead, discriminating against conservative Christian, Jewish, and Islamic students who speak out against homosexuality and feminism and other issues. National Christian groups have also taken up the cause of challenging "politically correct" tolerance policies at several schools. And suits similar to the one at Georgia Tech have been filed across the country by nonprofit defense funds like the Alliance Defense Fund, which represents the Tech students. Pennsylvania State University, for one, recently agreed to revoke its speech code after a similar lawsuit. (See the following Web site for further information: http://chronicle.com/news/article/859/georgia-tech-revises-speech-policies-in-response-to-).

These recent legal challenges against speech codes expose an unacknowledged truth on all college campuses: each of us, no matter how progressive, open minded, or flexible we think we might be, has our nonnegotiable, uncompromisable bottom lines when it comes to certain religious, social class, and political issues. Whether we identify as a social justice activist, civil liberties activist, religious pluralist, feminist, or gay rights activist, each of us has our own peculiar brand of intolerance. This is precisely what the Alliance Defense Fund argued in its winning brief. The Fund recognized well that even those who passionately espouse a policy of tolerance for difference can, at times, be among the most intolerant people on a college campus.

Here is a poem, written by an eighteen-year-old high school senior, George Davis, and friend of one of the authors, Robert, on the paradox of pluralism. He captures well how easy it is for tolerance to become intolerance, especially when the right buttons get pushed by those who think differently from us. Nobody is immune. Everyone, whether faculty, staff, student affairs professional, student, practitioner, or scholar, has the capacity to become an uncompromising monist instead of an open-ended pluralist—on almost a moment's notice:

> **"Let Ninety Nine Flowers Bloom:**
> **Sir Lovey Dovey Hugsalot"**
> Whether you think far left or right,
> Whether your thinking's dull or bright,
> He doesn't care just how you play,
> Or if or how you choose to pray.
>
> But just when you think Sir Hugs is neat,
> You find that he's a touch off:
> Beat on your neighbor's right to think,
> He will against you make a stink.
> Examine, if you would, this row—
> There's one small bulb He won't let grow.

Like it or not, there are no definitive empirical tests that can determine once and for all whether particular claims to truth are true or false, in the same way that there might be in some areas of science. In the end, when all the pluralistic conversation has stopped, and whether we agree or disagree with one or another of the contrasting points of view, opposing claims of one kind or another will always remain profound mysteries. Each of us has a "small bulb" of our own that is beyond compromise, as well as a small bulb that we refuse to let others grow. These small bulbs will need to be understood and appreciated on their own terms *before* they are refuted and dismissed on *our* terms.

Even though we in the university understand all too well the *downside* of closed and final proclamations of truth on a college campus, we make very little effort to understand their *upside*. Every small bulb, whether we like it or not, has an upside. Every small bulb actually conceals a profound truth for the believer. A commitment to intellectual pluralism demands that we make an all-out effort to identify this potential profound truth before we launch into a critique of its downside, no matter how valid and necessary the critique might be. We will illustrate this assertion in some detail in the three chapters to follow.

BOUNDED VERSUS UNBOUNDED CONVERSATION

Before the pluralistic conversation can begin in earnest, we maintain that on a college campus such conversation must become "unbounded." Stephen Carter (1998) introduces a concept he calls "bounded discourse." Bounded discourse—"[deliberately constructing] an arena in which some ideas can be debated and others cannot" (p. 134)—systematically excludes certain ideas from cross-university dialogue for a variety of reasons, some conscious, some not. We have mentioned a few of these reasons in previous sections—political correctness, ideological privileging, shying away from controversy, the fear of making enemies, offending a number of powerful campus constituents, and so forth.

What Carter (1998) is saying is that whether in the classroom, counseling center, campus coffeehouse, advising office, or residence hall, whenever we "take off the table" what truly matters to all of us, then we bind up discourse. The unintended, but no less tragic, result is that in our calculated efforts to avoid firing up people's hot or cool passions on the controversial topics discussed throughout this book, we severely narrow our mission, along with our effectiveness, as higher education leaders. Worse, we relegate those conversations, necessary for the vital functioning of a democracy, to the nether regions of the private realm (for example, to college bull sessions or to private e-mail exchanges) where they are not allowed to enter the public arena in any full, rich way.

Daniel Callahan's concerns (2000) quoted earlier in this chapter notwithstanding, the possibilities for "harmonization" of what is particular and what is universal grow more and more unlikely. The robust, pluralistic conversation necessary to examine and understand both difference and commonality in religious, social class, and political points of view rarely, if ever, gets off the ground. Callahan wonders how a community can respect genuine differences in values and moral perspectives and still find a way to transcend those differences so as to reach consensus on "some matters of common human welfare." The challenge for any community, in his view, is to find a way to resolve the conflict between particularism and universalism, a fight he wants to have end in a draw, as he puts it. So do we, and often this is the only alternative. This challenge has been pivotal for college and university communities, of course, in matters of race, class, gender, and sexual orientation.

Here is Callahan (2000, p. 44) on the central problems of harmonizing universalism and particularism:

> No society can be utterly multicultural: it must share some common values to even be a functioning, minimally humane society. Nor should any society be monolithic in its values, simply pushing aside cultural differences: those differences are not necessarily incompatible with a functioning society and are often an enrichment to it. . . . I contend that it is perfectly appropriate in a pluralistic society for the various cultures within it to comment on and criticize each other—and where necessary to attempt to change by persuasion each other's values when they seem harmful or mistaken. . . . Criticism and persuasion, yes; coercion, no. [Pluralistic discourse] may sometimes bring peace, but often it must disturb the peace. . . . All cultures deserve our presumptive respect, but none can claim a moral exemption from scrutiny and evaluation.

According to the principles of moral conversation that we have outlined earlier, we would add the following to Callahan's comment that it is okay for the various cultures in a multicultural polity to attempt to "criticize and persuade each other":

1. Whenever appropriate, encourage evenhanded, compassionate, and critical commentary from all sides. But make sure no culture is given an a priori special treatment.

2. When necessary, help participants identify, and possibly transform, those particular beliefs that appear to be harmful, mistaken, or coercive. But make sure that no participants get unfairly stereotyped, demonized, or stigmatized.

3. Be crystal clear as to the reasonable limits of moral conversation by establishing (ideally by consensus) strict guidelines for avoiding psychological or physical harm to each and every participant. But make sure that moral conversation doesn't degenerate into a rigid set of dos and don'ts. Allow flexibility to enter into the process whenever appropriate.

Once again, we resonate strongly with Eck's observation (1993) that effective pluralistic conversation requires direct, give-and-take participation with the "other." At times, it stirs up the "hornets' nest." It insists that we allow the "other" to get under our skins, to engage with us, to disturb us, and, if the circumstances warrant, even to change us. Simple tolerance, respect, and celebration of difference must always give way to the active seeking of understanding, and to a willingness to consider transforming or modifying our previous views. This is both the burden and the opportunity of pluralism. People need to take an active initiative, says Eck, to "build bridges of exchange and dialogue . . . and this must include constant communication—meeting, exchange, traffic, criticism, reflection, reparation, and renewal" (pp. 197–198).

When Should Intolerance Replace Tolerance?

All of what we have said regarding the promise of pluralism in the academy does not gainsay the following difficulty: whenever groups or individuals, in the name of one absolutism or other, overstep the line between a respectful listening and clarifying and a disrespectful pontificating and ridiculing, then there will be times when intolerance must replace tolerance *in order to preserve the principle of tolerance.* This is the most difficult challenge regarding the paradox of pluralism on college campuses. Who decides what is safe and unsafe? What are the acceptable limits of tolerance and intolerance of strongly held (and expressed) religious, social class, political, and cultural views? Again, who decides? What do we do when two or more implacable belief systems collide, and when all the learned conversation has led to one stalemated result? This is the unyielding conviction that the Whole Truth resides in only *one* point of view, and that therefore all competing truths are lies, heresies, or apostasies that must be repudiated and expunged, regrettably by any means necessary.

Is Rorty (1999) right when he says that we must always use "persuasion rather than force" to deal with "people whose convictions are archaic and ingenerate"? Who determines the guidelines for what beliefs are archaic and ingenerate? More important, what do we do when all the civil dialogue and attempts at persuasion end, and the shouting (or worse) begins? Unfortunately, we have no definite, once-and-for-all answers to such daunting questions that will please everyone. And neither does anyone else, including Rorty.

Here is Walter Lippman, writing in 1955 (cited in Hunter, 1994, pp. 238–239) on a guideline for pluralistic dialogue in a democracy, one that we find compelling even today:

> If there is a dividing line between liberty and license, it is where freedom of speech is no longer respected as a procedure of the truth and becomes the unrestricted right

to exploit the ignorance, and to incite the passions, of the people. . . . What has been lost in the tumult is the meaning of the obligation which is involved in the right to speak freely. It is the obligation to subject the utterance to criticism and debate. Because the dialectical debate is a procedure for attaining moral and political truth, the right to speak is protected by a willingness to debate.

Although, as we have said, we prefer the word *conversation* to *debate*, because it is less adversarial and dichotomous—guided more by a wish to reconcile and integrate than by a need to fight and win—we agree essentially with Lippman. We believe that in a democracy and on a college campus, people have a right to speak freely on the issues about which they care so deeply. However, this right carries with it the corollary obligation to allow others to converse and to disagree, and vice versa. Moreover, people's right to freely express their views also entails that they speak about their strong beliefs in a way that engages rather than enrages, so that others might hear them rather than fear them. This means that no single voice is to be granted special a priori moral privileges in the pluralistic conversation. All participants possess the same rights and must exercise the same responsibilities. The outcome of this type of conversation should always rest on the merits of the views expressed.

This means:

- Stop blaming and start affirming.

- Do more listening and less telling.

- Engage, don't enrage.

- Feel deeply and be passionate, but don't vent.

- Explain, don't complain.

- Let go, don't hold on.

- Request, don't command.

- Turn down the volume and turn up the sensitivity.

- Be curious, not furious.

- Inquire, don't require.

- Appreciate the process as much as the product.

- Remember that in the moral conversation less is sometimes more.

- Let generosity trump animosity.

Furthermore, we must always be prepared to repeat this conversational process over and over, as often as necessary. If any one of us refuses to accept mutually agreed-on rules of moral conversation on a college campus, then, sad to say, we must be sent into exile. Why? Because we have freely chosen to forfeit our right to be part of the ongoing conversation about any number of controversial topics on a pluralistic college campus. We have chosen to communicate via conversation stoppers rather than conversation starters. We have elected to silence others.

Finally, it is vitally important to have a clear understanding of what type of speech might be considered extremist enough to justify exiling or marginalizing a particular participant in the conversation. What does one do, for example, with the infamous Holocaust denier, whose opinions might threaten the "safety" of some others in the moral conversation? Actually, extreme cases like the Holocaust denier are relatively rare in our experience in leading moral conversations. We try to be clear up front in moral conversation that "extremists" of all kinds will be relegated to the margins of conversation if their speech continues to be corrupt, immoral, incorrect, cruel, or harmful, especially if it persists after participants have made a number of gentle, respectful interventions that might include challenges, clarifications, and valid counterexamples. Such moral descriptors as "corrupt," "cruel," or "harmful," of course, represent value judgments that, at the very least, ought to be contested. Thus each descriptor will need strong justification on the part of the conversational leader.

But who exactly are these "extremists"? Does this group include, along with Holocaust deniers, members of the Jesus seminar (and Thomas Jefferson), who deny the existence of an historical Jesus; speakers against white privilege who deny their own intellectual, aesthetic, and Judeo-Christian privilege (along with their wealth and fame earned from doing "multicultural guilt gigs"); atheists who deny the existence of Jerry Falwell's and George W. Bush's God; those members of Congress who at the outset denied the existence of WMDs in Iraq; or Rush Limbaugh, who denies the threat of global warming; and who knows who else? The Holocaust deniers are actually an easy case because they are so extreme. They choose to ignore sound, irrefutable historical evidence, they possess patently harmful ideological agendas, and they function primarily to incite hatred against Jews, against whom their animus knows no bounds. But as our examples here show, there are other deniers whose rights to free speech, no matter how inflammatory, are not so easy to dismiss.

Philosophers have a saying: moral positions based on extreme cases make poor candidates for generalizability, because they are relatively rare and, at first glance, seem to be clear-cut. In contrast, the devil resides in the details of less extreme cases where moral ambiguity and honest differences of opinion are the norm. The principle of the paradox of pluralism is bothersome precisely because it provides no easy, one-size-fits-all answers to the question of how to deal with the controversial views of a variety of contrarians, True Believers, and controversial thinkers, some of whom might actually be on the cutting, albeit unpopular, edge of an issue. This is one of the reasons why pragmatists and postmodern philosophers eschew sweeping generalizations about truth and, instead, approach each truth claim on a case-by-case basis.

A POSTMODERN APPROACH TO PLURALISM

The first step in opening moral conversation about the difficult topics is for us to listen intently and nondefensively and to respond in a spirit of active engagement. This approach conveys the unmistakable message to the entire campus that students, faculty, student affairs professionals, and administrators have a right to be heard on all matters, no matter how controversial. Free speech on a college campus should be alive and well to all people and in all areas of human interest and conviction. We should encourage and respond to it, anywhere and everywhere.

The second step, in the interests of academic integrity, is to listen critically and, whenever appropriate, to change or modify our own previous positions on these topics, given the intellectual and emotional force of what we hear. We expect this outcome, for example, in political, economic, philosophical, religious, and educational conversations in the seminar and lecture hall. Why not in faculty senates and in other cross-campus conversations? Anything less than this potentially self-transforming response on our part trivializes and, worse, consigns to the outer regions of academic dialogue the deepest convictions that shape the lives of millions of people everywhere.

The third step is to construct what Nicholas Wolterstorff (cited in Wilson, 1999) calls an "ethic of conversation": "Thou must not take cheap shots. Thou must not sit in judgment until thou hast done thy best to understand. Thou must earn thy right to disagree. Thou must conduct thyself as if [all your friends and enemies] were sitting across the table—the point being that it is much more difficult to dishonor someone to his face" (p. 3). An ethic of moral conversation, therefore, ought to begin with the principle that, at all times, one needs to refrain from going on the attack. It must proceed to the principle that a genuine attempt to understand another's views must always be a prerequisite for critique and judgment of those views. Honest disagreement is a right to be earned, rather than an entitlement to be expected; and one earns this right by demonstrating the capacity to honor, rather than dishonor, a competing point of view, even while challenging it.

The fourth step, therefore, in encouraging unbounded moral conversation on college campuses is to start the process with candid, personal disclosures on everybody's part concerning where they currently stand on the most controversial issues and where they would like to end up. Putting our cards on the table early is a good way to set the stage for enlarging the conversational space for everyone.

We predicate all these steps on the postmodern supposition that each of us lives in religious, social class, and political narratives that are cultural and historical in origin. As yet, we have no Final Answers as to whether the Ultimate Truth of any or all of these narratives actually exists outside of a humanly constructed culture. Although the itch to locate a Final Answer to all the crucial problems that beset human beings is important, what is more important is for all of us on college campuses to engage in an ongoing, vibrant conversation with others about just this sort of question.

We are convinced, however, that if our individual truth narratives were indeed connected to some context-free, objective reality outside of us, it is highly unlikely that we could formulate a universally accepted method of determining which narrative was The True Narrative. For philosophers, this is called the problem of *incommensurability* (there is no unchallengeable, standard measure of truth that all of us can ever agree on). As authors, we do not deny the possibility of a commensurable truth. We remain genuinely open to this, even while we are skeptical. We can only assert that it appears highly unlikely that anyone will ever be able to construct or discover an Objective Truth, one accepted by every living person, except through an infinite array of interpretations or mediations. And this, in turn, is irrevocably blurred by the personal, historical, and cultural contingencies that shape our individual and communal humanness. We appreciate Friedrich Nietzsche's observation, made in 1870 (Breazeale, 1979) and still timely today: "Our truths are those illusions without which we cannot live."

Don Cupitt (2005), the philosopher-theologian from Cambridge University, puts the postmodern conception of incommensurability this way: "We need to remember that we, and we alone, invented language, and we projected onto nature, the world, and people, all the ideas, the order, and the feelings that we see in them. So it is scarcely surprising that every little breeze seems to whisper *Louise!* For we are hearing our own voices, echoing back to us. We made the world, our poets and our physicists, our weather forecasters, and our philosophers and theologians. We did it to familiarize our environment, adapting it to ourselves, naming things and describing them in terms of what they can mean to us" (p. 51).

In other words, our world is inescapably pluralistic in its every facet, because in the most profound sense, it is always invented by each and every one of us, on every single day, for all our days, until there is a point in our lives when there is simply no more time left. In Sartre's memorable phrase, there is "no escape" from the responsibility each of us has to engage actively and continuously in the narrative reconstruction of our lives. And this is why moral conversation seems aptly suited for communicating effectively on a pluralistic college campus. It is here that there is no escape from encountering difference in others, and where we can learn to hear others' voices echoing back, not only to themselves but to us as well. It is here that all of us can practice the art and craft of a type of pluralistic conversation that the world itself needs in order to get beyond the clash of worldviews that historically has led to armed collisions between and among groups and nations.

Finally, in William Butler Yeats's words, we believe that we can never escape the "rag and bone shop of our messy lives" (cited in Natoli, 1997). We know of no grand truth narrative that definitively transcends the rags and bones of particular times, places, and psyches. So, in the end, we on college campuses everywhere are left with three options: telling our rags and bones stories to others and listening to theirs as well; foisting them on others in order to save or educate them; or keeping our stories to ourselves. We believe that sharing stories is the best educational strategy for all those who choose to spend their time together in a learning community.

RECLAIMING TRUTH TALK FROM THE ABSOLUTISTS: ASKING PLURALISTIC QUESTIONS

A good pluralistic question is one that effectively draws out a person's most intimate background beliefs without judging them . . . at least initially. A good pluralistic question gets people to reflect on what is really important to them as they live in the details of their rag and bone shops. Although for postmodernists there may be no more grand beliefs that soar above our messy rag and bone lives, we know from firsthand experience that people's individual background beliefs still matter to them, even if many are very difficult to retrieve, and even if most are ultimately unprovable.

What follows are some "pre-questions" that we, as pluralistic educators, ask ourselves even before we attempt to construct effective pluralistic questions for others. We want all our questions during a moral conversation to be both evocative and fair, respectful yet honest and challenging. The following pre-questions help us examine our motives with candor and sharpen our inquiry regarding the presence of pluralism on a college campus. (We have been inspired to think about these pre-questions by Juanita Brown and David Isaacs, in Brown, 2005):

> Which of our questions promise to be probing enough to produce some type of breakthrough in a person's, or group's, thinking—including our own? Why ask these questions in the first place?

In what ways are our questions relevant to the actual reflections and thought processes of the people we are working with in moral conversation? Do we know our audience well enough to know their general slant on the controversial topics we are discussing?

To what extent do our questions conceal our own pet assumptions and biases? Are we willing to be honest about exposing our agendas to others for feedback and critique?

Are our questions calculated to get at the issues we are trying to explore more deeply in the moral conversation? Or do they tend to be off-the-track distractions from the real issues?

Will our questions lead naturally to a number of other questions that participants in the moral conversation can generate for themselves, and for us in turn?

After we get clear among ourselves about why we are asking the questions we do, we are then able to formulate a number of more general philosophical questions about the epistemology of pluralism. We ask these questions in order to get moral conversationalists to dig a little more deeply into their background beliefs, their taken-for-granted assumptions about knowledge and truth. We find that these starter questions, and others like them, tend to get us to the heart of the matter with participants very quickly. What is the heart of the matter in this case? As Callahan (2000) notes, it is the predictable conflict that always surfaces in our groups between the more abstract, *universal* truths of people's moral, religious, political, and social class beliefs and the *particular* truth systems each person actually lives in, believes, and fights for each and every day:

Do you think of your "truth" as something "out there"? Or as something "in here"? What are some of these "background truths" that keep you afloat when you think that everyone else seems to be sinking?

Why do you think of your truth as an "it"? Or as a "process"? Or as a "personal preference"? Or as a "negotiated compromise"? Or as an "absolute"? Or as a "myth"?

Is it possible for you to possess multiple truths, some of which might even be contradictory? If so, how is it possible for you ever to stand for something without wavering, if everything is always up for grabs?

How do you arrive at your truths in the first place? What makes a truth *true* for you?

Is it ever possible for you to extricate your truths from the way you were raised, trained, and socialized, or is this impossible?

On what grounds do you privilege some of your truths over others?

In the event that your individual liberty were ever to be in irreconcilable conflict with your community responsibility, what side would you come down on, and why?

When was the last time you made a compromise regarding one of your basic truths that might have been in conflict with someone else's basic truth? Can basic truths be compromised and still be basic truths?

What are some of your fears regarding the presence of pluralism on your college campus? What are some of your hopes and expectations? Are these mutually exclusive?

How is it possible to emphasize respect and compromise in pluralistic conversation, yet still hold fast to personal beliefs and perspectives that might be so critically different from those of others? How would you define the expression *paradox of pluralism*? For some, a paradox is only a *seeming* contradiction. For others, it is a *real* contradiction. Where do you stand?

We now move on to the next three chapters, where each of us, in our own way, will translate and apply the principles of moral conversation to our unique educational situation and practice. In each of these three chapters, we intentionally speak, not with one voice, but with three distinct voices. We speak as jazz musicians who, despite our individual differences—our signature melodic variations, improvisations, and dissonances—will still agree on a central thematic motif: that there can be no enduring human connection on a pluralistic college campus unless and until we learn to respect each other by listening deeply and compassionately to one another's stories. This will call for a new chord progression. In the words of Welch (1999), this human connection will require "self-criticism, an awareness of our own weaknesses and flaws, openness to conflict, critique, and change, but, above all, compassion, energy, creativity, and a delight in the surprise and unexpected gifts of life" (p. 25).

Part II

Practicing the Moral
Conversation

A Faculty Member's View on Moral Conversation from the Classroom

Robert J. Nash

My purpose in writing this chapter is to show how one faculty member uses the principles of moral conversation in teaching highly controversial, potentially provocative subject matter. I teach an elective course each year called Religion, Spirituality, and Education, which is open to undergraduate and graduate students in a professional college of education and social services in a medium-size secular state university. This was the first course of its kind to be offered in a professional school in the United States; hence, in the early days, there was no precedent in creating and teaching this course to undergraduates and graduates preparing to be education and human service professionals. My students and I made it up as we went along. The one constant throughout the years has been that we always talk about this difficult material according to the principles of moral conversation.

I begin this chapter with a description of an actual scene that took place in my course a few years ago. The purpose of presenting this scene is to show how I handled a major in-class conflict by using moral conversation strategies. I go on to develop a rationale for teaching such a course in a professional school and to describe the types of believers and nonbelievers who make their way to this course each year. I end the chapter with generalizable lessons I have learned during the fifteen years I have been teaching this course.

THE "AMBUSH"

My elective course Religion, Spirituality, and Education was falling apart. Halfway into the semester, the class had become dysfunctional. I did not directly address the problem during class time, as I ordinarily would, because many of these students had taken courses with me before and knew all about the protocols of moral conversation. I was confident that they would eventually come together on their own to resolve the difficulties, as my students often do. I also thought that they liked and respected each other enough to make the effort. I was wrong. It seemed that all they were willing to do was to be aggressive with one another, and my impatience and self-doubts were growing with each hour I spent with them. I felt that I had lost control—and would never get it back. After a very difficult, often contentious, class conversation on Islam, several members of my course confronted me outside the classroom. They were angry and frustrated. Their words were confrontative and direct. I felt ambushed, and, truth to tell, sick to my stomach. An unexpected student ambush is every professor's worst nightmare, and here I was experiencing it firsthand.

Marty: "Robert, why on earth did you pass out that piece on Islam that you wrote [reprinted in Appendix C]? There was enough in it to piss off everyone, including me. What were you thinking?"

Jane: "Where the hell is the respect for other religions that you always talk about? I never heard so much hate in a seminar before. What did you call it one day—*Islamophobia*? Well, it was alive and well in our class today, wasn't it? I can't believe what a bunch of bigots there are in our class."

Paul: "Is this what our discussions are going to be like every week from now on? If they are, I'm totally withdrawing. I'll just sit with my mouth shut, and let others go on the attack. Why did you have to provoke us so?"

Ruth: "Did you see what they did to poor John? They leaped all over him when he started to defend Islam, and how he claimed that Americans just don't understand Muslims. When he said that women are actually treated more fairly and respectfully in Islamic countries than in the United States, I thought some of our so-called feminists were going to do him bodily harm."

Larry: "I didn't think you'd be able to do moral conversation in this class given the volatility of the subject matter, Robert. There are just too many egomaniacs in the group for us to communicate well with one another this term. If you turn this resistant bunch around, you will really be a miracle worker. We're just not at a place where we can study Islam with any kind of objectivity. The Christians and Jews in the room are too closed minded."

Dennis: "Why didn't we go into more depth in the readings? Why aren't people even doing the reading? Why is it that nobody wants to share their personal writing reflections with one another? Why is everybody making speeches and being critical? Have we forgotten everything we learned about moral conversation? Everybody is out to look like an expert. Maybe this is just human nature whenever people talk about what's really important to them, especially if it's religion. Did you ever think of that?"

Gabe: "I'm beginning to think that moral conversation is a pipe dream when it comes to the real world. Try doing your moral conversation with Palestinians, Jews, and Christians in the same room! Or even with Sunni and Shia Muslims! Try it with Hindus and Muslims in the same space! My grandfather, an orthodox rabbi, told me that he would consider me a 'sell-out Jew' if I ever tried to make peace with Palestinian Muslims, as one of our authors appears to be advocating. The history of enmity between our peoples is just too long and destructive. Yeah, as I said, moral conversation is a pipe dream. Easy for us sitting here in the ivory tower to talk about our religious differences when nobody is holding a gun to our heads, or bombing our families, or desecrating our temples."

Elizabeth: "How can I ever talk honestly about my Christian evangelical beliefs when the atheistic bigots in the room are ready to rip off my head? Why do you let some people get away with rudeness and snideness? You wrote such great things in your syllabus, and in your articles, about having mutually respectful conversations, but I haven't seen any evidence of it yet in here. I'm sorry, but I'm beginning to think that you just use a bunch of nice-sounding words that don't pan out in the real world."

Aaron: "It's obvious to me that you favor Islam over Judaism, Robert. Your essay is so slanted that it makes all the other religions we're studying this semester seem inferior to Islam. Why did you feel the need to let Muslims totally off the hook? My own Judaism is just too brittle at this stage in my life to expose it to people like you."

Molly: "Why do we all have to be so defensive in this course? Why can't we just be more politically correct? I admit that in our PC diversity courses, our conversations are pretty tame most of the time, but nobody has to fear being verbally attacked for saying the wrong thing. Why should religion be more difficult to talk about than sexual orientation, or race, or gender difference anyway?"

Louise: "I'd like to interject my two-cents worth here, and I'm not seeking favor. Why are we attacking our instructor, Robert? It's true, he's the course leader, and the so-called religious studies scholar, but he can only do his job if people are willing to make an effort to loosen up a little bit and join him in real moral conversation. Where's the good will and mutual support in this group? We've been brawling with one another since the first day we started our unit on Islam. At first, everyone was polite. But eventually when Robert passed out his now infamous essay—'Western Stereotypes About Islam from Both the Left and the Right'—everyone seemed to have an ax to grind. Everything we've learned about moral conversation in this course we set aside outside the seminar door the last few weeks. Why? Can't we handle this subject matter without looking to 'Big Brother' Robert all the time? I don't know about you, but I'm getting fed up with this class, and I'm really disappointed in myself. Why the hell are we ambushing Robert? We're as much to blame for our screwed-up class as he is. If you ask me, he looks pretty lost!"

Vivian: "I agree with Louise. Everything was okay as long as we were being nicey-nice about our reactions to the assigned readings on Zen Buddhism. But, frankly, at one point our unit on Buddhism got so boring that I almost fell asleep on one occasion, and it wasn't because I was meditating. And then along came our unit on Islam. Sure, people started to get upset when Robert claimed in his essay that Christians, not Muslims, were the first terrorists. Or when he showed that Islam is more than just an Arabic religion, and, in fact, has an international presence that threatens all the major religions, including Christianity, in its rapid growth. Or that Islam does not oppress women as much as feminists in this country think. Or that Islam is not a cruel, backward religion whose notions of social justice, criminal justice, and theological proselytization are the most inhumane in the world. In fact, the case could be made that Judeo-Christianity is all of these things and then some. And when Robert went on to say that in actuality there is as much cruelty in the Hebrew and Christian Bibles as there is in the Qur'an, so many of us went ballistic and blamed him. Why?"

Why indeed. Yes, I was pretty lost, and filled with more than a little bit of self-doubt too. How in the world did I ever get involved with creating, and teaching, a course on religious pluralism in the first place? I was trained as a philosopher of education, although one of my graduate degrees was in religious studies. Was I kidding myself about being able to get college students of all ages to talk about religion in a secular classroom without hurting too many feelings? Did I finally go over the top by passing out a provocative essay I had written on the issue of Islamophobia in the United States? Admittedly, the moral conversation in our course that semester was growing less and less robust by the week, but why did

I want to deliberately stir things up, when, in my mind, the process seemed fairly harmless?

Were my colleagues right when I told them a decade earlier that I wanted to create an applied religious pluralism course? I remember many of them saying to me that it would be impossible to deal with this subject matter without ruffling feathers and causing trouble. Students in professional training, they said, tended to be too "conservative" and "provincial." Besides, why would educators and human service professionals care about such an *impractical* course? More important, because of decades of terrorist actions by jihadist extremists, it would be foolhardy, they said, for anyone to focus on Islam in a religious pluralism course, and doing so would no doubt cause anger and pain, and confirm all the usual anti-Islamic stereotypes. I hated to admit it, but during the ambush outside of class that late afternoon, I begrudgingly had to agree with my colleagues. At least on that day, teaching this course was probably the most foolhardy thing I'd ever done. (More on the ambush later in this chapter.)

COSMOPOLITANISM

For a long time, I have been influenced by the work of Kwame Anthony Appiah. His latest books (2005, 2006) represent an attempt to rescue the concept of cosmopolitanism from the "sneering elites" who use it primarily to put down what they disdainfully call provincialism. For Appiah, cosmopolitanism is the awareness that one is not only a member of a particular community of belonging but also a citizen of the world—what the ancients used to call a *cosmopolite*. Therefore, each one of us needs to have a profound sense of our obligations to others beyond our kith and kin.

This means, among other things, that we need to take the trouble to understand the cultural practices and beliefs of particular human beings everywhere, including their religious rituals and doctrinal teachings. This also entails that we develop a sense of obligation to be kind, even hospitable, to these "religious strangers" so that we might learn from them. One way of doing this is to explore in depth, and with an open mind, what others might hold to be religious truth. It is in their religious narratives, according to Appiah, that we can best make a real human contact with the strangers in our midst. I could not agree more strongly.

For me, a cosmopolitan person is someone who is knowledgeable about, and receptive to, the complexity and richness of religious diversity throughout the world. This is an informed and respectful person able to avow what is good about religion and to disavow what is bad. This person is liberally educated and knows that it is impossible to understand the history, culture, or politics of most modern societies today if one is ignorant of the fundamental role that religion has played in every country. Most important, this would have to be an ethically discerning person who realizes that much of what we in the United States believe to be moral or immoral is largely a legacy of the Judeo-Christian heritage, as well as of the European Enlightenment. Similarly, what much of the rest of the world believes to be the crux of morality for themselves is based on the teachings of their own endemic religions and philosophies.

Thus a cosmopolitan citizen is a person who is fully aware of the tensions in all religions throughout the world—tensions between "tradition and modernity, community and individualism, consensus and pluralism, faith and reason, and religion and secularity" (Nord, 1995, p. 380). Above all, this is a person who is able to distinguish clearly between the corruption *inherent in* the very nature and structure of religion (for example, inflexible and literal doctrines and readings of "sacred scriptures," identifying the "other" as enemy, and so-called divine claims of exclusivity in behalf of the possession of a final and absolute truth); and the corruption *imposed upon* religion by unscrupulous, extremist adherents who use religion to advance their own distorted goals.

In reaction to increasing religious strife throughout the globe, long before what happened on September 11, 2001, I had become convinced of the necessity of experiencing ourselves as interconnected citizens of the world. No longer should any of us continue to think of religions outside the Judeo-Christian axis to be unimportant or inferior in the global scheme of things. No longer could we be content to ignore the need for religious and spiritual understandings on our college campuses. No longer could we, as professors and campus leaders, afford merely to intellectualize religious and spiritual differences in a bemused, dismissive, or detached manner; or to adopt a folkloric approach with students wherein we do some superficial ceremonial "sharing"; or to mention this content only in passing, if we bother to do so at all.

No longer is it enough for those of us who might be more cosmopolitan in our worldviews to do a whirlwind, textbookish tour through the three major monotheistic religions in a world history course, and let it go at that. In the global society we live in, we no longer have the luxury of thinking about religion as merely a private affair, something best left to the home, church, synagogue, mosque, or temple. And no longer can we marginalize the teaching of religions in our colleges and universities.

For the last few decades, the reality of religious pluralism has hit each of us where we live. We must learn to deal with the phenomenon of religious pluralism with openness, respect, and critical understanding, or all our unexamined religious stereotypes could very well kill us. For Americans to be ignorant of militant Islamic fundamentalism or of ultranationalistic Judaism or of radical Hinduism or of the proliferating extremist, evangelical-fundamentalist denominations of Christianity throughout the world, for example, is to court international disaster. Religious illiteracy in today's global community is simply unacceptable (see Nash, 2007).

Closer to the present, the events of 9/11 have thrown our triumphalist American worldview, particularly its religious, political, and cultural elements, into turmoil. We have seen firsthand during the last few years what happens whenever starkly opposing religio-political conceptions of the world and human life collide. Whatever our views on world religions such as Islam might have been in the past, at the present time these religions signify something dramatically different and real for all of us. Whenever these religions remain true to their original, humane ideals, they are a force for good in the world. But whenever they serve as engines for the escalation of cruelty and violence, they are an indisputable force for evil.

Religion as a Political Force for Evil

Teaching about religious pluralism in an intellectually respectable way means that we need to be scrupulously honest about both the good deeds and the misdeeds committed in the name of a variety of religions throughout the world (for example, see Nash, 2005). Here are some up-to-date statistical reminders of how, globally, the religious world is radically changing: by the year 2050, India's population alone will reach 1.5 billion people, of whom 1.2 billion will be Hindus. By 2050, Muslims worldwide will outnumber Jews by over a hundred to one, and will even outnumber Christians. At the present time, Buddhism is the fourth largest religion in the world, and at one time in the twentieth-century claimed 20 percent of the world's people. By 2050, Buddhism will be the main religion of East and Southeast Asia, in such populous nations as China, Vietnam, and Thailand. In the United States, by 2050, one hundred million Americans will claim Hispanic origin, and upwards of sixty million citizens will claim Chicano descent.

At the present time, 70 percent of Latinos are Catholic and 30 percent are Evangelical Protestants in the United States. Moreover, very conservative forms of Christianity are on the rise in Latino America. In European nations, the figures are quite different due to an increasing secularization—44 percent of the British claim no religious affiliation whatsoever. In France, only 8 percent of the population identify as practicing Catholics. And in

Italy, despite the hegemony of the Vatican, religious identity has declined steeply in recent years, as less than 10 percent of Italian Christians claim to be active practitioners of their faiths. In Africa at the present time, there is a stunning growth of Christianity, especially its most conservative evangelical and Pentecostal forms. Eight-and-one-half million people on that continent convert to Christianity every year, an average of twenty-three thousand a day. Finally, it always shocks my students whenever I cite current statistics from a number of sources that roughly one-third of the world's population, close to two billion people, identify as nonbelievers. (Two references from which all these data were drawn are the Web site www.religionfacts.com/big_religion_chart.htm and Jenkins, 2002.)

On the global scene, whenever we mix fundamentalist and extremist forms of religion with politics, geography, economics, and the military, we get something volatile and lethal. Even a partial list of present-day religio-political conflicts is daunting in terms of the obvious threats to human life. To cite but two specific examples, the war against the imperialistic West waged by Wahhabi Islamic extremists like Osama bin Laden, and the war waged against al-Qaeda and political terrorism by the United Nations and the United States, continue unabated throughout the world. There are some who see the American war against worldwide jihadist terrorism as a righteous Christian war with the almighty Christian God on its side. According to many of these believers, the war against al-Qaeda and terrorism will be a war that could very well continue throughout the twenty-first century, reaching into all corners of the world. Direct military action began in Afghanistan in 2001. It threatens to continue throughout, and even beyond, the infamous so-called axis of evil, including Iraq and, possibly sometime in the future, such countries as Iran and North Korea, and who knows where else?

A dramatic example of what happens whenever religion mixes with politics has been the continuing deadly strife occurring in

India and Pakistan between Hindus and Muslims. The most recent wave of violence started in 2002, when a group of Hindu zealots, returning home by train to Gujarat from building a temple at the birthplace of Ram in Ayodhya, precipitated a fight with Muslim vendors on a station platform. The train was set on fire, and fifty-eight Hindus died. In response, over the next several days, Hindus throughout northern India killed more than six hundred Muslims. With the ongoing struggle to regain control of Kashmir, the violence between Muslims and Hindus will probably continue to simmer for years to come. Hundreds of thousands of soldiers from both sides, for example, amassed on the Indian-Pakistan border in 2002. For a while, the world stood transfixed in fear of the prospect of nuclear war taking place between two of the most militarily powerful, nuclear-armed nations in the region. The *New York Times* proclaimed that if war had broken out, twelve million people would have died (Kimball, 2002; Nash, 2005).

Similar threats exist throughout the world. To mention just a few: decades-old armed attacks flare up frequently between Israelis and Palestinians, the former supported by the United States, the latter aided and abetted by such allies as Lebanon and Syria. In New Delhi, militant Hindus of the Save Dara Singh Committee often harass and kill Christians. On the island of Cyprus, Muslims and Orthodox Christians have been engaged in thirty-five years of armed standoff. In Armenia, Shi'ite Muslim Azerbaijanis and Christians kill each other. In 1993, in Bosnia and in Kosovo, Serbian Christians engaged in organized mass rapes, summary executions, and ethnic cleansing of Muslim women and children. All too often, Sikhs in India bomb Hindu aircraft, and Hindus open fire on Sikh temples.

One religious studies scholar has estimated that more wars have been waged and more people injured, killed, captured, or missing for religious reasons alone throughout the first and second millennia than for political, geographical, and military reasons (Kimball, 2002). Even if this is not completely accurate, a convincing case can be made for its partial truth. Whenever war reaches the point that it is waged as a holy cause, whatever the original reasons for going to war, then, even to objective observers it might seem that religion and war are inextricably linked, and maybe even inevitable. (For a ringing defense of this view, see Harris, 2004.) This inference, of course, is a terrible mistake, because at the heart of all religion is the promise of reconciliation and peace. Our students need to understand that whenever war throughout the world is conducted in the name of religion and declared "holy," whether by Christians, Muslims, Hindus, or members of any other religion, it is a good indication that the purity and goodness of that religion has been corrupted.

Religion as a Spiritual Force for Good

Although this lineup of human atrocities committed in the name of religion is a compelling enough reason for college students to develop some basic literacy regarding the structural tensions within, as well as the differences among, many of the world's major and minor religions, it is not the whole story. Students also need to understand that religion and spirituality have the reconciling power to call forth that which is universally generous and decent in human beings everywhere. There is a common framework of positive values and ideals that bind all the religions of the world together, even though this common ground is often difficult to locate amid the competitive strife of so many exclusivist religious claims.

For example, most of the world's religions teach compassion toward the poverty stricken, persecuted, enslaved, aged, and infirm. Most of the world's religions encourage charity and almsgiving to those less fortunate. The notions of social service and social justice have their origins in early forms of Judaism, Christianity, and, later, Islam. Moreover, all the world's religions have engaged in some forms of moral uplift and humanistic social reform. Christianity, Islam, Hinduism, and Buddhism have produced such world-transforming ideas as forgiveness, pacifism, peace, nonviolence, and compassion. Martin Luther King Jr. was an ordained Baptist minister. Mahatma Gandhi was a Hindu and peace activist. The Dalai Lama, a Nobel Prize winner, and Thich Nhat Hanh are devout Buddhist monks and advocates of social justice who have put their lives on the line to advance the cause of peace in their respective countries, Tibet and Vietnam. Clearly, all religions have the potential to contribute to world peace.

Also, on a more spiritual, less institutional, level—and in spite of our cultural, religious, and political differences—all the world's religions teach us that we are enmeshed in the same human experience together. We are all brothers and sisters. There is just no way out of the human condition, with its incessant ups and downs, its struggles and disappointments, and its unending reminder that we need to discover deeper meaning and transcendent purpose if we are to weather life's storms. The world's religions have in common the understanding that we all share a similar drive to make and find meaning. We also have similar values, rooted in what secularists in the West call the principle of reciprocity, and what Judeo-Christian believers call the Golden Rule: do unto others as we would have them do unto us.

The world's religions remind us that regardless of our social position or our wealth, we all hurt, and we all cry. During times of personal crisis and disillusionment, we live in the same dark cave of confusion and futility. Even when things are going well for us, we sometimes fear the impending loss of our good fortune, the imminence of some unexpected catastrophe that will befall us and destroy our lives. Whether North American, European, Asian, Middle Eastern, or African, all of us strive to locate the larger meaning that we hope actually exists in the midst of our broken dreams and unreachable aspirations.

For example, in the West, we are faced everywhere with a sterile hedonism and a competitive individualism that, too frequently, pits us against one another in the marketplace. This lonely state of affairs leads inevitably to a widespread numbness and despair, giving rise to runaway substance and alcohol abuse and record sales of antidepressants and antianxiety drugs. Also, faced with the grim prospect of volatile stock markets and an unpredictable economy, corrupt multinational corporations, massive job cuts due to downsizing, an overreliance on foreign oil supplies, and a decaying natural environment, we experience very close to home the insidious worm that exists in the core of capitalism. It is important for our students to know that one of the major functions of all the world's religions is to offer a more enduring, personal meaning to those who have experienced the spiritual poverty that often exists in the midst of affluence.

In many less developed, Third World countries, there is grinding poverty and little hope for social justice and upward mobility. As we have seen over and over again in recent years, poor and oppressed people who live their lives in a constant state of hopelessness run the risk of being seduced by fundamentalist versions of all the world's major religions and the assurances of salvation delivered by theocratic rulers. Of course, there are many oppressed peoples who resist the enticements of easy religious answers to complex social and political problems.

In an existential sense, we human beings everywhere seek consolation and comfort whenever we feel that we suffer inexplicably, or whenever we feel that we stand alone in an indifferent universe. This quest for an enduring spirituality is endemic to the human condition. It is what sustains us, what inspires us, what gives us hope, what ultimately binds us together in a pluralistic world. Spirituality is the name that we give to the omnipresent quest for meaning that helps us make sense of our finitude and our uncertainty. Spirituality is the breath of life that has the power to bring love to the world. It is the force that makes us truly human. For three thousand years or more, human beings have experienced this animating force to love, create, and believe, in a number of venues, only one of which has been organized religion. (An excellent account of the wonders of spirituality can be found in Gallagher, 2001.)

Our students must realize that religion, on both a national and a global scale, is always a mixed bag. It is capable of delivering so much that is beneficent and enduring, yet so much that is maleficent and short lived. Spiritual literacy begins with helping our students understand that the cry for both proximate and ultimate meaning has been the one constant for human beings in all times and places. The words of Dorothy Allison are incisive: "There is a place where we are always alone with our own mortality, where we must simply have something greater than ourselves to hold onto. [We need] a reason to believe, a way to take the world by the throat and insist that there is more to this life than we have ever imagined" (1994, p. 181).

ADDRESSING THE REALITY OF RELIGIOUS PLURALISM IN THE COLLEGE CLASSROOM

And, so, here is where I found myself a decade ago, and where I still am today. What could I do as a teacher in a professional college to promote a cosmopolitan understanding of religious difference—the one difference of all, I believed, that could become the precipitating cause of global warfare in the twenty-first century? With all my heart, I believe now, as I believed then, that unless we become genuine cosmopolitan citizens, as knowledgeable about religious difference as we are trying to be about all the other cultural differences that too frequently turn us into paranoid xenophobics, we can only look forward to a dismal and tragic century of continuing religious slaughter throughout the world.

A decade ago, when I first began to create my course, I asked myself some very practical questions: Is this material too controversial, too value loaded, for secular colleges? How could I avoid offending a number of constituencies, particularly campus ministry, devout students, parents, and potential donors? Why stir up the hornet's nest of fundamentalist special-interest groups of all types in the community, who will resist what they see as the encroachment of religious, even secular, pluralism in colleges and universities? Would administrators back me up, or would they sell me out at the first signs of trouble? Is it possible to teach about religion in such a way that I don't take sides?

Also, what religions and spiritualities do I teach, and how do I do this? Won't I need a Ph.D. in religious studies if I am a philosopher of education? What if I myself am a nonbeliever? Isn't it inevitable that no matter how scrupulous I am, my own biases about this very provocative subject matter will get in the way? How can I get students to look critically at religions? Won't some believers, and even nonbelievers, feel disrespected? Just how far can I take the principle of academic freedom? Why not just avoid all these troublesome questions by putting the issue of religious pluralism on college campuses throughout America on the back burner? Why not just leave well enough alone? Why was I so set on becoming a religious-pluralist masochist? All these questions came back to me as I faced the ambush on that terrible afternoon after the class on Islam ended.

A PERSONAL DISCLOSURE

Here are some very personal responses to some of the questions that I just raised. I have been a professor at the University of Vermont for almost four decades in a professional college of education and social services. During this time, I have worked with thousands of social and human service professionals, teachers at all levels, and higher education administrators. Too many times in the past I have had to bite my tongue whenever religious questions have come up in my seminars, and, make no mistake, sooner or later in all my philosophically based courses, talk about religious and spiritual differences makes an appearance. Whenever I ask my students to consider what is truly important to them as educational leaders—what pivotal values and principles they base their practices upon—religious and spiritual responses are unavoidable, if students are being honest. I push them to dig deeply even when they do not want to. I ask them what, in the end, gets them up every single morning, especially when their personal burdens are heavy.

This is the primary reason why I developed my religious pluralism course. I myself have been a restless, existential atheist for years, but I have always wanted to come out of my own closet of religious denial and confront these questions openly with students. I wanted to enlarge my understanding of multiculturalism to include religious pluralism. I wanted to help those students who were preparing to be educators to find a way to include the issue of religious pluralism in their own work with students, along with such issues as racial, ethnic, gender, and sexual orientation differences. I wanted my students to understand that if Americans choose to remain ignorant about what gives religious and spiritual meaning to people's lives throughout the world, then they open themselves up to the charge that they are completely out of touch with contemporary global realities.

I knew from teaching thousands of undergraduate and graduate students over the decades that a large number of students want to know much more about those religions that are different from the Judeo-Christian heritage within which most were raised in this country. They want to understand what would drive some people to die, or to kill, for what they believe. They want to know why so much violence is committed in the name of religion, why so much hate is manifested under the guise of God's love, why religions can't seem to get along with one another instead of having to dominate all the rest. They want to explore alternative religions and spiritualities for themselves. They want a chance to find convincing spiritual answers to their worrisome, existential questions about meaning, love, relationships, autonomy, careers, higher education, faith, peace, patriotism, and violence.

I find that I am most comfortable teaching about religious pluralism from a narrative perspective. What does this mean?

Religions are most captivating, I believe, when they are understood at the level of story, because they feature unforgettable characters, momentous events, and luminous ideals. The languages of religious narratives are often sonorous and seductive. At its best, religion as narrative, as a powerful storytelling device, reaches out and captures our imaginations, because the vitality of its message and the vividness of its language are potentially life transforming. We are moved to fresher understandings of the deeper, previously concealed meaning of our lives.

I hold that we are more likely to get college students from a variety of religious backgrounds to open up publicly about their guiding beliefs when we are able to de-emphasize the revelational, doctrinal, and corporate-institutional elements of religion in favor of the aesthetic and the poetic, the philosophical and the literary. I make the case to my students that the best way to approach conversations about religious beliefs is to understand them as compelling and useful narratives that people have constructed for thousands of years in order to explain life's tragic anomalies as well as its gratuitous gifts of grace.

Even though I experienced my usual moments of agonizing self-doubt during that group ambush I described earlier, I know of no better way to mine the richness of a growing religious pluralism on secular college campuses throughout the United States than to get students to exchange their religious stories with each other in a nondoctrinal, mutually respectful manner. Remember, though, that this is an ideal, not a foregone conclusion. The hazards and failures of talking about hot topics, both inside and outside the classroom, are always just one, often very tiny, misstep away. I have never failed to make either a tiny, or huge, misstep in teaching my religious pluralism course. Knowing this, therefore, I always declare at the beginning of a semester that there will be no money-back guarantee that all will go well in our seminars, regardless of how praiseworthy the method of my instruction might be. I let it be known right off that I, and my students, will screw up often.

THE RELIGIONS WE STUDY AND THE STUDENTS WHO STUDY THEM

Each semester, I try to create my religious pluralism course anew, based on previous feedback and also on what has most recently been exciting my own passions for this topic. During the past decade, I have explored such religious narratives as mystical Judaism, evangelical Christianity, Tibetan and Zen Buddhism, Hinduism, Afro-Caribbean spirituality, Islam, secular humanism, neo-paganism and Wiccan, Taoism, Shinto, Sikhism, Quakerism, and a host of others. I limit my coverage to three or four in any given semester. Realistically, I can offer only a relatively brief introduction to these religions, with the hope that students will decide on their own to explore them more deeply later. Most do, if I am to believe their feedback to me long after the course is over.

What I have learned about students' personal relationships to their respective denominations, however, is that even though some identify strictly with one or another of the aforementioned religions, there is as much diversity of belief *within* each religion as there is *between and among* the various religious groups. I have met few students through the years who can be neatly typecast in religious terms. We really do not know very much about the actual beliefs of anyone who self-identifies simply as a Catholic, a Baptist, a Jew, a Muslim, a Hindu, or, for that matter, an atheist or Wiccan. We need to know *what kind* of Catholic, Baptist, Jewish, Muslim, Hindu, atheist, or Wiccan believer each is. For example, I often ask atheists in my seminars to talk about the particular god whose existence they refuse to believe in. The responses will be different according to their earlier religious training and family upbringing.

For this reason, therefore, I have identified several types of students who come into my course each and every year (see Nash, 2001a; Nash and Bradley, 2006, 2007). I have found all the types, to a greater or lesser degree, represented within each distinctive religious grouping. Thinking about the variety of ways that my students actually experience their formal religious affiliations has helped free me, and them, from constructing pat stereotypes of one or another of the religions. Each of the religions actually represents a great mansion with countless rooms. What follows is a brief description of the several types of believers who tend to inhabit each of these particular religious mansions and who show up in my course time and time again:

• *Orthodox believers* come in all religious and philosophical stripes. With only a few disturbing exceptions, they usually remain humble but unyielding in their claims to be in possession of an absolute, revealed truth that most of their classmates and I obviously lack. The core leitmotif for the orthodoxy story is this: there is a Truth that is unimpeachable, immutable, and final, and it can only be found in a particular book, institution, prophet, or movement. The mission of the orthodox believer is to deliver this Truth to others as an act of love and generosity.

• *Mainline believers* constitute a very large group of college students. These students are neither excessively conservative nor avant-garde. They dislike authoritarianism in religion as much as they dislike faddism. They prefer a life of worship that balances traditions, standards, self-discipline, and moral conscience with a degree of personal freedom, biblical latitude, and the *joie de vivre* of close community life. Often they remain in the Catholic and Protestant churches (and temples) of their parents and grandparents. They are the proud holdouts against postmodernity and the religious experimentation and deconstruction that so often accompany it. The controlling theme in the mainline narrative is this: people need an organized, sacred space, one that provides clear boundaries between the sacred and the profane, a stable support community, a sense of order, and a moral bulwark against the excesses of secularism.

• *Wounded believers* include those students who define their religious experience mainly as a reaction to the physical and mental abuse (often perpetuated in the *name* of religion) that they have suffered at the hands of hypocritical, overzealous clergy, lovers, parents, relatives, and friends. Wounded believers, for the most part, are more than willing to share their self-disclosing narratives of suffering, denial, reconciliation in some cases, and eventual healing. The thematic thread that winds throughout all wounded belief narratives is this question: If there is a good, all-loving God, why has there been so much unbearable pain in my life?

• *Mystics* remind us continually that more often than not a genuine faith requires a discerning silence on the part of the believer, instead of a learned, theological disquisition. Some turn to the East, some to alternative American religions, some to folk religions, and some to private forms of spirituality. Most express a love for mystery, stillness, and attunement that eludes those of us who too easily fit the stereotype of the fitful, ambitious, hard-driving Westerner. At the heart of the mysticism narrative is this motif: the transcendent is best experienced, not through idle chatter or abstract concepts, but by way of meditation, mindfulness, and, above all, a pervasive calmness.

• *Social justice activists* urge us throughout the semester to consider the possibility that believers must be responsible for building the Kingdom of God in the here and now, rather than waiting for some distant paradise to come. They advocate an activist faith dedicated to the liberation of oppressed peoples, equal rights and social justice for all, and radical social transformation marked by full democratic participation in decision making. For them, religious leaders are judged to be effective only according to their commitment to bring about massive social reform in behalf of the least among us. The common theme in the activism narrative is this: religion makes the most sense whenever it tells a story of human rights and social transformation, whenever it invites believers to criticize existing structures of power and privilege, such as the wealthy, white, male hierarchies in the churches, universities, businesses, media, and government.

• *Existential humanists* refuse to turn to the supernatural in order to escape from the difficult responsibilities of individual freedom. For them, a humanistic, "self-centered" ethic can stand on its own as a defensible way of a person's being in the world and living an authentic human life. What is necessary is that all of us confront the inescapable fact of our human finitude and make a conscious choice to create ourselves through our daily projects—that is, through our courageous strivings to make meaning in an absurd universe. The recurring idea in the existential humanism story is this: the stark truth is that God has forever disappeared—if He ever existed in the first place—and now it is up to us to get on with our lives.

• *Postmodern skeptics* are also deeply suspicious of any and all religious claims to absolute truth. But unlike the existential humanists, they reject the existence of an unsituated, context-free self or soul. As committed moral relativists, they openly challenge religious and moral certitudes, ethical universals, and grand spiritual narratives. The leading theme in the postmodern skepticism narrative is this: an informed sense of contingency, irony, and doubt, and a willingness to repudiate religiously grounded, patriarchal systems of social domination are what make us truly human and our lives truly worth living.

• *Scientific empiricists*, though genuinely open to the possible existence of a cosmological God who created the universe, nevertheless argue that the evidence of astrophysics, organic evolution, biology, and the brain sciences effectively contravenes this hypothesis. No empirical evidence is able to establish incontrovertible proof of a supernatural power greater than nature or ourselves. But neither can the alleged existence of a transcendental power be controverted scientifically. The core of the scientific empiricism story is this: we are utterly alone in the universe, beyond final divine revelations and interventions, and are left to our own human devices, accompanied by the findings of science, to create a better world for everyone.

Individual representatives of each of these types always have a powerful religious story to tell throughout the term. I try to honor their narratives as respectfully as I can in every class that I teach. I feel privileged that I am able to spend fifteen intense weeks each semester with such stimulating people. Each of these truth seekers demonstrates in every class meeting that the search for meaning is never ending and persistent, even though at times it might exist just below the surface. This multidimensional search also shows that it is virtually impossible for any analyst to adequately capture the complexities and nuances of the distinct religious narratives in an easy, catch-all way. Thus it is my double intention in offering my course to try to maintain the wonderful distinctiveness of my students' religious stories while also encouraging them to recognize the uniqueness of the religious views of others. This, for me, is what religious pluralism should be about in the university classroom.

RETURNING TO THE AMBUSH

What did I do to get us back on the moral conversation track in the seminar that I described at the beginning of this chapter? Once I got out of my perseverating, self-punishing, teacherly funk, I went directly to the students at the very next class meeting. I wanted us to talk honestly together about what was going wrong in our group process, and how we might correct it. I also wanted us to talk about what was going right. In short, I decided to accentuate the positive initially before we accentuated the negative. For a very long time in my teaching, I have believed that *how* we talk to each other about the content in a seminar is as important as the content itself. I have had students who sound as if they have read everything in the religious studies universe, but if these people are intent merely on wielding their knowledge like a deadly rapier in order to pile up the bodies of other conversationalists, they will be no help to us or to themselves. This holds also for the cynics, the True Believers, the ridiculers, and the Unbelievers who manage to show up in my course each term and want to use it mainly as a platform for promulgating their own brands of absolutism.

They, like all the rest of us, must learn to talk softly and let their behavior, not their rhetoric, reflect their knowledge and passion for the content. I often say to these people, "Ask a question; don't give a lecture. And make sure that your question doesn't conceal your answer. Keep it genuinely open ended. You will only look good to the rest of us to the extent that you make us look good. Make *us* look bad, and *you* look bad. And please know that I am giving myself the same advice even as I give it to you."

And so without hesitation, I started the conversation the following week with these comments (see Nash, 2001b):

"We will be spending many more weeks together talking about religious pluralism. I, for one, do not want to engage in mortal combat with anyone during this time, and I do not believe any of you do either. I also know that most of you genuinely want to be here, but you may not know how to address this material without inadvertently harming yourselves or others. Perhaps you fear the volatility of the content. I know I do in some ways. But I am convinced that we can salvage a great deal from the time we have already spent together, and that it will only get better if we renew our commitment to be here.

"What, in your opinion, might we do to make the last half of our course something we can look forward to? I know that many of you do not like the way things have been going with us, especially during our unit on Islam. What do you think, if anything, might already be working in our seminar, and what, in your mind, needs some more work? We have two more religious narratives to cover, each of which has its strong proponents and opponents—evangelical Christianity and secular humanism. How can we talk about each in the best spirit of moral conversation without hurting one another in the process?" (p. 179).

I worked very hard that class to get the entire group into a problem-solving mode. I wanted them to understand that the only way our remaining weeks together would be satisfying and productive would be to arrive at some general guidelines and ground rules for engaging in moral conversation during the remaining weeks of the term (I discuss these guidelines in Nash, 2001b, pp. 171–172). Here is what collectively we came up with:

- Revisit the principles of moral conversation during each and every class, if only briefly. These principles are at once the most important guidelines for constructive exchange of ideas about religious pluralism, but also the easiest to set aside when the conversation gets heated and the stakes get higher.
- Remember to ask these four questions at all times while others speak:

1. "How do the speaker's own background beliefs influence the religious story being told?"
2. "What exactly is the religious story that the speaker is telling?"
3. "What do I think is the religious narrative's special appeal to its believers?"
4. "What, in my opinion, are the narrative's strengths and weaknesses as I listen to the speaker's account?"

- Refer to specific passages and proof texts from the assigned readings as often as possible during class conversation, and always with an intention to "unpack" these in your own language.
- After the midclass break, where appropriate, remind us to revisit issues raised during the first half of class. Understand, however, that because of time and content constraints, several issues each week will necessarily be left up in the air for you to explore on your own time.
- Remember always to talk to each other, instead of having a two-way conversation with the instructor during class time. But do not forget that the instructor is also a member of the group.

Occasionally a conversation with him is appropriate, particularly when reacting to something he says, and vice versa.

• Keep this in mind: we are all responsible for each other's success. One of our duties during the conversation is to make each other look smart, not stupid, and this includes you, the authors, and me. Who among us is truly an expert in this material? Scholars write in order to become more learned; at its best, the act of writing leads to learning, which may or may not lead to expertise. Students read, talk, and write in order to learn more about the things they do not know but would like to. Instructors write, read, talk, and above all listen, because they have as great a need as anyone to dig more deeply into what they think they know, and to be able to voice this a little more clearly and with a little more compassion and humility.

• E-mails outside of class time can be considered an essential part of our moral conversation this semester. E-mails are one way of extending and enlarging the conversation beyond the three hours of class time each week, particularly when they do not degenerate into insidious gossip and chronic complaining. Learn how to use the listserv when you want to include all of us in the conversation. A good rule of thumb for e-mails: Would you want the comments in your messages to each other to be printed on the front page of the *Burlington Free Press* the next morning?

• Understand that each of us is a genuine seeker, even though, at times, it might appear that we have already made up our minds. Here is another rule of thumb: the more heated someone's comment, the more intense someone's search. Few of us have made up our minds once and for all on religious matters. Thus we need to treat each other with exquisite respect and sensitivity. Critique and feedback, when appropriate, ought always to come out of a framework of generosity and empathy, and always with an intention to make the other person look good. Faith, whether sacred or secular, is always delicate.

• Realize that spirited and candid religious inquiry is more likely to occur when conversationalists feel safe and supported to speak their truths to others. In matters of religion and spirituality, the *receptive mode* of listening and responding in moral conversation is far more effective than the *attack mode*.

CULTIVATING A CLASSROOM CLIMATE FOR MORAL CONVERSATION

"We listened, and through that listening a dynamic of its own developed. The end result . . . was a group spirit and group coherence stronger than any I have ever known, yet it was a 'dance with many dancers,' a group of individuals who had found an emergent reality drawing our differences into a meaningful whole" (Zohar and Marshall, 1994).

In moral conversation, creating a climate of safety is everything. Understand that by "safe" I do not mean dull, comfortable, wishy-washy, touchy-feely, anything goes, or involving no risk. Rather, safety is more about offering my students a "safe-conduct pass." This pass promises that no matter how unpopular or unorthodox their views may be, my students can always expect to be respected, listened to, and, even, in many cases, affirmed for their courage in taking the religious road less traveled—whatever that might be. A climate of safety, then, frees up conversationalists to take some risks, to be forthright, but, most of all, to express an honest feeling. Sadly, too often the academy considers feelings to be mere illnesses, following Immanuel Kant's advice that rationality always and everywhere trumps emotionality because it is the "wiser course of action." Kant also said that emotions were illnesses.

I did not pay as much attention to my principle of safety as I usually do, before I handed out my essay on Islamophobic stereotyping. I moved away from the bedrock moral conversation strategy of creating a sense of group safety to a strategy of all-out provocation with little warning. For that one class, I made a decision to set aside the qualities that I believe are essential for having effective moral conversations: empathy; generosity;

examining assumptions and stories nonjudgmentally; building a spirit of trust, respect, and group cohesiveness; and, above all, fostering an ethos where expressing multiple points of view on religious topics is the group norm at all times.

Was there a way that I could have used my essay to better pedagogical advantage? Of course. Could I have worked harder in choreographing a conversational "dance with many dancers"? Yes. In reflecting on that class, I decided to return to some basic assumptions that I usually make about moral conversation. I will discuss them here as a series of reminders to myself: what follows is what I wish I had done the first time around in my ambush class, but managed to do later by giving myself a second chance:

- *Build group trust, first and foremost, and avoid creating mistrust.*

I restarted the conversation about my essay by telling students why I wrote it. I said that I wanted to stimulate them, because I thought our conversations were becoming too placid and impersonal. I also felt that there was an obvious tilt against Islam in the conversations, especially from the feminists, skeptics, humanists, and social justice activists. Anti-Islamic clichés were growing more and more predominant. I wanted to stir things up a bit. I also acknowledged that it was highly possible I had made a poor judgment in writing, and handing out, what some considered to be a one-sided diatribe against all other religions except Islam. I then asked them to comment.

Generally, the comments were supportive of what I did, but critical of how and when I did it. Many students wished I had acknowledged my strategy for provoking them *before* I distributed my essay, rather than waiting until later, after the damage had been done. In a sense, in publicly second-guessing my own teaching tactic and admitting my mistake, I was becoming vulnerable to the group. I was also ceding some of my professorial control by showing that I was not a perfect teacher. My pedagogy, while well intended at times, was also full of holes. On this occasion, it might have leaked badly. I was human after all.

My confession of pedagogical fallibility gained a measure of empathy from the group. I believe that without empathy for one another, there can be no honest, trusting conversation between and among students and faculty. I repeated my signature aphorism: "Before there can be any *learning* in a seminar there must first be *relating* in a seminar. If there is no genuine effort made to forge relationships, then there will be no genuine conversation about religious differences. We will have only an exchange of monologues without dialogues."

- *At the outset, explain as many key assumptions as possible*.

One of my major assumptions that I disclosed was that there is an eightfold (at least) typology that I think exists within all religious narratives (see my earlier section in this chapter). This disclosure worked very well for my students. It clarified for them some basic assumptions that I was making about the heterogeneity of beliefs that exists within, as well as among, a variety of religious groups. It made the ensuing conversation about Islam an open, rather than closed, process. Students realized that Islam is as multilayered and pluralistic as any other religion, including the other two monotheistic religions, Judaism and Christianity. I meant my essay to get this message across. It did, but coming clean with some of my own assumptions helped even more. This time I exposed my hidden agenda and biases at the outset.

I admitted without apology that my own philosophy of religion was close to postmodern skepticism and existential humanism. In fact, if anyone wanted to call me an atheist, I would not be offended. I did stress, however, that I was a "gentle, affirming atheist," not a "militant, antagonistic atheist." I told them that I had four minimalist criteria for what constitutes religious or philosophical "truth": a belief should help the believer, should not harm others, should not be imposed on others, and should not harm the believer. Meeting all four criteria results in what I call a "pragmatic truth." Nietzsche calls truth nothing more or less than a "useful fiction." Obviously, these four minimalist truth criteria prove nothing more than the fact that you and I will be able to live together without fear of being hurt or humiliated by one another. This "fiction" is enough for me.

One significant content learning that emerged for students, according to their feedback later, was that it is almost impossible to understand what someone believes by simply hearing a conventional religious term used to describe a particular affiliation. In fact, some believers are mystics; some are orthodox or mainstream; and some are even postmodern skeptics or wounded believers. Those students in my class who were pluralists got my intent immediately. Others were patient enough to give me a chance to make my case, because no longer did they think I had a special agenda to impose on them. And, equally important, we were able to expose those simplistic stereotypes that abound in the American press whenever it emphasizes one or another distortion of Islamic belief and practice.

- **Be up front at the very beginning about the purposes of the course.**

I was very clear with my students that for the duration of the semester, we were not going to shut off difficult conversation or come to final, unquestioned conclusions or be pressured to forge concrete solutions or engage in consensual decision making (unlike the Interfaith Peacebuilding Objective described in Smoch, 2002). Our course would be primarily self-interrogating, self-disclosing, and, as important, self-informing. The course would ideally include equal amounts of personal discovery, content learning, and interpersonal relating.

I reiterated my belief that learning is best understood as an ongoing process, a flowing series of open-ended questions, and a resistance to anyone who tries to force premature closure on all the great existential issues of meaning. Most students appreciated such an explicit public statement of my pedagogy and course objectives. I also included this statement in my rewritten syllabus: "There will be times when we must let differences stand. Or in the words of that famous Zen philosopher Trebor J. Hsan [my name spelled backward]: 'In moral conversation, we must learn how to flow, glow, and, when necessary, let go.'"

- *Find the stories, and you find the person. Find the person, and you find a particular take on religious truth. Find the particular take on truth, and you will find a way to live with the one commonality we all share that actually makes a difference: the inescapable influence of our personal narrative filters.*

We decided to work hard to listen for the personal stories each of us was telling that were probably being concealed by the speeches each of us was making. If we heard someone claiming a strong allegiance to one religion or another, we tried to get a sense of how one or more of the eight typological differences might have framed that allegiance. We also attempted to find the religion's emotional as well as intellectual meaning for the believer. We encouraged one another to show a little feeling for others' religious beliefs or nonbeliefs, and we promised never to question, ridicule, or make light of these emotions.

We also decided to take the time during the second half of the course to hone our storytelling skills, but, as important, to sharpen our story-*listening* skills. We learned from the failures of the first half of the course that the extent to which each of us feels safe enough to tell an honest story about our religious beliefs is the degree to which we will be able to engage others in the ups and downs of our unique meaning-making quests. Stories are magical. They are capable of enchanting. They are demystifying. They reach out and seize listeners. They make us appear both strong and vulnerable at the same time. What makes us human is our ability to frame and narrate a compelling story that draws people in instead of shutting them out. Storytelling skills confer survival benefits on all of us, if for no other reason than that they have the potential of maximizing, rather than minimizing, the number of friends and supporters in our lives.

One very special advantage in approaching a course in religious pluralism from a narrative perspective is that it drives home for students the force of one's personal context in interpreting a particular religion's representative teachings, practices, and traditions. Deborah L. Flick (1998) identifies some key elements in everyone's personal context, and these emerge more clearly as we listen carefully to the unique stories behind the formal declarations of religious beliefs. These elements include our special genetics, education, family influence, hopes and dreams, jobs, desires and ambitions, health, social class, politics, familiarity with other cultures, sexual orientation, travel, significant life events, and cultural "taken-for-granteds" (p. 60).

Another advantage is that the focus in a moral conversation is as much on the storyteller as it is on the storyteller's beliefs, on the storyteller's interpretive filter as much as it is on the storyteller's grasp of a particular religion's dogmas, rituals, or history. Although these latter three elements are important pieces of information for all students to have in a religiously heterogeneous world, what is equally important is for students to learn how to make human connections with those who have differing beliefs. They need to do this before they begin to judge the worth of those beliefs. Out of this exercise comes a strong sense of generosity and sensitivity. Out of it also comes the possibility of finding some narrative overlap in conflicting religious stories.

- **Be scrupulous about avoiding the usual conversation stoppers in a classroom.**

Daniel Yankelovich (1999) is very helpful in pointing out what he calls the "potholes" that make the road to mutually respectful conversation almost impossible to travel. These include, in my own words and from my own experience, the following: intentionally withdrawing from the group out of fear, embarrassment, or boredom;

rolling one's eyes in disgust; rudely whispering to others while someone else is speaking; giving and expecting predictable, knee-jerk responses to every question; calling for immediate action on issues (what I call the "action faction" that tries to derail genuine conversation by doing everything it can to circumvent analysis [what it disdainfully calls "analysis paralysis"] and unilaterally "calling for the question"); showing off by strutting one's "expert" stuff at all times instead of listening to others with an intention to learn something new; limiting one's role to being a cynic, contrarian, or devil's advocate; and engaging in special pleading at the drop of a key word or phrase.

There are many other potholes, of course, but these will do for now. What all these have in common is that each is reversible. None is so firmly imprinted in the mind that it becomes an irreversible, reflex response. Group training in how to identify and avoid these damaging mind-sets has proven to be very effective in my classes. Practice makes near-perfect in my experience. Most of the time it takes nothing more than for me to call attention to a pothole (including, most of all, my own), explain it, and then model its opposite. I also ask students to practice doing likewise—with one another and with me.

But all of this takes time, patience, and commitment on the part of every single person in the class to work on our own worst listening behaviors. For my money, however, working early on these potholes can frequently lead to greater rewards later. I only wish I had started the pothole training earlier in this particular semester, as I have deliberately done in other courses. But I also believed that despite my lapse, there was still time for each of us to recover and to learn the skills necessary for effective moral conversation around such a difficult topic as religious pluralism on a secular campus. Eventually, however, we did exactly this. And I am grateful beyond words. My class was too, if an avalanche of their postcourse e-mails was to be believed. And, in this sense, I became a believer . . . perhaps for the first time.

4

An Administrator's View on Moral Conversation from the Division of Student Affairs

DeMethra LaSha Bradley

In this chapter, I illustrate the need for, and benefits of, engaging in moral conversation as student affairs practitioners within divisions of student affairs. I speak from three professional perspectives: as a division member, as a student affairs practitioner with high student contact, and as a coinstructor. Thus I voice my opinions from a place of learning as well as teaching. I write this chapter from my own experiences, and I openly share insights on how to infuse moral conversation into the work many of us do as student affairs practitioners.

I begin this chapter by recounting an actual conversation that took place during a divisional leadership training I attended. I present this conversation to remind each of us of the importance of examining our own opinions and biases as we embark on the work of moral conversation. I then prompt you to delve into some self-reflection and assessment regarding the topic of social class. I go on to describe what I have encountered as nuances associated with the controversial topic of social class, particularly in the higher education setting.

I describe several social class types of the students I have encountered over the years, and I explain the social class narratives they often live within. I go on to share suggestions for cultivating a climate for moral conversation in cocurricular settings, and I introduce moral conversation as a communication tool in those settings. I then revisit two social class concepts viewed through the lens of moral conversation. I end the chapter by offering a to-do list for student affairs practitioners who desire to incorporate moral conversation into their divisional cultures.

"EVEN THOUGH I KNOW I DIDN'T DO ANYTHING WRONG, I FEEL BAD"

Each month, members of the Division of Student and Campus Life at my university come together for a daylong session as part of the division's curriculum on diversity and social justice awareness and education. The group consists of those individuals who have been identified as departmental leaders (separate from front-line or direct delivery staff). I always attend these training sessions with a bit of excitement and anxiety. I believe that when a person is educated on topics of diversity and social justice, there is bound to be an emotional response—and my response tends to be one of nervous expectancy mixed with a little concern.

During one of our trainings, our guest facilitator guided us in an exercise of recognition and acknowledgment of what voices were and were not present in our group that day. He instructed us to step into the middle of the circle after hearing any prompt with which we identified. Regardless of whether we were in the middle of the circle or still standing as part of the circle, we were instructed to look around and notice the voices present or not present in the room. He opened the exercise with prompts that I would categorize as "general group identification," such as racial and ethnic identity, age, gender identity, and highest degree obtained. As the exercise progressed, the prompts became more "personal-emotional" in nature, including socioeconomic status, learning disabilities, and exposure to alcoholism or abuse while growing up. Prior to this training, I had participated in many exercises similar to this one, but what struck me that day regarding this particular facilitator was that he inserted prompts that were asking for people to share information that was generally not visible.

His prompts shifted to disclosure of information that we may have only known about people by listening to their personal stories. He asked us, by our own choosing, to identify with narratives that many of us disguise quite well. There were disclosures during that exercise that evoked a number of emotional responses, with the majority of these outward responses expressed during the last group of prompts. Of the twenty or more prompts, only two did not provoke someone to enter the middle of the circle. The first was a prompt in the racial and ethnic identity category, and the other was a prompt from the socioeconomic and social class group. The facilitator stated the following: "Step into the middle if you grew up affluent–owning class–wealthy." No one in the entire group of sixty stepped into the middle of the circle. Later on in the training, during our debriefing of the exercise, the following dialogue occurred:

MANDY: I would like to share something with the group. I was going to step out when you asked about growing up affluent–owning class–wealthy, but I didn't, because I didn't like the way it was phrased.

FACILITATOR: Say more about that, Mandy.

MANDY: I live middle class now, by choice, but I was raised owning class–wealthy. I listen to the way my office colleagues talk about the owning class–wealthy, and I feel bad. Even now I feel like I'm "outing" myself as coming from an owning class–wealthy family.

FACILITATOR: You said you "feel bad." Unpack that for us, so we are clear on what it is exactly that you "feel bad" about.

MANDY: I feel bad, ashamed even, that I grew up that way because of how my colleagues talk down about people who grew up like me. I choose to live a middle-class life now, but when I was growing up, I grew up in a rich–wealthy environment. And sometimes I feel ashamed, even though it was no fault of my own. Even now, I'm talking about my growing up as if it were bad. But it just seems easier to be accepted if you grew up poor or working class or even middle class. "Outing" myself as having grown up rich is hard because of the stereotypes I hear from my own colleagues.

Facilitator: Mandy, thank you for being willing to share your feelings with us and basically challenging us to think thoroughly about who may be feeling silenced in our group, whose voice we choose to listen to or ignore, and perhaps whose voice we feel is less valid in our group when we talk about certain issues.

As Mandy was speaking, I began to think about all the comments I have either heard or said that could have contributed to how Mandy was feeling. As I looked around the room at my colleagues, I wondered what people were thinking. I wondered if there were other people who grew up like Mandy but were unwilling to step into the middle of the circle. I thought about what were the typically accepted social classes within the field of student affairs. Had I ever heard class-biased comments from colleagues toward the working or middle class? Or just toward the affluent owning class? What is the atmosphere around the topic of social class within our division and the field as a whole? How many of our students feel the way Mandy felt—silenced, ashamed, as having experienced some sort of social class bias—regardless of their social class status? I went home that evening replaying Mandy's words in my head, and hoping that as our training sessions continued throughout the next year we would have an opportunity to focus on the topic of social class.

WHO AM I, AND TO WHOM AM I TALKING?

I have held positions in student affairs for over thirteen years, as an undergraduate, graduate, and full-time professional. I have held, or currently hold, administrative leadership positions within areas of student affairs that are considered "high student contact," including, but not limited to, residential life, student life and student activities, and judicial affairs. The first two areas typically produce a large amount of student leaders at many colleges and universities. I also coteach a course addressing issues of higher education in the United States, and this course includes a unit on social class.

As I stated, I speak from the "high student contact" professional lens. I interact with students on a variety of levels, in a number of ways. As I address how to facilitate moral conversation, I keep in mind that many student affairs professionals supervise student leaders, as well as advise many other students. This mix of supervision and advising often creates a unique challenge for those of us who want to facilitate moral conversation. Our "face time" with students is not always consistent (unless they are employed by us, or perhaps are dedicated members of an organization we advise). Most of our interactions with students are over the course of one, two, or sometimes three meetings.

When seeking to understand how to facilitate moral conversation with student leaders (for example, the resident adviser, club executive board member, or student union leader), I believe that we can learn much about how to facilitate moral conversation from colleagues, like Robert, who do this in the classroom. Robert describes his moral conversation facilitations with consistent groups of students, who convene on a regular basis. He has the wonderful opportunity to build rapport with his students over the course of fifteen weeks or longer. As student affairs professionals, however, we know that many of our interactions with students (in the residential hallways, at the activities festival, or in the judicial hearing) are shorter term, less structured, and less academically focused. Our interactions must therefore be of high quality in short bursts of time. Having said this, though, I know from firsthand experience that moral conversation can be taken out of the classroom and applied to the work I do.

Silent but Damaging

In 2004, the National Association of Student Personnel Administrators (NASPA) authored the report *Learning Reconsidered: A Campus-Wide Focus on the Student Experience*. It urged educators to give high priority to student identity development (what it called "education for transformation") and the changing ways in which students orient themselves within the larger society. (See Appendix D for an examination of this document vis-à-vis moral conversation.) The objective of the report was to help student affairs professionals produce an ethos of "intentional learning" for their students. The report went on to assert that those approaches to teaching and learning that create empowered, informed, and responsible students cannot occur solely inside or outside the classroom. NASPA's call to emphasize identity development challenged me to do an audit of what aspects of student identities receive the most support on our campuses. Sad to say, exploration of social class identity was near the bottom of the list, as it probably is at most institutions of higher education. Too often, social class languishes in the shadow of the more conventional multicultural topics, such as race, sexuality, and gender.

The reason I am concentrating on social class as the "difficult topic" for this chapter is that time and time again in the work that I do, I observe that although social class issues can be silent, they can also be extremely damaging. Even worse, the damaging experiences students undergo due to their social class status are too often endured in private and kept secret. These injurious situations can be as simple as a student's not having money to participate in an impromptu hall pizza night, or being viewed as "elitist" because of the new car a parent just bought him or her. Students also experience those crushing feelings of anxiety over not being able to fit into college life, because it soon becomes apparent that they lack certain experiences shared by so many of their peers. How many of our students walk around daily with hidden wounds received from not knowing how to deal with social class issues? How many of our more class-privileged students inflict wounds on others and do not even know it? How many of us well-meaning student affairs leaders harm students (and even colleagues) through ignorance of social class identity characteristics?

Many of the wounds I speak of come in the form of unstated assumptions, as well as out of a beneficent desire to help. We make certain assumptions about what our students have access to (for example, cell phones, e-mail when school is not in session, fully loaded laptop computers), or how they live their lives away from the college or university. We also wound with our efforts to help those we see as less fortunate, for those efforts tend to be based on our own unexamined attitudes regarding social class status. Some of our most praiseworthy actions can end up alienating and damaging the very population for whom we hope to be resources. Authors have written about the "hidden injuries" of class (Sennett and Cobb, 1993), the ways in which "class matters" (Correspondents of the *New York Times*, 2005), the feelings of living in "limbo" associated with upward class mobility (Lubrano, 2004), and how social class in the United States protects some students from harmful judgments but dangerously exposes others (hooks, 2000). Despite the increasing mention of social class in the literature, it is still searching for its discussion spotlight on the college campus.

As we student affairs leaders strive to create cocurricular settings that are welcoming and affirming to all students, we tend to give less immediate attention to classism than to other isms (for example, racism, heterosexism, ableism). I believe that a large part of classism on college campuses is a result of its relative invisibility in the larger social dialogue. I am not saying that issues of class receive no attention at all, but my experience at two major state universities indicates that large campus dialogues around the tough topics of social class and classism range from infrequent to no-show. This continues to surprise me, given the growing amount of literature that links social class and its attributes, such as cultural capital, to student achievement and educational access (Anyon, 1980; Heyneman, 2005; Lee and Bowen, 2006; MacLeod, 1995). Who is helping our students understand classism and social class issues? Is classism less important, less vital, than other isms present on our campuses? Is it briefly addressed as an issue, but otherwise totally obscured by other issues concerning social justice and equity?

ADDRESSING THE REALITY OF SOCIAL CLASS IN THE COCURRICULAR SETTING

So how, if at all, is social class talked about among our college students? Where do these conversations take place, if they take place at all? How does one bring up social class in a conversation? When is social class recognized or acknowledged? The reality is that our students encounter social class on a daily basis in the college environment from the very beginning of their time with us. We can look, for example, at those students who come to our summer orientation sessions. In addition to all those who attend these sessions, how many are unable to attend, and why? On move-in day at the beginning of the academic year, what types of cars are parked on the lawns? Who has already preordered their books? How many, if any, electronic devices does a student own? Who has limited, or even unlimited, credit card access? Who can draw on a savings account? Who has already purchased furniture?

Many of my examples stem from the thirteen residential life move-in days I have observed through the years. In my opinion, move-in day is one of the best illustrations of social class membership on the college campus. (Tom Wolfe's novel *I Am Charlotte Simmons* captures this moving-in process extremely well.) Judging from the comments I hear from my colleagues, as well as from parents and students during every move-in day, I know I am not the only one who notices this vivid illustration of the "haves" and the "have-nots." It is during move-in day that students, along with their parents, receive their initial social class stereotypes. Some, sadly, never recover.

How then do we begin to bring up the issue of social class without offending people, without embarrassing our students, without making anyone feel guilty for having or ashamed for not having? How do we do this without pointing a finger at certain student organizations that we might think are biased in terms of social class? Why even bring up a topic like social class that, by default, touches (or curses) everyone who lives in the United States? Why not just wait for students to come to us with an issue around social class and then, as good cocurricular educators, simply listen and sympathize, and change the subject? What makes us so uneasy about addressing social class in the cocurricular setting?

Could it be because we really do not know anything substantive about social class content? Have we been taught that talking about social class is taboo, so we keep it in our cocurricular closet of denial? As bell hooks states, "Nowadays it is fashionable to talk about race and gender; the uncool subject is class" (hooks, 2000, p. vii). Or perhaps it is because social class is "America's forbidden thought" (Blumberg, 1980). Is it the last tough topic still fashionable to ignore on college campuses, because it diminishes in importance compared to all the other crucial identity issues that face us as a nation? Whatever the reason for its relative obscurity, I maintain that unless we begin to actively address the problem of social class in our cocurricular settings, it will remain a silent but dangerous enemy of our students.

When, I ask, was the last time you openly confronted an issue that touched on social class? When was the last time you heard a classist comment? How did you react, if you reacted at all? If you have never heard these discriminatory comments or have never openly addressed an issue around social class with students, why do you think you have somehow escaped the omnipresent curse of classism? I ask these questions because for all of us to benefit from moral conversations about social class identity, prejudice, and privilege, we have to start with an awareness of where each of us stands on the issue of social class. There are days in my work when I wonder if we really know anything at all about this subject matter. Or worse, whether we really care.

Defining Social Class

Recently I posed the question, "What is social class?" to twenty-one graduate-level students whom I coteach, and they responded with a flurry of answers. Most of their answers referred to a person's or family unit's access to income. But as I probed deeper and prompted them to look past the easy answer, I heard some astounding insights. We came to see social class as comprising specific mannerisms, vocabulary, and ability to access and use information—what might be called *social class capital*. Possession of social class capital means that one knows how to move about and get what one wants in this society. Lack of it leaves one powerless and disenfranchised. It soon became apparent to all of us that social class is the fuel that drives one's overall experiences in the world.

I began to talk with my students about the disconnection some of them felt from their family-based social class beginnings. We talked about their feelings as they began to delve into this topic. Many were shocked to realize that they actually had less social class capital, or more, than they had originally thought. We started to clarify a number of social class concepts, and we did so for the entire, very intense three-hour seminar. Whenever I address this topic with undergraduate students, as well as with other professionals and with individuals outside of higher education, the responses are pretty much the same. Some people tend to focus on access to income as a primary definition of social class; others readily speak to the idea of social class capital.

In the United States, the terms *social class* and *socioeconomic status* are used interchangeably. Although there are academic schools of thought (such as sociology) that see one term as analytical and the other as empirical, most of us think the terms are indistinguishable (see, for example, http://en.wikipedia.org/wiki/Class_system). Economic status and social mobility are seen as "kissing cousins" in the United States, and the perceived close relationship of these two concepts makes perfect sense, at least at first blush. After all, the majority of advertisements, television programs, and films scream the message that the more money you have, the more status symbols you are able to buy. And the more you own, the greater your success and thus the more worthy you are. Loretta Alper and Pepi Leistyna (2005) illustrate this assertion in their film *Class Dismissed: How TV Frames the Working Class.*

Even though scholars are unable to agree on a common definition of social class, if I were to amalgamate the answers from my students, colleagues, and others, I would say that social class could very well be the most significant determinant of who each of us is in the United States. It is a way for all of us to sort ourselves into dozens of microclasses based on lifestyles and careers, to position ourselves in pecking orders. The social class construct is an excellent predictor of how people vote, what religious groups they belong to, what schools they attend (kindergarten through graduate school), what health care they receive, what jobs they hold, what recreational experiences they enjoy, and how long they live.

Social class is so intrinsically a part of us that it is extremely difficult to tease out the differences between our particular social class—along with its unique modes of socialization—and what constitutes our very life. We live in social class narratives, and any revision of these narratives is indisputably affected by our previous socialization in them. Is social class, therefore, destiny? No. Although social class is an extraordinarily powerful determinant of our behavior, we all believe that we can modify crucial elements in every single one of our affiliation narratives. But we can do this only if we receive appropriate information and education, and only if we are motivated to do so. Socialization is powerful, it is true, but so too are consciousness raising, insight and discernment, transformative life experiences, and a resolute will to rewrite our primary narratives of identity.

If it is true that social class takes the form of access to money, language, education, looks, fashion, possessions, services, and work ethic, then who exactly are we when social class influences are removed from our identities? What all of us in higher education need to understand is that social class shapes us indelibly, because it is so deeply imprinted in all of us. It is the ultimate silent divide, often an invisible cage, in a country and in a national educational system that still advertises that we all can "make it to the top if we really try."

Before moving on, I invite you, as student affairs professionals, to ponder the following questions:

- When was the first time you became aware of social class?

- What feelings do you have about your current social class, or the social class of your family while you were growing up?

- What are the characteristics of one of the social classes with which you clearly do not identify?

- With whom, if ever, do you talk about social class?

- Does social class matter? If so, why? If not, why not?

- What expectations do you place on people from working-class, or middle-class, or owning-class backgrounds? What experiences, if any, do you assume they have had that might be similar to, or different from, your own?

I pose these questions because I believe that before we can move forward in teaching and conversing about such hot topics as social class, we must be willing to address some of these basic questions ourselves. We need to be open to the answers and *feelings* that come as a result. Some of these responses might not be pleasant. Whenever we raise these types of questions with our students, feelings are intense, tears are sometimes shed, and self-disdain or self-congratulation is often the rule of the day.

The Social Class Baggage of Our Students

Our students arrive on our campuses with many attributes and identities. They arrive with excitement, nervousness, and some degree of awareness (albeit small or almost nonexistent for some) about race, gender identity, and sexual orientation. They come from a variety of educational and social class backgrounds. What aspects of our students' identities are we likely to address at opening weekend programming? Or at the first residence hall meeting? Or during passive or active programs in our residential learning communities? Or on our campuses in general?

What I have observed from my own work in student affairs is that social class identities do not get addressed as deeply, or as openly, as other identities. Why is this? Have the negative connotations surrounding social class in the United States—where nobody is supposed to be any better than anyone else, regardless of their money, position, or education—contributed to its notoriety as a taboo topic? It is my opinion that as we look to make identity development a priority with our students, social class must become one of the primary identities that need further, deliberate exploration. This is going to be difficult.

When our students grow up thinking that social class is an out-of-bounds topic—or one that maybe doesn't even exist in an equality-and-justice-for-all vision of American life—why should the subject ever come up in conversations on the college campus? Hence we are left with yet another silent aspect of student identity, one that disappears almost completely from the cross-campus identity conversation. Occasionally, of course, conversations about social class do happen, but we rarely hear about them in student affairs, nor do we know how to facilitate them on a regular basis. This is a shame, because one of the terms that we so often use in student affairs is the guilt-inducer: *white privilege*. A more accurate term, in my opinion, is *social class privilege*, yet this phrase has yet to make a regular appearance on the cocurricular radar screen.

Our students are thus left to their own devices. They face alone—some in fear and trembling, some in total ignorance—those lethal stereotypes of certain social class groups that circulate silently on every college campus in the United States. Many of our students are dealing with the shame they feel because of their social class status, while others are coping with the newness of the topic altogether. America's forbidden thought (Blumberg, 1980) is also fast becoming the college campus's forbidden thought.

Victims and Villains of Social Class

When it comes to social class issues, who is the victim and who is the villain? One may immediately say that the person from a lower social class standing is the victim and that the person from the higher social class standing is the villain. This popular rationale is based on the assumption that someone, or some group, is to blame for social class prejudice and discrimination. Thus, as in many social justice programs, there is someone, or some group, for whom our sympathy is sought. In these programs, we are taught to name the oppressor as well as the oppressed. We learn how to liberate the oppressed from the oppressor by expanding consciousness through something we call "intergroup dialogue." We are often tempted to punish the oppressor by inducing guilt and requiring penance. I want to get away from this labeling mentality. After all, victims and villains are cardboard characters that society has labeled as being good or bad, right or wrong, innocent bystander or not so innocent aggressor. The real world is not this simple.

According to Merriam-Webster Online (www.m-w.com/dictio- nary.htm), a victim is "one that is injured, destroyed, or sacrificed under any of various conditions." A villain is "one blamed for a particular evil or difficulty." Using these stipulative definitions, couldn't all students be considered potential victims? Couldn't they all be potential villains? I put the victim and villain perceptions out here because these are the perceptions of our students that are common to the student affairs profession. After all, we are only human, and although highly trained to do laudable social justice work, we still come at it through the prism of our own histories, injuries, and stories. I know I do. I therefore challenge each of us to look into our own experiences with social class and to acknowledge where our own hidden injuries lie. I ask this of us as student affairs practitioners, because those hidden injuries (often manifesting as hidden biases), along with our political agendas, covertly guide our work as educators.

How then do these victim-and-villain perceptions play themselves out in regard to classism on the college campus? Who is alienated? Who is shunned? Who is made to feel shame? Are there heroes in any of these perceptions? Is it really fair to say that there are victims and villains of social class? Whom do we see, or ignore, whenever social class issues come to the surface on our campuses? It seems that one of the agreed-on myths in American life is that the United States is a classless society. According to this myth, anyone who works hard can make it to the top, thanks to the self-justifying assumption that we live in a meritocracy.

bell hooks (2000) asserts that the problem with thinking the United States is a class-free society is that no one stops to acknowledge that in a truly classless society, there is no top or bottom, as there is in a meritocracy, where those with more merit are in control, and those with less are the controlled. For meritocrats, this is almost an article of faith. Several authors have pointed out the irony of meritocracy, in that it is a system easily manipulated and dominated by people who already have access to wealth and affluence. For example, how many politicians are millionaires? How many are supported by the wealth of gigantic corporations? How many could ever get elected without the tens of millions of dollars that contributors with vested interests make to their campaigns? Who was the last genuine blue-collar, working-class person to be elected president of the United States or to the Senate or to the Supreme Court or even to leadership positions in most of the U.S. elite colleges and universities?

How we think the system of success works is informed by the "meritocracy myth," and its perpetuation makes most of us feel good—righteous, fair, and just. After all, if one or another of us is successful, then it is simply because of our merit. If we are unsuccessful, then it is simply because we lack the merit. Work hard, and we succeed. Work less, and we fail. Success is a matter of moral strength; failure, a matter of moral weakness. And if this is true for us, then it is also true for "them." Right? Wrong!

My Own Social Class Labels

While exploring the literature on the topic of social class, I have come across numerous microdesignations of social class—lower class, blue-collar class, working class, middle class, affluent class, professional class, leisure class, and owning-wealthy class, to name just a few. Yet I've also found subtle stratification within each of these classes. What I notice about these class standings is that most of them have to do with access to wealth and privilege, which is not surprising, considering that as I said earlier, many people in the United States tend to see social class and socioeconomic status as one and the same. I, however, see social class more holistically. Social class encompasses much more than financial means. It is a whole array of life experiences. This array of experiences in our students' stories rarely, if ever, gets addressed in conversations about social class in the academy.

In Chapter Three, Robert creates several religio-spiritual types of students who enter his religious pluralism course each year. Likewise, in this chapter, I will introduce some representative categories describing the social classes of students with whom I have worked during my years as a student affairs administrator in the university community.

Listening to the ways in which students endure the hidden injuries of social class, and challenging students to think about what feelings get intensified whenever it comes to social class conversation, I am able to evoke a wealth of social class stories. From these stories, I have developed my own categories of social class groups, all of which exist within and between the different social class standings. I do not intend for these categories to box in our students. Rather, I wish to broaden their perspectives, and ours, on social class identity in the higher education community. What follows is a brief description of the types of student identities that I have encountered whenever I listen carefully to students' narratives on social class.

• *Embarrassed students* do not want anyone to know what their social class narratives entail, and some students go to great lengths to hide them. They often leave out certain facts about the geographical area in which they grew up, what jobs they and their parents may have held, and other general experiences of their upbringing, including their schooling and recreational activities. These students tend consciously to omit pertinent details from their narratives that would expose their social class status. They carry feelings of guilt, or even self-mortification, because of the stereotypes that swirl around them regarding their social class.

These students strive to escape any stereotypes associated with their social class status by blending in as much as possible with the majority of their peers. For example, some acquire a cell phone because everyone else has one (even if they cannot afford it); some become fans of a certain style of music (while omitting their real preferences for other styles of music); and some do not invite family or friends from back home to visit them at their colleges and universities (for fear that their actual social class will be exposed by their guests' appearance or behavior). At the center of the embarrassed students' narrative is silence. This is a pity, because all too often, we never get to know the "real them." They are people in social class disguise, and this is the way they travel through their college experience.

- *Comfortable students* are just that—secure and confident in their social class narratives. Regardless of what their narratives entail, these students make no apologies for what was or was not available to them on the basis of their social class standing. These are the students who have very little, if any, angst regarding their social class narratives. They share their personal stories frequently and without any critical self-analysis of their life experiences based on their upbringing. Some of their comfort is due to their lack of knowledge about social class issues, but even when they begin to explore the concept of social class in any depth, their comfort level tends to remain the same.

These students are proud of where they come from, and they cherish the experiences they have had because of their backgrounds. Unlike embarrassed students, comfortable students enjoy sharing their narrative, because it is a significant part of who they are, and they are more than willing to proclaim it. The leading theme of the comfortable student is this: I am proud of my experiences; they made me the person I am; and whether I had a lot or only a little, I make no apologies, nor expect any sympathy, for my upbringing.

- *Straddler students* are torn between two or more social classes. Lubrano (2004) defines straddlers as "born to blue-collar families and then . . . [having] moved into the strange new territory of the middle class" (p. 2). Some of the straddlers that I encounter fit Lubrano's definition, because the upward mobility of education has placed them in a strange new territory—a different social class circle from the one in which they were raised. But other straddlers, though having been born into one social class, feel far more comfortable in another. These straddlers differ from those in

Lubrano's designation, because they *choose* to associate themselves with another social class. It is there that these straddlers feel a greater sense of comfort and belonging.

The dominant, recurring theme in the straddlers' narrative is the feeling of social class alienation. Rarely, if ever, do these students believe they fully belong in any of the social classes to which they are exposed in college (Rodriguez, 1982). They are often coping with guilty feelings of having abandoned the social class in which they were raised, or suffering awkwardness and embarrassment in navigating their new social class circles, or constantly having to prove themselves in order to be accepted in their new social class milieus. At times they might feel like imposters or posers, living their lives on the edge of being found out. At other times they experience a nagging despair, triggered by feelings of social class marginalization and ennui. Most of the time, straddlers are people without a "home."

- *Multiclass lingual students* function well in multiple social class circles. In addition to their familial social class experiences, they have had other experiences that have helped them in navigating multiple social class milieus with ease (for example, gifted and talented school programs, study abroad, community service, or preprofessional work experience). The cultural and social class capital they have acquired facilitates their seamless navigation through multiple class circles. This has much less to do with money and more to do with the ability to access a wide range of social class experiences. They have learned well how to exploit those different experiences as they move through various social class categories.

Unlike straddlers, these students feel as though they can belong to and participate in more than one social class. Thus they learn to speak the various class languages. They become multilingual in a variety of class strata. They pick up social class cues very quickly. At the center of the multiclass lingual narrative is this: the ability, as well as the desire, to be social class chameleons, living here, living there, changing class colors whenever and wherever this might be necessary. But unlike the chameleon, multiclass lingual students rarely consider themselves to be fickle or phony. Instead, they pride themselves on their superb adaptability.

- *Escape artists* select a moment in their lives (often the college years) to reinvent themselves in terms of the social class into which they feel they should have been born, the one with which they feel the most natural connection. Unlike embarrassed students, they do not carry around any guilt over separating from their social class origins. They openly acknowledge where they came from and, in the same breath, are likely to express never having had a full sense of belonging to their social class of origin. They just flat-out believe they would be much happier, and fit in better, with a different social class affiliation.

It is the longing to be totally comfortable in their surroundings that motivates these students to take on a new class identity. Unlike straddlers, these students do not look back or feel as though they have abandoned anyone. They embed themselves deeply into the world of their newly chosen social class. They readily and happily change their class identity. The recurring motif of the escape artist's narrative is captured in this assertion: I have always felt more comfortable with a social class that just happens to be different from the one I was raised in. I am not ashamed of my upbringing, but I feel that it is time for me to become who I have always felt I was.

I encounter students who represent all these narratives in the pluralism course that I coteach with a faculty member, in the residence halls and apartments I have managed, in the Greek letter organizations that I have advised, in the numerous judicial hearings that I have held, and in countless other areas where I have been privileged to listen to these stories. Each time I hear a story related to students' failures or successes with the continuing saga of social class, I cannot help but wonder how their narratives will continue to shape their college years and beyond.

I am compelled to share these types with you because they further illustrate the ambiguities and complexities of social class identities. My wish is that these types will remind all of us in student affairs to ask nonjudgmental, clarifying, genuinely inquisitive questions in our interactions with students around social class issues. In order to evoke the real stories of students' social class journeys, however, we must ask the open-ended questions, rather than give the closed-ended answers, regarding the difficult, sometimes ambiguous, travails related to social class identity.

CULTIVATING A CLIMATE FOR MORAL CONVERSATION IN THE COCURRICULAR SETTING

Addressing social class in the cocurricular setting is a unique challenge to take on because of the inconsistent, time-intensive relationships we have with students in our high-student-contact areas. However, the topic of social class deserves an environment (whether in the classroom, the judicial meeting, or residential life one-on-one meetings) where students can feel safe and be heard from all sides. For me, this is what moral conversation is all about—creating a space for dialogue across the vast differences of opinions and perspectives without setting up one opinion for victory and another for defeat. How, I ask, can we create an atmosphere that invites moral conversation, when the conversation may happen only once or, at the most, a few times? What are some ways in which student affairs leaders can employ a method of dialogue (that for the faculty is rooted in lengthy and consistent contact with students) and make it effective? In this section, I offer ways to cultivate moral conversation in cocurricular settings.

- *Be able to identify the teachable moments.*

In this field, we use the term *teachable moment* a lot. According to the definition from the MSN-Encarta online dictionary (http://encarta.msn.com/encnet/features/dictionary/dictionary-home.aspx), there are two parts to the teachable moment: the first has to do with the "responsiveness [of the student] to being taught or made aware of something"; and the second is when educators actually take the opportunity to further challenge a student about a certain way of thinking. These teachable moments can happen anywhere at any time, but they are most effective when we recognize them as grand opportunities to further develop our students. These moments do not need to be moments within a lengthier, sustained relationship (supervisor-supervisee), although they can be, of course. As the definition suggests, they are moments in time that provide an opportunity for us to foster greater learning and to gently challenge our students.

I caution you not to disregard the presenting agenda with which the student may have come to you in the first place. It is best to acknowledge that the opportunity for a teachable moment seems to be there, address the student's needs (for example, finish the hearing, attend to the budget request), and then invite a conversation. Remind the student later of the initial comment that triggered the possible teachable moment, and ask to hear more. Listen with empathy and openness, and then gently teach. Should the student elect not to accept your invitation of dialogue, gently teach anyway by planting the seed.

- *Plant the seed and let go!*

During a moral conversation training at the American College Personnel Association's Conference on Religious and Spiritual Difference, held in Burlington, Vermont, in October 2006, one of the presenters shared a wonderful story about planting a seed and letting go of the outcome. She spoke about how she addressed a lack of diversity among religious holiday decorations at her local gym with the gym manager. The presenter expressed to the manager that there are multiple religious holidays during the winter season, but the decorations at the gym illustrated only one. After diplomatically sharing her thoughts, the presenter went back to her workout, fully understanding that this was a private gym and that the manager had the right to decorate it in any manner she wanted.

A year passed, and it was winter again. The presenter told us that one day when she came into the gym, the manager approached her with the following question: "So what were those other religious holidays you were talking about last year?" The presenter had planted a seed, let go of the outcome, and, to her pleasure, the seed blossomed. Soon other religious decorations began to appear. In relation to social class, sometimes all that is needed from us is simply a brief but genuinely curious comment about social class background. This works best, of course, only after picking up key social class cues in our conversations with the student.

- *Learn to hear the unsaid.*

In his work, *A Week on the Concord and Merrimack Rivers*, Henry David Thoreau said, "In human [interaction] the tragedy begins, not when there is misunderstanding about words, but when silence is not understood." One of the major components of facilitating moral conversation is not just being aware of what is being said, but learning to hear the unsaid. If you have never heard a student make a comment about social class issues on your campus, does that mean those issues do not exist? No. It probably means that they are not being talked about in your presence. Or, perhaps, what is being talked about does not act as a trigger for you to interject another perspective for students to think about.

Through the years, I have learned to take mental audits of the opinions that are verbalized in my classrooms, in my staff meetings, and in various other campus arenas. I do this in an effort to figure out whose opinions, and what opinions, are being silenced. I listen particularly for safety issues. I look for anxiety and fear in the faces and voices of students.

Learning to hear the unsaid should not be confused with playing devil's advocate. Mental auditing is a skill to be learned for the major purpose of bringing multiple points of view into the discussion. Playing devil's advocate, more often than not, is a subterfuge for attacking an idea and dominating a conversation with show-off, argumentative behaviors. Remember the metaphor that Robert cited in Chapter Three about moral conversation as a "dance with many dancers" (Zohar and Marshall, 1994). In my experience, learning to hear the unsaid invites more dancers to the stage to enrich the performance. Playing devil's advocate invites one other dancer to the stage in order to out-dance those already participating in the performance.

- *Make it a habit to invite honesty into your discussions.*

As stated earlier in this book, moral conversation begins with an assumption that there is nothing inherently erroneous or immoral about any initial presumption of a particular truth. Therefore, we must be willing to invite all truths to the discussion, and actually listen to them when they arrive. Not listening seriously to an invited opinion, no matter how erroneous it might at first seem to us, is a guaranteed conversation stopper. Hence, while I ask you to promote honesty in every interaction with students, I also remind you that regardless of how it makes you feel, you need to listen compassionately to the truth you invited in the first place.

- *Speak up about what you notice.*

One of my favorite ways to engage in conversations about hot topics is to report on what I have been "tracking" during the conversation. Tracking is an activity that involves selecting a particular phenomenon in a conversation, perhaps a key word, an opinion, or a set of observations, and then actively paying attention to how that phenomenon unfolds in students' daily lives (Washington, 2006). Whereas the tool of learning to hear the unsaid focuses on general ideas that may not be vocalized during a conversation, tracking, and speaking up about what you have tracked, focus more on the individual narratives and opinions that are being vocalized but that go unheard in our conversations. In the case, for example, of tracking dominant voices, I find it necessary sometimes to simply say, "We have heard a lot from some people in our group, and I would like to invite those who have yet to speak to add to the conversation." This immediately clears a path for people who do not like to fight for airtime, and it also gently reminds the dominant voices in the group to leave some time for others to speak their minds and hearts.

- *Remember, safety first!*

Moral conversation, as we have written earlier, is a way to share vulnerabilities, make connections, and enlarge and deepen worldviews and perspectives. How can these things happen in an unsafe environment? An unsafe environment is a sure conversation stopper. I offer the following observations about safe environments: a safe environment encourages listening to all ideas, with the understanding that listening to an idea is not the same as agreeing with an idea; a safe environment invites everyone to treat each other as he or she would want to be treated. It is not always free of stress or disagreement, and moral conversations do not always have happy endings. There are no money-back guarantees when students talk about what is truly important to them, such as matters of social class. Passion sometimes has a way of creating tension. Remember, however, that tension in a learning environment can be creative as well as stressful.

A safe environment does not mean that we walk lightly and choose to play in the shallow end of the conversational pool. In a safe environment, we can play in the deep end, without feeling the need to be expert swimmers. Safe environments invite us to play hard without fear of being injured. And because an atmosphere of conversational safety can suddenly change, depending on the emotional volatility of the topic being discussed, we should make it a point to assess the safety of our teaching-learning environments frequently.

INTRODUCING MORAL CONVERSATION IN COCURRICULAR SETTINGS

The best advice I can give in regard to introducing the moral conversation in cocurricular settings comes from a phrase I heard growing up: "inch by inch is a cinch, yard by yard makes it hard." This mantra was used by many of my teachers when we were learning new or difficult concepts. I am using the mantra in this section to remind you that introducing moral conversation is best done in manageable steps, not giant leaps. I offer the following advice as "inches" for introducing moral conversation in cocurricular settings:

- *Invite colleagues to be "moral conversation companions."*
Begin talking publicly about your desire to introduce moral conversation into your work, and take note of who seems interested. Consider sharing literature (for example, Chapter One of this book) with your colleagues in an effort to further introduce potential allies to the moral conversation. Express your desire to work with a few people in hopes of introducing this concept to your students, department, or division. Do not worry about the number of past dialogue trainings you or your moral conversation companions have had. Although prior training can be helpful, a positive, willing attitude is perhaps one of the essential "skills" required to do this work. Having moral conversation companions also provides you with a cohort, so to speak, of individuals from whom and with whom to learn.

- *Early on, use moral conversation in a group with whom you already have a relationship.*

Test the conversational waters with a group that you already know and where mutual respect is already established. Introduce colleagues and students to the concept of moral conversation, demonstrate how it could be beneficial for their group, and be sure to express your own reasons for being drawn to this type of dialogue tool. Try to have the group identify an internal issue that needs discussion, and guide them in discussing the issue by way of moral conversation. Starting with a concrete social class issue, for example, would be more helpful than just talking abstractly about the concept of moral conversation. This can also serve as a great recruitment tool for moral conversation companions, because they will be able to see it in action.

- *Start with small issues.*

Moral conversation is a dialogue tool for all sorts of topics, not just the hot ones. It can aid in conversations about group disputes and in processing group decisions, to mention only a few uses. I suggest that in the initial introductions of moral conversation, if possible start with issues that seem to be manageable to you and your moral conversation companions. Bite-size social class conflicts are a good place to begin. I do not recommend that beginning runners just lace up their shoes and run a marathon; similarly, I do not recommend that beginning moral conversation facilitators take on huge issues. As you become more versed and comfortable with moral conversation, you can of course help others tackle hot topics, but I advise you to "start small and grow tall" with the topics you facilitate.

- *Practice, practice, practice.*

Each semester, when Robert and I introduce the concept of moral conversation to our students, I always remind them that there is no perfect way to engage in moral conversation. We must practice, again and again, the art and science of moral conversation in order to feel comfortable with it. We speak of the practice of medicine and law, because we know that practice makes for competence in these fields. We rarely use the language of practice in higher education, though. Is it because we think we are above practice? Whether we are faculty, staff, or administrators, aren't we all practitioners? As a facilitator, you should seek a diversity of out-of-classroom arenas in which to practice. Some days you will find that your practice flows smoothly (dare I say, it will go almost perfectly); but on other days, you will long for just one more chance to practice in order to work out the kinks, so to speak.

- *Solicit feedback, and use it.*

Remember to solicit feedback from your moral conversation companions and any other groups with which you work. Ask them to think critically about the moral conversation process, and engage in continuing conversation with them in order to make it a better process. Early in this book, we stated that the moral conversation is still evolving. Therefore, do not forget to solicit feedback and use it at every opportunity to improve your skills. Encourage the sharing of what worked well and what did not work well. Reflect on the process for yourself, and be willing to share your observations with others. This includes exposing your failures as well as celebrating your successes. Know that we are all rank amateurs when it comes to fostering consistently good moral conversations about the hot topics.

REVISITING TWO SOCIAL CLASS CONCEPTS

Earlier in this chapter, I explained two concepts that I have encountered in my work and observations regarding social class: the silent but damaging effects of social class dynamics and the victim and villain dichotomy. I would like to revisit briefly each of these concepts to illustrate how moral conversation can help in enhancing and, for some colleges, completely transforming, the conversational environments on those campuses.

Silent but Damaging

As we stated earlier in this book, moral conversation is an excellent way to engage in dialogues about controversial topics because it forces participants to come face-to-face with the ubiquity of pluralism in all aspects of their lives. For example, the dynamics of social class are present everywhere on the college campus. They are in the air that all of us breathe. None of us escapes the influence of social class by ignoring or downplaying its impact on our lives. Whenever we do this, it looms even larger. In a community that practices moral conversation around controversial topics, there is no room for silent and damaging enemies.

No matter how outrageous, or hidden, a point of view might at first appear, we must always grant it the right to be heard and understood. To prevent an open airing of all social class issues, either out of ignorance or out of the well-meaning intention to avoid harm, is to end up encouraging environments of shame, distrust, and disregard. We do not need these environments on college campuses; they are directly antithetical to the principle of free and unabashedly open intellectual inquiry in the academy.

Moral conversation has a unique way of drawing attention to the squelching of particular points of view in college discussions. Shared stories that echo one another do not always mean that we have a homogenous group of students. Often this sameness is an indication that we have wittingly or unwittingly silenced certain individuals in our groups. Listening for the unsaid and speaking up about it are ways to avoid silencing unpopular points of view.

Victims and Villains

If there were a primary agenda behind moral conversation, it would be to eliminate the need to oversimplify or dichotomize the narratives of opposing viewpoints. The victim and villain dichotomy is not exclusive to social class, of course. There are a number of other hot topics in the pluralistic curriculum that feature dichotomous thinking. An atmosphere of moral conversation challenges us to deal with issues on the complex level they deserve. As moral conversationalists, we need to take every step possible not to breed either-or, right-or-wrong, black-or-white type thinking.

The temptation to reduce complex topics such as social class to a series of oversimplified dichotomies stems from our fear that complexity will make our interactions with others even more difficult. We fear that complexity will forestall expeditious decision making. Complexity will keep us from arriving at simple solutions. We will be immobilized by our spinning wheels, and we will get frozen in our analysis paralysis.

Standing against these rudimentary fears, however, I hold that moral conversation is conversation for the real world. What issues around social class actually lend themselves to simple formulas of understanding? Social class lines too often get blurred. Formulaic definitions of social class always fail to capture important nuances, and they privilege particular points of view. Nothing is ever simple about social class, because so much is invisible to the naked eye.

Challenging dichotomous thinking is a major implication of the golden rule of moral conversation: be willing to find the truth in what you oppose and the error in what you espouse . . . at least initially. Failing to follow this rule creates a breeding ground for simplistic, dichotomous thought. Our golden rule encourages an environment of open-minded, investigative listening. It urges us to question one another for further understanding and, at the very least, to be open to the possibility that even a kernel of truth might be found in a position one firmly opposes.

PREPARING A DIVISION OF STUDENT AFFAIRS FOR MORAL CONVERSATION: A TO-DO LIST

To establish a strong foundation for the introduction of moral conversation, I suggest that we look at our divisions in three ways: as the individuals who make up the division, as the departments within the division, and as the division as a whole. I offer the following suggestions as part of a "to-do list" for preparing our divisions for moral conversation.

- *Foster a sense of belonging within the division.*

As we have stated numerous times in this book, safety is a vital tool for moral conversation. Creating safe spaces within our divisions and fostering a sense of belonging go hand in hand. Be mindful of how individual voices are heard or not heard within the division and within departments. There may not be enough room for every voice to be actively heard at a division meeting, but if departments are also fostering a sense of belonging, the collective of voices should have a place to be heard. One way to foster a sense of belonging is to develop an overarching theme that invites the voices within the division to be heard. The University of Vermont's Division of Student and Campus Life developed the theme "Unique Voices Matter" to further promote their commitment to developing a divisional culture where individual voice is cultivated, valued, and appreciated.

- *Create a moral conversation curriculum for departmental use.*

It is important not to assume that the leadership within our divisions is already equipped with the knowledge to facilitate conversations or teach others about the controversial topics we encounter. I make the assertion that many of our divisional leaders are diversity and social justice *advocates*, but they are not all diversity and social justice *educators*. The former role speaks to a leader's willingness to express and support social justice beliefs, whereas the latter role speaks to a leader's ability to help others learn about and understand the meaning and implementation of social justice. Creating a moral conversation curriculum for our departments provides those leaders who are not social justice educators with the tools they will need to start social justice conversations within their departments. By the same token, such a curriculum will provide those leaders who *are* social justice educators with a sense of the hot topics the division hopes to emphasize, so that they can better help others facilitate conversations about them.

- *Address the power dynamics.*

In preparing our divisions for moral conversation, we must directly address the power dynamics within them. Although moral conversation is a dialogue tool that encourages all voices to enter the conversation, we cannot ignore the power dynamics that may deter some voices from entering the process. This will require the exploration of such questions as these: Who feels comfortable speaking their truth to those in upper leadership in your division? How are those voices outside of department leadership (for example, frontline staff) encouraged to participate in the process? Answering these questions will help divisions assess where they will need to start in performing moral conversation work. Although it is true that power dynamics will always exist within the political realities of higher education, it is also true that directly addressing them will help reduce their impact.

- *Frame feedback as a tool for improvement within the division.*

How is feedback used within your division and department? Is it used as a tool for improvement, or is it a voice of power? Is feedback solicited in your division as a way to assess a process and improve it, or is it used selectively merely to justify divisional and departmental decisions? Framing feedback as a tool for improvement, as opposed to a rubber stamp for maintaining divisional power, is crucial when preparing for moral conversation. Assessing, and even adjusting, how we will use the feedback we solicit in our divisions will assist us in creating a culture in which every unique voice matters. Being proactive in demonstrating how feedback has informed and improved our processes toward the facilitation of moral conversation builds a stronger commitment from all leaders within our divisions.

- *Be realistic.*

If, as some behavioral research claims, it takes twenty-one days for an individual to form a new habit, imagine the amount of time it will take to change or realign an entire divisional culture. Being realistic also comes with the caveats of being patient and understanding and of daring to be different. Most important, the idea of being realistic allows for us to be gentle with ourselves as we prepare for this kind of work. It also reminds us to develop clear benchmarks in order to assess our progress. As we strive to be realistic in our work, we should seek outside consultation to help us agree on the shared meaning of what ought to be realistic. Outside voices can challenge us to be more aggressive with some of our goals and more realistic with our benchmarks.

The work of creating environments of moral conversation is not easy. It takes dedication, affirmation, and a willingness to think far outside the box. What makes me passionate about this work are the possibilities that unfold when there is a climate and a culture of open, accessible, and inviting conversation. Our students will reap the benefits, and so will we as student affairs professionals.

5

A Senior Administrator's Systemic View on Facilitating Moral Conversations Across Campus

Arthur W. Chickering

This chapter must differ from the previous two in a fundamental way. Robert Nash says that the ideal outcomes for his teaching are "equal amounts of personal discovery, content learning, and interpersonal relating." For him the critical need is to create conversations that encourage those outcomes for each individual. So the focus, and rightly so, is on helping each of the diverse persons in his courses examine their own prides and prejudices and expand their understandings as other share their own explorations. For DeMethra LaSha Bradley, the concern is to help students participating in various student affairs activities to expand their self-understanding and better their understanding of others who differ. Staff development aims to increase their ability to work with students toward that end. But for administrators, at whatever level, the ultimate concern is the institution—not the personal discovery, content learning, and interpersonal relating of themselves or their fellow administrators.

Now let me quickly recognize that personal learning will be necessary for all of us administrators, but that will not be sufficient. The challenge for administrators—educational leaders—is to create an institutional culture that welcomes and nourishes those difficult conversations. And this challenge needs to be addressed not only "at the top" but throughout the organization, within each administrative unit. It needs to pervade the entire organization.

Our ultimate responses need to be decisions for action that create an institutional culture where "constructive conversations" are the norm, not the exception. In reaching those decisions and in taking those actions, we will doubtless encounter challenging personal discoveries. We will need plenty of "content learning" about pertinent research and about promising practices and instructive mistakes at other institutions. We will learn about the particular internal strengths and weaknesses, resources and roadblocks, concerning varied initiatives that characterize our particular institution. We will need to become highly sophisticated about strategies for change concerning these emotionally loaded areas. We will need to build and nourish trusting, candid, open relationships among ourselves and with others that support creative ventures, risk taking, and personal vulnerability. But while all this is going on, we need to be making tough decisions and acting on them.

That is the systemic challenge I am trying to address. Not only do we need to learn better how to talk with each other—rather than at each other—we also need to learn how to articulate achievable outcomes, build strong working relationships, and create processes that result in timely decisions and effective initiatives.

From this basic perspective, this chapter next shares two calls for action. One comes from a broad range of presidents supporting the Ford Foundation's "Difficult Dialogues" request for proposals. The second comes from a Wingspread meeting on religion and public life. Then I turn to the complex of intellectual, emotional, and political issues related to addressing hot topics at home, with all the time pressures and varied constituencies involved. Strategies for uncovering and understanding the mental models built into each of us diverse actors comes next, followed by specific suggestions. I close with a bit of historical perspective and some personal comments as to why I think we must address this critical arena for nuts-and-bolts competence and more broad-gauged personal development.

CALLS FOR ACTION

Let's think back on the concerns of the college presidents who signed the opening letter for the Ford Foundation's "Difficult Dialogues" request for proposals. They emphasized the "challenge of sustaining informed political and civil discourse" and the need to promote "open and honest dialogue . . . [in an] atmosphere of mutual respect, in which diversity is examined and seen in the context of a broader set of common values" and to promote "new scholarship and teaching about cultural differences and religious pluralism, while supporting academic freedom." They went on to say, "It is no longer adequate for student affairs staff to bear, largely alone, the responsibility for sponsoring and overseeing difficult dialogues." Rather, all constituencies on college campuses, including students, will need to know how to engage one another "in constructive dialogue around difficult religious, political, racial/ethnic, and cultural issues."

One "constructive dialogue" occurred in July 2005 when scholars from public and private colleges and universities came together at the Wingspread Conference Center to examine the intersection between religion and public life and to define the role that higher education must play in response to these conditions. They created the *Wingspread Declaration on Religion and Public Life: Engaging Higher Education*. It calls for improving religious literacy, for creating standards and ground rules for civic discourse on matters of religion and public life, and for responding to students' search for purpose and spiritual meaning.

Making timely decisions and implementing effective initiatives are first and foremost political processes—in the fundamental sense of that word. *Politics* and *political* derive from the word *polis*, which originally referred to the Greek city-state. More broadly, polis refers to "a state or society, especially when characterized by a sense of community." Thus one fundamental definition of politics is "the total complex of relations between people living in society." When we administrators create policies and encourage varied practices consistent with our mission, we are concerned with the total complex of relations within our institutions. And we are concerned as well with how those policies and practices may have an impact on the people living in our local, regional, national, and global societies. So the conversational and decision-making processes and practices discussed in this chapter are rooted in that basic orientation.

Political conversations, as we point out in Chapter Six, are often emotionally loaded, because they frequently touch on long-held and deeply felt attitudes and values. Changing those orientations may imply changes in our daily lifestyles, our friends, our community activities. The maxim, "Don't talk about religion and politics in social situations," has a good bit of logic behind it. Most of us have good friends and relatives with whom we avoid one or both of those topics so that we don't threaten the relationships. Yet in this book and in this chapter, we propose that under our current social and educational conditions, we will have to discuss those issues, and we must therefore learn how to do so more effectively.

A WINGSPREAD CONVERSATION

We are at the Johnson Foundation's beautiful, well-run Wingspread Conference Center in Racine, Wisconsin. Twenty of us have come to this fine facility, with its comfortable accommodations, fine food and drink, and all the resources necessary for meaningful, constructive, conversations. We are a diverse group. One wag notes that there are mixed nuts at every table—professors from varied disciplines, Senior Scholars from the American Association of Colleges and Universities (AAC&U) and the Carnegie Foundation for the Advancement of Teaching, and the presidents of AAC&U and of the Society for Values in Higher Education. We come from public and private colleges and universities, faith based and secular.

We gather under the topic of "Religion and Public Life: Engaging Higher Education." We will be here for three days to address the increasingly complex interactions between religion and public life and to define the role that higher education must play in response to those interactions. The increasingly potent and volatile forces flowing from tensions among groups with diverse religious and spiritual orientations in the United States have powerful implications for higher education. As we are all well aware, we are tangling with a politically loaded set of issues.

Our group has been put together by Nancy Thomas and her colleagues at the Society for Values in Higher Education, the sponsoring organization. With her leadership and facilitation, our task is to create a statement that articulates the challenges and opportunities and makes specific recommendations for follow-up activities. Our aim is to frame this statement so that all of us diverse folks can sign it. We adopt a three-stage agenda: survey the "landscape" here in the United States, describe higher education as it relates to and interacts with this current landscape, and spell out some basic action recommendations.

(An editorial note. All quotations are paraphrases of participants' comments. The transcript does not give the speakers' names, so no attributions are given except for the facilitator [Nancy]. In the interest of parsimony, these statements often come out as flat assertions, whereas the oral versions were more qualified. Indention and quotation marks indicate a new speaker.)

We begin by discussing how we will talk.

Nancy: "Do we need any ground rules for this conversation? The one I had a question about was whether people want any kind of confidentiality or protection about what is reported and how it is used?"

"Normally, if people are going to have direct quotations in a document they are asked if it's OK. Let's just do that."

Nancy: "OK. Anything else? Any other general ground rules for the conversation?"

"I hope we can be very conscious of how much time we are taking. If you think you have a lot to say, cut it in half and in half again, and then say it. We need to make sure everybody has an opportunity to talk."

Nancy: "One of the concerns I have is that when somebody is talking about the problem, and somebody else is talking about the solution, and somebody else is talking about what the vision is, and somebody else is talking about next steps, it would help me if we stayed on one or maybe a combination, to the extent possible. If it's OK with you, can we parking-lot other points and come back to them?"

"You made me think of another one. I am wondering if there is a way to determine who's next in line to speak. I don't know if there is a protocol or natural way to do it."

Nancy: "One way is to have one of us call on somebody each time, but I am a little hesitant to do that. I really want this to be a dialogue, not something where all the comments are directed back to me and then they pivot from there."

"It's a tough call. This size group is right on the cusp of having a queue and being more free flowing. At times people jump in when it is advantageous to the conversation because it was directly related to the point that was just made. If you don't allow that, then you undermine the quality of the conversation."

"I'm looking for a balance. Probably we need to be mindful that others may be in the queue for a period of time and check before leapfrogging over them. Or just yield the floor."

"I actually think that if we keep an eye on the trail on the floor at the moment, then that will help a lot."

Nancy: "All right. So there is not going to be a formal queue system. There will not be hands raised and being called on. But please try to be cognizant of what topic we're on and stick with it. Write in your own margins—'I've got a good idea for the next session'—and then be sure to come back to it."

We find these ground rules helpful as we twenty diverse and highly verbal college and university professionals tackle a daunting agenda. In our numbers, diversity, and verbosity, we are not unlike faculty senates many of us have experienced, nor unlike many administrative councils and retreats we have lived through.

Not surprisingly, the first thing that surfaces are our different perspectives, professional starting points, and sources of wisdom in how we view the landscape. The following comments give some flavor of those.

"Public discourse haas sharpened the split between the forces of religion and the secular forces in the society, where there is an individual culture."

"For a long time liberals happily accepted the distinction between public and private spheres, identifying religion as in the private sphere. It's not that they weren't religious, but they distinguished between what they were doing in public life and what they might be doing privately."

"Some lines of division that were literally taught and accepted by a lot of people have broken down. Some people have moved to shape a new framework, and others are still struggling, inarticulately, to function in that new environment."

"Religion doesn't belong to the right. We need to be careful how we align the traditionalist-conservative-cultural mores and not identify that as religious. Sure, it's religious, but so are convictions on the other side. People are not philosophers. They don't sit around thinking about public reasons as distinct from religious reasons. For most it's a seamless whole."

"But the rhetoric, I think, is religious versus secular. Many people on the right identify people we call liberal religious as secular humanists. That's how the rhetoric goes."

"When we talk about religion, we talk about it in the singular as opposed to the diversity of religions. Even within denominations and religious traditions there are various ways of looking at and practicing those religions."

"The black church in the U.S. has never been singularly a place for individualism or individual reflection absent of politics, absent of social impact. It's been used certainly as a place for personal salvation, but throughout the history of this country, faith among African Americans has been used for political purposes. So when we talk about religion, I would caution us not to look at it monolithically. I hope we can address it in its vast diversity and how different traditions interpret and make meaning out of this thing in their lives and their communities."

"The only way that individual particular religions have a space at the table is to have some ground rules that don't privilege one religion over another."

"Bill Moyers, in 2006, said, 'One of the biggest changes in politics in my lifetime is that religion is no longer marginal. It has come in from the fringe to sit in the seat of power in the Oval Office and in Congress. For the first time in history, theology and ideology hold the monopoly of power in Washington. Theology asserts propositions that cannot be proven true. Ideologues hold stoutly to a worldview, despite being contradicted by what is generally accepted as reality. When theology and ideology couple, their offspring are not always bad, but they are always blind. And there is the danger: voters and politicians alike oblivious to the facts. . . . An unconscious people that indoctrinate a people fed only Protestant information and opinions that conform to their own bias, a people made morbidly obese in mind and spirit by the junk food of propaganda, is less inclined to put up a fight, to ask questions and be skeptical. That kind of orthodoxy can kill democracy.'

"I agree with Bill Moyers, and I think that describes the challenge we face in higher education. We need to be a strong force fighting that kind of mentality and know-nothing simplistic opinions."

"One of the worrisome things is that democratic life needs to be characterized by dialogue, negotiation, compromise, and disagreement. Dissent is a critical feature of responsible citizenship. I worry that religious beliefs are crowding out what it means to be an engaged citizen."

"The religious symbolism and language, the apocalyptic moralizing, carries a huge amount of anger and resentment. There is an emotional vehemence that is very powerful and violent."

During this conversation we generate much more light than heat. We are enjoying each other and learning from the wide-ranging sources of wisdom among us. After sharing those diverse and complex perspectives on the current landscape concerning religion and public life, we turn to the landscape of higher education.

"I am wondering whether in our colleges and universities, and in the system, we do things that shut down these folks. Are there symbols, policies, procedures, expectations that tell them you are not welcome? You are not part of this. Like we did to African Americans and women, saying, 'Why can't you just be more like us?'"

"Yes, more like me."

"I think we operate out of a whole different set of assumptions that we are not even aware of. They are taken for granted and have been operating in an uncontested way for a while, and now they're being contested."

"Religion is very much a living tree for me, a living vine; it's not a dead letter. I contrast that with the way it sometimes looks dead in our society. We profess that one can find truth and goodness universally, and that's the basis of my teaching. But one can also find evil and corruption ubiquitously within religion as well as outside. So it's that kind of depth of perception, or moral values, that I reach for, not ignoring moral values. We were taught to do more than to describe. We make judgments, hopefully judgments that give evidence of knowledge, wisdom, and care for the world.

We do not serve special interests. We are to serve the world as a whole. Serving a broad constituency should be our aspiration."

"I think we need to defend the value, honor, and integrity of our vocation. I came out of my education thinking it gave me the right to have an informed opinion, and it enabled me to make some moral judgments in my area of expertise. Then I went forth into the world to teach and advise, and I discovered that the left didn't want my moral judgments and the right didn't trust my knowledge because they thought it undermined faith. So, one of my fears for higher education is that we are facing the loss of freedom to exercise the professional judgment we have worked so hard to attain. It's analogous to the way medical doctors lost some of the ability to exercise professional wisdom as they have to subscribe to HMO rules."

"We are accused of ignoring religious perspectives on topics that are important to society and the world, like intelligent design, for example. But not all faith-based arguments are going to be treated with the sort of respect given to scientifically documented realities. We need to bring the spirit of intellectual tough-mindedness to these issues. And I'm a little nervous about this "search for meaning" argument. It may be that students will find personal meaning in rigorous academic study. It may be that they won't. It may be that's not what they are looking for. But our job, frankly, is not necessarily to give students the meaning they are looking for or meaning that makes them happy or whatever. It's to be rigorous, serious scholars, and to pursue the truth. Students coming to school looking for meaning and not finding the liberal academy sufficiently meaningful may exist in great tension with serious intellectual questions."

"On UCLA's Higher Education Research Institute national survey, 75 percent of the students say they are interested in some kind of spiritual quest or meaning-making concern. We have students bringing more interesting questions than many of us have thought. Some of them are looking to reinforce their religious commitments. Some of them are engaged in religious struggles. Some of them are genuinely interested in a pluralistic environment. And so, as we're thinking about the role of religion in public life and our responses, we need to recognize that students are coming from very different places. The pluralism of their quest for meaning is very much part of what we have to take into account."

"My observation is that we not only addressed the religious divide but another internal divide in higher education. The divide surfaced when we talked about the goals of liberal education. We went through knowledge and intellectual skills, inquiry, analysis, communication, and so forth. We all agreed with that. We agreed that it is the moral obligation of the teacher to ask inconvenient questions, that this is the heart of our vocation. Then we moved to issues of social responsibility and civic engagement, and some of us became increasingly uneasy as we went down that list. Then we talked about students' spiritual quests and search for meaning. There were references referring to addressing this as 'therapeutic' and not our concern. So we are divided as to whether the academy should address the students' hunger for meaning."

So as we come to the end of this part of our agenda, it is clear that we have differing orientations toward higher education and its legitimate goals. We see different ways we are challenged by the current landscape of religion in the United States. But by the end of our time at Wingspread, we agree on the general contours of our declaration. We also agree on three basic action areas:

1. Religious literacy: What do graduates need to know about religion in a diverse democracy and global society? How well are we educating students for a religiously pluralistic society?

2. Standards of intellectual inquiry, reason, and academic freedom: How do academics preserve standards of intellectual inquiry, public reason, and academic freedom when faced

with religiously grounded assertions? How can the classroom be open to religious insights without promoting or denigrating specific religious beliefs? What are the ground rules for civic discourse on matters of religion and public life? How do we encourage civility, candor, and diversity of perspectives through our educational programs?

3. Students seeking purpose and spiritual meaning: What is the responsibility of colleges and universities to respond to growing spiritual concerns among students? To the extent that a college or university enables students' search for purpose or spiritual quest, how does it simultaneously hold to standards of intellectual inquiry and academic excellence? If an institution's mission includes a commitment to educating students for personal and social responsibility, is a spiritual framework an appropriate template for student development?

How do we manage to agree? Well, first, and perhaps most important, we create some simple ground rules for managing our conversations to ensure that everyone gets time to speak and to help us stay on topic. We do stay on topic—pretty much. We seldom interrupt. We try to be succinct and to the point. As we go along, we synthesize what we have heard and understood, as did the last speaker quoted above. We speak only for ourselves, avoiding putting words in other people's mouths. We do not make assumptions about others' beliefs or motives. We seek first to understand and then to be understood. We commit to the process, arriving on time and staying until the end. In short, we are competent, experienced participants in an intellectually challenging enterprise.

Second, interestingly, a process observer would find that we behave consistently with the underlying assumptions about moral conversations that we discuss in Chapter One of this book, as well as with the ground rules and strategies for moral conversations that Robert describes in Chapter Three. We do not pontificate.

Everyone, and every perspective, has the right to be heard and understood. We look for the truth in what we oppose—at least most of us do. We certainly do not have either-or, all-or-nothing attitudes. We share, and listen to, our subjective stories. We establish a safe space for discussing and then writing about very controversial issues. We keep open minds, and respect the diverse views expressed. We check whether we have understood correctly before adding our own elaboration or disagreement. We listen generously and do not question others' motives. All of us, apparently, feel that we have been heard and understood.

We also have an excellent facilitator and leader. Nancy papers the walls and windows with newsprint. She accurately captures—in our own words, not hers—the points we make. She checks and makes sure she has it right. This behavior recognizes and validates our contributions. The sequential sheets help us avoid repeating ourselves and help the conversation build even though the trail may wind and meander. At the end of each session, she scans the newsprint and offers an oral summary. When there is an overnight break, the next session starts with a newsprint summary for all of us to examine, amend, qualify, clarify, and sharpen.

Sharpening our focus for action is the most difficult challenge. During our various sessions, ideas for action recommendations pop up. Nancy parks these until we get to that point in our last session. As we repeat them, she lists each idea on a separate newsprint sheet. Then each of us walks around with a set of sticky paper dots, pasting them on the three action items we most support. After this little exercise, we take ten or so minutes in silence to reflect on what we have done. Then we discuss ways to aggregate some of the items, agree to eliminate others, and reach our final set. Nancy adds these newsprint sheets to her large roll from earlier sessions as the basis for creating the first draft of our declaration. We discuss final arrangements for the disposition and distribution of all the session tapes. We congratulate ourselves and part with widely shared hugs and handshakes.

We succeed in addressing politically and emotionally loaded topics to which we bring very diverse professional perspectives and personal orientations. Our success, in large measure, comes not only from excellent facilitation and group processes but also from our ability to talk about these hot topics in ways consistent with the underlying assumptions about moral conversation we spell out in Chapter One.

After we return home, most of us critique several drafts. Nancy, with great patience and understanding, creates multiple revisions, and we do end up with a solid document that is nationally distributed. That document is much more powerful because of the very broad and diverse perspectives brought to bear as we addressed the implications for higher education of the current landscape concerning religion and public life. The action recommendations provide the basis for seeking financial support from varied sources, and participants volunteer to help with some of that fundraising.

HOT TOPICS AT HOME

As I said earlier, I submit that the diversity we worked through at Wingspread will be present in our two- and four-year colleges and universities—except perhaps in narrowly focused, faith-based colleges—among administrators, faculty members, student affairs professionals, and staff. We need to learn how to work with these complexities. Unfortunately for us, we will not be facing them in the benign, elegant Wingspread Conference Center environment. We will not have the luxury of the emotional and intellectual detachment that characterized that time and place and the kind of work we did together.

Remember some of the hot topics we've described:

- Political correctness: outside "watchdogs," controversial faculty speeches and publications, student desires

for hard-hitting speakers, challenges to foreign and
domestic policies and local mores

- Identity politics: curricular content that questions
deeply held beliefs; scholarly research that probes inconvenient, politically loaded issues

- Ethics and morality: relativism and faith commitments,
opportunism, materialism, social responsibility, human
dignity

- Social class: exclusivity, selectivity, academic excellence, rigorous teaching, silence, prejudice

As we have noted, each of these hot topics is an umbrella
for politically and emotionally loaded issues: abortion, stem cell
research, family planning, intelligent design, civil union and gay
marriage, equal pay for equal work, health care, social security,
affirmative action—make your own list.

We have a lot going on within our institutions. It is hard to
anticipate when some policy, practice, well-researched scholarly
product, or inadvertent off-the-cuff comment will trigger principled
opposition or a personal grievance—and often a mix of both—from
a trustee, administrator, faculty member, student affairs professional, staff member, student, or parent. When this situation is not
resolved quietly and in a mutually agreeable fashion, when it esca-
lates and hits the street, it quickly becomes enflamed and politicized.

These conditions are far from the calm, cool, relatively dispassionate deliberations, lubricated with fine food and drink, we
experienced at Wingspread. That's why it is critical that we have
already learned how to reason together, how to talk with each
other, in the ways this book advocates. We in the university love
to debate, but the kind of dialogue we are talking about here is not
that. So we need to change our habitual culture. If we do not do so,
if we have not practiced, if we have not developed the discipline,

trust, norms, and habits—and especially the competence—called for, we certainly will be handicapped in our ability to cope.

Almost every significant institutional decision is made by a group. And follow-up action typically involves, or has an impact on, a variety of stakeholders. Leading group decision making that brings about changes in policies or practices is very different from leading conversations in classrooms or residence halls. As we have noted, those conversations aim to expose and explore different points of view to increase individual insights and understandings. They do not aim for, nor do they need to reach, closure. In fact, as Robert notes, it is important to realize that there is no bottom line, no final truth on which everyone must agree. But organizational groups do need to reach some kind of closure, even though it be tentative and temporary. We hope that group members and group leaders listen and interact with the kind of openness, respect, and forbearance that our underlying assumptions suggest. But that is not sufficient. We also need to hone the skills that Nancy Thomas so well demonstrated at our Wingspread gathering.

INSTITUTIONAL CULTURE

Faculty teaching and classroom conversations do not occur in a vacuum. The varied programs and activities of student affairs professionals are shaped by the larger institutional context. One of the most important roles for administrators and educational leaders is to help shape and sustain an institutional culture that supports and is consistent with the group decision-making processes and interindividual conversations we espouse. This is an "aerial view" of institutional change, and it is foundational to getting off the ground those cross-campus conversations about hot topics that we identify in this book.

In *Encouraging Authenticity and Spirituality in Higher Education* (Chickering, Dalton, and Stamm, 2005), my coauthors and I describe Beverly Daniel Tatum's approach to creating "a community where we will affirm and hopefully understand each other, not seek to convert one another" (p. 262) for Spelman, an historically black college for women. She believes that effective functioning as a religiously and ethnically diverse community can be achieved only through the practice of dialogue. She recognizes that this is particularly challenging where "many young people have come from religious communities that have claimed the 'Truth' as their exclusive property" (p. 262). She describes four critical ingredients:

1. *Living in proximity.* "When we live with people different from ourselves, we have the opportunity for personal connection through friendship. But proximity can also lead to conflict, so while it is a necessary condition, it is not sufficient by itself to lead to mutual understanding" (p. 262).

2. *Sharing personal narratives.* The sharing of stories, "witnessing" to one another, is a highly valuable pathway to seeing another's perspective, as we note in our opening chapters. Tatum calls for colleges and universities to seek opportunities in our curricular and cocurricular initiatives for this type of personal sharing and urges institutions to challenge students to take advantage of these opportunities.

3. *Creating models of cooperation.* Tatum observes that although students have often heard about and even witnessed acts of bigotry and racial and ethnic hatred, they generally are less familiar with active efforts to overcome this bigotry. To remedy this situation, she advocates creating and highlighting campus initiatives of multiracial, multiethnic, and multifaith cooperation. Such initiatives can occur in the classroom, through cocurricular activities and programs, and particularly through community service.

4. *Experiencing diversity.* Students can truly learn the power of a pluralistic community only through direct experience. Although the previous three ingredients provide frameworks

to create such experience, ultimately the students themselves must own the lesson. Tatum indicates that the greatest learning often occurs through the experience of "border-crossing," entering spaces where we are uncomfortable but have opportunities to learn through this discomfort. She gives the example of "minority" students' organizing programming at their cultural centers and inviting "majority" students to participate. Through such experiences, "the invited students are required to shift their cultural lens 'from the center to the margin'" (p. 262).

We also share President Diana Chapman Walsh's orientation at Wellesley College. She strives to create an institutional "ecosystem" that fosters "transformational growth, intellectual mastery, social consciousness, and spiritual depth" (p. 262). She defines her challenge as doing "all that I can to hold open space in which a community of growth and self-discovery can flourish for everyone" (p. 263). Because "in education the process is inextricably bound up with the product," Walsh asserts that "learning is nothing if not a messy process of discovery and unfolding. That means that how we as educators and educational administrators do our work—where we put our emphasis, what values we embody and express day in and day out, how we respond to the relentless pressures of time, of projections, of expectations, of conflicts . . . is fully as important as the outcomes we actually seek to produce. In fact, the process is the outcome in a very real sense" (p. 263).

To ensure that the institutional ecosystem provides "an education that liberates the mind and spirit from parochialism, and from ideology; an education that opens doors for a lifelong journey of learning . . . [and] of questioning assumptions and shaking loose of prejudice in an expanding world and in an expanding worldview" (p. 263) requires a special kind of leadership. This is a leadership that is humanistic, collaborative, and respectful, and that values and rewards individual autonomy and initiative;

leadership that supports the dignity of every person; and leadership that "authorizes, inspires and frees everyone in the organization to do their best and most creative work" (p. 264). This is a lofty aspiration. Walsh outlines some key elements from her own experiences to assist the work toward becoming such a leader:

• *Addressing adaptive challenges and accepting conflict.* In higher education, we are faced with significant challenges for which there are no ready solutions because they involve the unknown. We need to view and assess these challenges from multiple vantage points. Because we cannot solve these challenges without the inherent conflict of multiple perspectives, conflict becomes a resource for learning and for change. The leader's responsibility is "to guide the organization toward an understanding of its opportunities, to guide people into awareness of their resourcefulness in the face of ambiguity. . . . And to do so the first task of the leader is to clarify the values and the vision, holding the light of the organization's positive future, holding a vision of true health for individuals in the organization" (Walsh, quoted in Chickering, Dalton, and Stamm, 2005, p. 264).

Reflecting on her own experiences, Walsh concludes that to ensure that the inevitable conflict resulting from change is ultimately constructive, the leader needs "to gauge whether there is too much or too little pressure on the system, on individuals, and the organization, to gauge whether differences are being heightened in a way that opens up the field for a new, larger, more encompassing, more integrative vision of the future. . . . When faced with conflict, it helps to pay special attention to maintaining bonds: within oneself, bonds with others, bonds with the larger culture" (p. 264).

• *Overcoming resistance.* Walsh observes that when faced with personal and organizational change, some people are ready for it and embrace the challenges, and others put up resistance and attempt to subvert the process. The leader's task is "to look for the creative edge, the possibility of engaging the problems that people bring in, calling people into partnerships, . . . getting them to think about what it is that they are accountable for doing, gently confronting the avoidance of the difficult work of change, helping the community integrate and digest the ways in which the work that they are doing is enabling them and enabling the organization to learn and to grow" (pp. 264, 265).

• *Cultivating inner resources*. A crucial aspect of being a leader is that "it forces one to focus energy specifically on increasing one's own internal capacity for learning and for growth." The process of leadership can be personally draining, and it is essential for a leader "to cultivate access to regular nourishment from one's own spiritual roots and through working partnerships and systems of mutual support" (p. 265).

These two presidents exemplify the kind of leadership that helps create and sustain an institutional culture where the fires of conversation are constantly kept alive and where hot topics can be discussed without participants getting burned.

Mental Models—Meaning Making and Action

Before we turn to specific suggestions, we need to recognize and emphasize the importance of a basic human process. We all are meaning-making creatures. From birth we are trying to make sense of the often confusing, contradictory, paradoxical sights, sounds, tastes, smells, and touches that characterize our particular world. From our earliest years we create our own meanings, the emotional reactions that accompany them, and our behaviors in response to them. These meanings, emotional reactions, and behavioral responses create a complex of neural patterns, reflexes, and actions that become built in over time. The older we get, unless we encounter experiences that seriously challenge these patterns, the more solidified they become. Some researchers call these patterns *mental models*. That term is accurate insofar as it describes brain functioning. But it is important to recognize that these models also have associated visceral, emotional responses and that this combination of mental and emotional response drives behavior.

I call this interaction between our mental and emotional responses the "meaning making–action cycle." It works like this:

1. We experience external stimuli through our five senses: sight, sound, touch, taste, smell. (There are research, theory, and experiential vignettes concerning clairvoyants and seers that suggest we have other paranormal senses that we cannot yet identify and measure, but we will ignore that here.)

2. Depending on our preexisting patterns, we selectively accept some of those stimuli and reject others. That selectivity can operate at the level of the synapses, the bridges that link various neural pathways.

3. Input from the eyes and ears first goes to the thalamus and then, across a single synapse, to the amygdala. The amygdala has an extensive network of neural connections that allow it, "during an emotional emergency, to capture and drive much of the rest of the brain . . . to begin to respond *before* the neocortex . . . fully perceives and finally initiates its more finely tailored response" (Goleman, 1995, p. 17). The amygdala "mobilizes the centers for movement, activates the cardiovascular systems, the muscles and the gut. . . . Additional signals . . . tell the brainstem to fix the face in a fearful expression, freeze unrelated movements the muscle had underway, speed heart rate and raise blood pressure, slow breathing" (p. 17). So in terms of brain functioning, some emotional memories and reactions can operate without any conscious cognitive participation. That's why we sometimes act without knowing why we do, because the shortcut from the thalamus

to the amygdala bypasses the neocortex. "In the first few milliseconds of our perceiving something, we not only unconsciously comprehend what it is, but decide whether we like it or not: the 'cognitive unconscious' presents our awareness with not just the identity of what we see, but an opinion about it. Our emotions have a mind of their own, one which can hold views quite independent of our rational mind" (p. 20).

4. The neocortex responds. It processes the perceptual input through several neural circuits, analyzing, sorting and sifting among preexisting pathways, looking for appropriate meanings and responses. "Within moments the prefrontal lobes perform what amounts to a risk/benefit ratio of myriad possible reactions and bet that one of them is best" (Goleman, p. 25).

5. We act on the basis of the bet that results from this combination of external inputs and internal neural processing.

6. That action triggers another cycle of external stimuli and internal processing.

Thus, through these cycles over the course of our lives, we create our own realities and, for better or worse, have an impact on our relatives, friends, colleagues, and world.

These insights from the fast-moving research under way by neuroanatomists and brain researchers have powerful implications for learning to talk about hot topics without getting burned. At the most fundamental level, we need to become aware of and sensitive to our own particular meaning making–action cycles. We need to better understand their origins and how they operate in our daily lives.

Self-reflection, accompanied by "metathought"—thinking about how we think and why—is the basic route to increased awareness and self-understanding. We can try to walk ourselves back through the steps in the cycle. What was I thinking when

I said what I said or did what I did? What feelings accompanied those thoughts? What is there in my own history that is pertinent to this particular situation, these conditions, these persons, these emotional dynamics, that influenced my reactions and my responses? (The ten pluralism questions at the end of Chapter Two that aim to help us distinguish the *universal* from our *particular* belief systems are very applicable as we walk back through this meaning making–action sequence.)

It is rarely possible to do this reflecting when we are in the middle of any ongoing conversation, group discussion, or action sequence. The pace is too fast. There are too many things going on at once.

But it *is* possible to reflect afterward, preferably as soon afterward as possible. Use what I call a three-column exercise. Take a piece of paper and create three columns with the following headings: What I Said or Did, What I Was Thinking, and How I Was Feeling. Start with a very specific event and fill in each column as best you can. Then try to identify similar or analogous situations and see how those cycles may have influenced this one. The more we learn to do this as we encounter particularly challenging conditions or interactions, the more we will increase our understanding of the mental models and meaning making–action cycles that influence our perceptual processing and resulting actions.

BALANCING INQUIRY AND ADVOCACY

We academics, especially administrators and faculty members, have worked hard to learn how to be articulate and persuasive concerning our own points of view. We know how to share our reasoning. We are good at deflecting or shooting down challenges. Some of us are very adept at quick responses that leave an adversary groping for a comeback. We also have finely honed analytical skills. We know how to penetrate others' points of view and to ask questions that not only demolish the counterargument but lead others in our direction. Organization development and learning professionals like Chris Argyris, William Isaacs, and Peter Senge note that in group decision-making sessions, 80 percent of the comments advocate a particular position—and, further, that 80 percent of people's questions are really disguised advocacy. Most of us are not very skilled at asking nonleading questions—questions that truly seek additional information, that are neutral in their point of view, that try to understand at more complex levels without implying a particular orientation or answer.

True inquiry is especially difficult in the emotionally loaded contexts where we discuss hot topics. But to respect and act on our ground rules for moral conversations, we need to be on high alert for this distinction between inquiry and advocacy. The point is not that advocacy is out of order. We need not totally avoid expressing our own views. But if our first duty is to understand what we oppose before we advocate what we espouse, then we must know how to pursue genuine inquiry. Senge, Kleiner, Roberts, Ross, and Smith, in their *Fifth Discipline Field Book* (1995), developed a set of protocols for balancing advocacy and inquiry. They are consistent with our ground rules: make your thinking process visible, publicly test your conclusions and assumptions, ask others to make their thinking process visible, compare your assumptions to theirs, face a point of view with which you disagree, and deal with an impasse (pp. 256–259). The great thing about this part of the *Field Book* is that following each of the protocols are detailed statements of "What to do" and "What to say." They are very concrete and helpful for those of us who are not used to making clear distinctions between advocacy and inquiry. Check out this book and the cited pages if you would like help with this.

SOME SPECIFIC SUGGESTIONS

There are some concrete things all of us can do to help our institutions create the kind of culture Presidents Tatum and Walsh strive for:

• *Create a policy statement of ground rules for talking together and decision making.*

I believe that one of the best ways to start tackling these issues is to formulate a policy statement. Involve the full range of institutional stakeholders: students, staff, student affairs professionals, faculty members, administrators, and trustees. Give the process plenty of time. In this case, there is no urgent external force creating serious time pressures. Broad-gauged participation in wrestling with the major elements and fine-tuning the language creates serious engagement with the underlying issues, current problematic dynamics, and areas for potential future intervention. Expect to have—and welcome—multiple revisions; ensure that working drafts are widely circulated and that (where it makes sense) various forums react to its different elements. The final product, of course, needs to be jargon free, readable, and as tight and brief as possible, given the particular complexities that characterize your institution.

Policy statements laying out ground rules need to share some basic elements. Ensuring that our statements incorporate these elements will help us maintain our focus as we work to construct pluralistic conversations on our campuses.

Here, for example, are basic elements for a policy statement regarding religious pluralism.

1. They make a formal institutional commitment to supporting religious pluralism.

2. They recognize the educational value of open sharing and examination of diverse views, and promote interfaith dialogue.

3. They emphasize the importance of respect and civility.

4. They spell out expected behaviors, both positive and negative.

5. They provide special places and opportunities for religious groups and practices.

6. They discourage the isolation of religious groups into enclaves, even as they recognize the need for groups to have their own places and opportunities.

7. They support celebrating various holy days.

8. They believe everyone should be a good student of others' religions and cultures.

9. They designate a clear locus of responsibility for encouraging the educational values of religious pluralism and for monitoring on-campus activities and behaviors.

For me, improving practice is the fundamental reason for tackling the difficult task of creating a policy statement. The process itself requires that the institution be clear about what its "intentions already were." Very often, that process will identify gaps between espoused values and values in use, between rhetoric and reality. It takes solid leadership and committed faculty, student affairs professionals, and staff to bring those gaps to the surface, own up to them honestly, and admit them publicly. When these key stakeholders have achieved those tasks, they will have laid the cornerstone for addressing the diversity issues we all face.

- *Articulate some principles for good practice.*

By the time all of us have involved diverse stakeholders in creating a policy statement, we will have recognized that it would be useful to have some "principles for good practice" for conversations about hot topics. We will also have learned that it would be useful to have similar guidelines about handling group decision making. Our underlying assumptions in Chapter One may be helpful for adaptation. Robert's chapter from the professorial perspective and DeMethra's from the student affairs vantage point also suggest more detailed applications in those domains. See the step-by-step, how-to-guide in Appendix A for more details.

Nancy Thomas's behaviors, as described earlier in this chapter, may also serve as models when it comes to group decision making. There is an extensive literature concerning group processes and organizational learning. Although most of it comes out of the corporate domain, the basic conceptual frameworks are very applicable to our colleges and universities. William Isaacs's *Dialogue and the Art of Thinking Together* (1999) is one of the most penetrating and useful perspectives currently available. So it is important for all of us, I believe, to check out this and other useful sources.

- **Use process observers.**

Once we have articulated some generally accepted principles for good practice, we can start using process observers. Because all my teaching relies heavily on group discussions and varied interactive exercises, during the first class meeting I distribute a page that lists constructive and destructive participant behaviors. (There are standard lists readily available, or you can create your own version to suit your course.) Then I ask for a volunteer for each class who will take responsibility for tracking how we perform, and we devote the last five minutes or so of each session to feedback from the volunteer.

When I have been in a position to do so on various boards, either as chair or as a member, I have inaugurated the same group-process strategy. In my experience, this has been a very positive addition to our work together. It elevates our self-awareness about how we are functioning as individuals and as a group. It helps catch problem behaviors early, before they trigger unfortunate reactions.

- **Be careful about pacing; make time for reflection.**

For me, an important process issue is pacing. I have been powerfully influenced by experiences with the consequences of differences in the speech patterns of Inuits in Alaska with Anglos from the lower forty-eight. Alaskan natives typically let three to five seconds intervene after someone has spoken before responding, whereas Anglos typically respond instantly, as anyone who has sat through faculty meetings can attest. What actually happened as a consequence of this small difference when Inuits and Anglos came together in group settings—school classrooms, community meetings, decision-making groups, even in social settings? The Anglos believed that the Inuits did not know what they thought, could not finish complex statements, and had little to offer. The Inuits experienced the Anglos as rude, overbearing, and uninterested in what they had to offer.

So I take pains to legitimize silence and emphasize reflection. A fairly recent experience is etched on my mind. I was asked to give a keynote speech titled "What We Know About Learning" to open a three-day conference for administrators and faculty members from the U.S. Army defense colleges and universities. About 350 professionals sat in an elegant theatre space. Many participants had flown in the day before, and others had come from their offices there in Washington, D.C. I suggested we start with five minutes of silence to make the transition from their busy lives to this special event, to reflect on what they wanted to learn from it, or just to relax. By the end of three minutes you could cut the atmosphere with a knife. It took a great act of will on my part to hang in there for the last two minutes. I also ended my presentation with another five minutes of silence. That felt easier. Perhaps I had said something worth thinking about. On the evaluation forms, the feedback about these periods of silence was almost evenly divided concerning the opening minutes. About half thought it was a wonderful way to start; the others thought it was a waste of time. The proportions were somewhat more favorable for the final period. Maybe I am a slow learner, but depending on the setting, I still start and end workshops and formal presentations that way.

I believe that the power of reflection, and making time for it, is seriously underrecognized and underused in our teaching and in our group decision making. Bodily metabolism is my favorite metaphor for reflection. The food we take into our mouths and swallow becomes blood, bones, muscle, nerve fibers, and bodily juices only when it is metabolized. What is not metabolized gets vomited or excreted. In most of our teaching, we force-feed students and ask them to regurgitate. Many experiential learning activities do not call for serious reflection, either singly or with other participants. So it is not surprising that there is little learning that lasts, little significant contribution to working knowledge and competence, and little contribution to other key areas of personal development. I think we need to give much more attention to reflective activities as part of our teaching, advising, student affairs programming, and administrative decision making.

So, in my classes, I usually start with a brief period of silence. I say openly that I am comfortable with silence. I discuss the pacing issue. During classes, I often ask whether a person has finished. Occasionally I will simply say, "Hold it a second; I want to think about that" or "Let's take a minute to reflect on what we have been saying." This helps people whose style is more deliberative and helps ensure that everyone gets a reasonable amount of airtime. Remember Diana Chapman Walsh's point: the process is often the most important outcome. Or, as Robert tells us, in the long run, how we talk together is more important than what we say on any given occasion.

- *Encourage using the three-column exercise.*

Introduce the three-column exercise and legitimize its use. When setting the agenda for a meeting, schedule time at the end for participants to select a particular interaction and fill in those three columns and reflect on pertinent history. There is no need for everyone to select the same thing. The important thing is to provide a safe space and time for this particular kind of self-reflection. In some contexts, where there is high trust and openness, it may be useful for participants to share these reflections. But that will come only after individuals have had a chance to practice for themselves and the exercise has become an accepted part of the culture.

- *Encourage improvisation.*

Recall our jazz metaphor in Chapter Two. That's a useful way to think about group decision making. It is especially useful when we are trying to navigate the rapids of emotionally loaded, urgent issues. We need to hear all the voices, with all their tones and overtones. We need to find the harmonics that turn apparent cacophony into recognizable themes. We need to achieve some kind of closure. But we do not need a grand finale. We do not need to arrive at the best possible response. We are tackling very complex issues. Most of us are exploring new terrain. We will experience many unintended consequences. We need to stay light on our feet—if I may mix my metaphor here—ready to adapt and refashion not only our particular provisional policy statement or action but also our underlying assumptions and apparently flawless logic.

As Robert said about working with his students, there is no bottom line. There is no ultimate solution that will work under all conditions, through time, for all the diverse persons who may be affected. This posture eases the path to initial decisions, keeps us alive and learning, and generates much better long-range results.

- *Support professional development activities.*

The capacity to listen and converse in the ways we have suggested or to lead groups as Nancy Thomas did is not genetically determined. These are learned skills. Robert has learned through forty years of teaching, and as his example in Chapter Three indicates, he is still learning by reflecting on the particular dynamics he experiences. The next time a similar situation occurs, he will be better prepared to respond more effectively.

Nancy also has wide-ranging experience in leading groups. She studied with Chris Christensen, one of the creators of case method teaching at the Harvard Business School. She studied the art of facilitation and its relationship to leadership, organizational change, social action, and policy development by working with the Interaction Institute for Social Change, National Issues Forums, and Study Circles Resource Center (see Appendix B). She practiced using these skills as a professor and as a volunteer in her community, facilitating conversations on race for the National Conference for Community and Justice. Most of us have not tried to sharpen these skills with this level of intentionality. If we take them seriously, professional development activities can help administrators, faculty members, and student affairs professionals become more competent.

In 1974, Chris Argyris, then at Harvard, and Don Schön at MIT, published a groundbreaking book called *Theory in Practice*. It provides an excellent approach for our own professional development. They focus on what they call our Theories of Action. These theories rest on the concepts, attitudes, values, and behavioral reactions that govern our lives. Argyris and Schön articulated two basic distinctions. One is the difference between "espoused theories" and "theories in use." The other is the difference between "single-loop" and "double-loop" learning.

If someone asks us why we do something or why we behave in a particular way, our response will typically be our espoused theory—the way we like to think about ourselves and about various issues. In contrast, our theory in use is what would be inferred from our actual behavior. If someone asks us what we think or how we feel about environmental pollution or global warming, we may say, "I think those are serious problems that urgently need to be addressed." But if the person looks at the kind of car we drive, the size of house we live in, and our consumption patterns, he or she may get a very different picture.

Someone said that if you really want to know about someone's values, look at his or her checkbook. Many professors will say that they firmly believe in equal rights and status for women, but as the "chilly climate" in classroom research demonstrates, women typically get much less airtime than men. Many professors will say that they actively encourage widespread discussion in their classes, but tape recordings indicate that most of the time the professor is talking and that the majority of contributions to discussions repeatedly come from only a few students.

A key way to modify our behaviors is to examine the gaps, or contradictions, between our espoused theories and theories in use. That examination calls for double-loop learning. Single-loop learning strengthens and reinforces our existing skills, knowledge base, attitudes and values, prides and prejudices. Single-loop learning is efficient and satisfying. We don't have to relearn every day how to handle all the predictable activities that make up our lives. But it does not challenge us to change. Often we become prisoners of those routines, of those mental models, of those cognitive and affective reflexes.

Double-loop learning, in contrast, involves feedback that changes our frame of reference toward particular situations and how we are responding. A household thermostat is a good analogy for single-loop learning. It maintains a steady temperature within a narrow range by turning on or shutting off the heat in response to feedback from the room. But it does not adjust itself. It takes outside intervention to change the setting if the climate of the room is going to be modified. Similarly, addressing the gaps between our espoused theories and theories in use often requires some kind of outside intervention. It requires some kind of experience or new information or serious encounter with a different kind of person to challenge our single-loop response.

That's why, if we are sufficiently open and reflective, we can learn much more from failure than from success. Success typically reinforces our existing strengths, our existing knowledge and skills, the behavior patterns that have served us well in the past. The more these are reinforced, the more difficult it becomes to recognize that conditions have changed and to fashion new responses. Trying something new that is not supported by our built-in "theory of action" is risky and anxiety provoking.

With these conceptual distinctions as background, Argyris and Schön described two different theories in use for administrative decision making. Model I has four "governing variables":

1. Define goals and try to achieve them.
2. Maximize winning and minimize losing.
3. Minimize generating or expressing negative feelings.
4. Be rational.

For each variable, the authors posit an "Action strategy," "Consequences for the behavioral world," and "Consequences for learning." The Action strategy for variable 1 is to design and manage the environment unilaterally through persuasion and appealing to large goals. Consequences for the behavioral world are that the actor is seen as defensive, inconsistent, incongruent, competitive, controlling, withholding feelings, manipulative, and overly concerned about self. For this variable, learning is "self-sealing." The Action strategy to maximize winning and minimize losing is to own and control the task or guard the execution of the task. The behavioral consequences are defensive interpersonal and group relationships, with single-loop learning. Minimizing generating or expressing feelings calls for unilateral self-protection, defensive norms involving mistrust, conformity, lack of risk taking, power-centered competition, and rivalry. There is little public testing of theories but much private testing. Being rational involves unilaterally protecting others from being hurt by withholding information, creating rules to censor information, and holding private meetings. This is accompanied by low freedom of choice, limited internal commitment, and minimal risk taking.

Sound familiar? Most of us experienced administrators have often encountered this kind of theory in use. Many of us have operated in ways consistent with these governing variables and action strategies and have experienced the consequences.

Argyris and Schön argue for Model II, which also has four variables:

1. Provide valid information.
2. Enable free and informed choice.
3. Encourage internal commitment to the choice and constant monitoring of its implementation.
4. Ensure bilateral protection of others.

The action strategy for valid information designs situations or environments where participants originate and experience personal causation. The actor is minimally defensive and a facilitator, collaborator, and choice creator. Learning occurs as attempted processes or ideas are disconfirmed, generating double-loop learning. For free and informed choice, the tasks are controlled jointly with minimally defensive interpersonal relations and group dynamics. Internal commitment and monitoring of implementation are sustained by an orientation toward growth and joint protection of participants. The aim is to speak to directly observable behaviors and results and to reduce blindness about one's own inconsistency and incongruity. Norms are learning oriented and are characterized by trust, individuality, and open confrontation of difficult issues. Thus theories, implementation strategies, and activities can be publicly tested and revised.

Argyris and Schön argue that Model II results in a quality of organizational life that will be more positive than negative, with high levels of authenticity and freedom of choice. There will be more effective problem solving and decision making, especially for difficult issues, and thereby greater effectiveness in the long run.

Sound familiar? Probably not. Unfortunately, few of us administrators have often experienced this kind of decision-making context or behavior. One fundamental reason is that few of us have had opportunities to learn how to function this way and little chance to practice.

For me, Argyris and Schön's Model II approach to administrative decision making is highly congruent with our approach to moral conversation and the steps spelled out in Appendix A. It is consistent with Nancy Thomas's leadership of our Wingspread meetings. How can we encourage and help more of us function in these ultimately more effective ways?

Argyris and Schön had extensive experience helping corporate executives learn how to be effective Model II leaders. Their initial approach was to have executives analyze various audiotaped examples of decision-making sessions. Those analyses revealed the sometimes subtle and often not so subtle ways that CEOs and others were exercising their authority, capitalizing on their status, and asserting their power. The next step in coaching was to have participants bring in tapes of their own meetings and scrutinize those with similar rigor. Over time, and with practice, participants learned to behave differently.

I see no reason why we folks in the academy could not do likewise. We could undertake such activities more or less formally. As individuals, we could simply periodically audiotape our own classes or administrative council meetings, listen to them, and make notes about particular things we might have done differently. And then try to do differently next time. This does not have to be a perpetual, constant effort. In fact, identifying one or two particular things to change and working on them for a while will be more effective than creating a long, unmanageable list.

At the next level, we could find two, three, or four trusted colleagues who are interested in pursuing this kind of competence and share tapes and reflections. We will always learn more from others' perceptions of our behaviors than from simple self-observation, which is always filtered through own well-developed self-protective biases.

At a more formal level, existing professional development or teaching improvement centers could add this component to their existing array of activities. Experienced faculty members, student affairs professionals, and administrators can be recruited to work with others. The work can occur one-on-one between individuals or in small groups.

Over time a resource bank of audiotapes that illustrate strong performances and that also illustrate key problematic behaviors can be generated. Obviously these would need to be appropriately sanitized to preserve anonymity and used only with the permission of each professional. These materials could then be used for professional development workshops that would increase awareness of this important performance area and encourage others to tackle these challenges.

If we support professional development activities like these, we will strengthen our capacity to address complex, politically loaded, hot topics effectively. But this support needs to be backed by our reward system.

- *Recognize and reward professional competence and improvement.*

If we really want to take this performance area seriously, we need to build it into the reward system. We can add it to the criteria we use to evaluate teaching, student affairs professionals' contributions, and administrative effectiveness. This need not be done institution-wide, across all personnel. In the first place, such skills are not necessarily called for by all professional roles and responsibilities. Second, an institution-wide change in the reward system would not be politically possible to undertake for all faculty members or administrators or student affairs professionals, despite its potential value. But it could be added on a voluntary basis. Interested persons could include audiotapes or videotapes in their portfolios or other materials used for periodic evaluation. These recordings could be perused and evaluated by colleagues who already have demonstrated this kind of competence. Formative feedback could be given. Remember DeMethra's teaching: "inch by inch is a cinch, yard by yard makes it hard."

This work would add a plus to whatever other evidence of professional excellence was in the mix. Over time, as this area of competence is explicitly recognized, other concerned professionals can gradually get on board as they are interested and ready. As competence in talking about topics gets built into the performance of key formal and informal institutional leaders, it starts to have an impact on the organizational culture until finally a critical mass develops that makes it difficult to ignore.

The Study Circles Resource Center and the Public Conversation Project, both operated by the Paul J. Aicher Foundation, are two excellent resources for this initiative.

A BIT OF PERSPECTIVE

In the early 1970s, support for higher education shifted from institutions to grants and loans for students. Many colleges and universities moved to "open enrollments." In a brief period of time, higher education shifted from a "meritocratic" to an "egalitarian" orientation. For the first time in our history, we were faced with sharp increases in the numbers of minority students—then mostly African Americans. And we were faced with large numbers of students with less well developed verbal and numerical skills. The "massification" of higher education was under way. The proportion of late teenagers and young adults entering our institutions became much higher than in our western European counterparts. We also experienced major increases in "nontraditional" adult learners. With the women's liberation movement that gathered new energy in the 1970s, we became more concerned about gender differences and about the gender biases pervading our policies, practices, and teaching behaviors. Then we became the hope and the future for increased numbers of international students.

We are still trying to become effective with all those different persons. We are trying to recognize and respond to the differences in learning styles and motivation, differences in the need for structure and the desire for independence and individualized learning, different perceptions of the importance of the group versus the importance of the individual, and differences as a function of age and developmental stage. And there are a multitude of conceptual frameworks concerning individual differences, such as David Kolb's Learning and Adaptive Styles Inventories, the Myers-Briggs Type Indicator (MBTI), field dependent–field independent, levelers and sharpeners, and neurolinguistic programming. We have only scratched the surface in developing our ability to respond to all these different persons, each seeking to improve his or her economic well-being and to become more complex, self-aware, and productive citizens and parents. Each one is seeking to become better able to take charge of his or her existence.

Now we confront serious differences in religious beliefs and spiritual orientations, with their related political and social class issues. The affective load, the emotional importance, of these personal characteristics certainly equals those of race, gender, and national origin. We cannot become effective educators for each of these diverse individuals unless we learn to discuss hot topics with them without anyone getting burned. We will not have a civil democracy unless we, our colleagues, and all our students learn to do so.

A PERSONAL CLOSING

I would like to end this chapter with a personal declaration. At this writing, in 2007, in my now nearly fifty years of work in higher education; of arguing for greater attention to "the affective domain"; of helping students address issues of purpose and meaning, integrity and identity, and now spiritual growth; I have never felt as strong a sense of urgency as I do now.

My international experiences traveling and consulting in Canada, Great Britain and Ireland, Latin America, Europe, South Africa, Australia, Russia, and the Far East suggest that things are getting worse, not better. Many people around the globe are experiencing life as more stressful and less meaningful, even compared to the Cold War period of the 1950s and early 1960s. Certainly that is very much the case in the United States.

The ability of multinational corporations to move jobs to sources of cheap labor create employment problems in the countries where jobs have left, and social disruption and dislocation in the receiving countries. Our global communication systems let hackers in one location cause widespread havoc across national boundaries. A SARS outbreak in Southeast Asia becomes an international threat. Starvation and disease increase despite dramatic increases in food production capacity. International, intertribal, interethnic, and interreligious conflicts flare up and seem immune to peaceful resolution. Politically driven disinformation and misinformation renders informed decision making and well thought out political activism almost impossible.

We live in a two-tier society in which the gap between rich and poor has grown dramatically. The pay ratio of the highest- to lowest-paid employee has gone from roughly 60-to-1 during the 1960s to about 250-to-1 today. We have recurrent violence and crime, some driven by drugs, some apparently random expressions of rage and frustration. There is recurrent corruption in politics, corporations, and financial institutions. We all have our own lists of troubling national and world problems.

Furthermore, issues of religious diversity and spiritual orientation, powerfully driven by the terrorist events of 9/11, have moved front and center in public forums and political decision making. Increasing our sophistication about these issues and framing these debates at the level of complexity they require are critical if we are to sustain a civil, pluralistic democracy. We are one of the most globally interdependent, multiethnic, and multifaith nations in the world. We command more economic and military power than any other nation or political bloc. How we lead our beleaguered planet during the coming years will determine the future not only for ourselves, our children, and our grandchildren but for most of the rest of the world's population.

That's why, from my personal point of view, learning better how to talk with each other about the difficult topics, the ones usually taken off the table, is crucial. This needs to happen not just throughout college campuses but in all the other important institutions that influence our lives. This entails, for all of us, the need to know how to make inclusive and thoughtful decisions based on our most important personal and institutional agendas.

Part III

Final Words on Moral
Conversation

6

Opportunities, Risks, and Caveats
for Moral Conversation

We start this chapter with a heated political scenario that took place during a campuswide, residential life–sponsored colloquium at a major university in a red state on how to deal with dangerously escalating political differences between Republican and Democratic students. We begin with this scenario because one of us, Robert, was asked to come to this university to facilitate civil discourse around political differences—differences that had burst into acrimonious, ideological name-calling in some residence halls and in the journalism office of the student newspaper. Tempers were frayed on campus, as the congressional election season in this state was getting under way. Some candidates from both political parties had already visited this institution, and they managed to whip students into a frenzy of partisanship. Then they left. In the troubled aftermath, the Student Government Association sought out one of us to facilitate a campuswide conversation.

We follow this scenario with an open letter to all our colleagues on secular and sectarian campuses throughout the United States. In this letter, we make general recommendations for thinking about, initiating, and actually implementing campuswide conversations. This letter also serves as a concise final summary of the main points we have been trying to make in our book about the possible benefits and risks of moral conversation as a strategy for talking about volatile topics. We address this letter to both faculty members and higher education administrators. Immediately following this chapter, in Appendix A (cowritten by Robert J. Nash, a faculty member, and Alissa B. Strong, a student affairs administrator), we present a succinct, step-by-step framework for preparing a campus (or a classroom) for moral conversation.

IS AMERICA SCREWING UP THE WORLD?

JAKE: In my contemporary political issues class, we're reading a book by John Tirman called *100 Ways America Is Screwing Up the World* [Tirman, 2006]. It's a great book, but nobody in the class seems to be getting it. I think one of the reasons why there is so much animosity between the Young Republicans and the Progressive Democrats on our campus is that these right-wing Republicans won't even listen to well-reasoned criticisms of the current administration in Washington and their backward policies. They're so defensive. Worse, they're so self-righteous and certain that the United States has become what the likes of Rush Limbaugh, Pat Buchanan, Jerry Falwell, and Bill O'Reilly think is a cultural wasteland and a moral sewer.

Tirman makes an airtight case that the United States is actually a "rogue nation." We are abysmally ignorant of non-Judeo-Christian religions (in fact, we'd like nothing better than to Christianize the rest of the world), contemptuous of international agreements, disdainful of the United Nations, evangelical about imposing a capitalistic, market-dominated system of democracy around the world, and more than eager to use preemptive force to bring ideologically resistant nations, along with their leaders, to their knees. One example of this is when the United States decides unilaterally to curb nuclear buildups in other countries. Countries that we've arbitrarily placed in an "axis of evil" have no right, according to the United States government, to experiment with an alternative form of energy like nuclear energy. Imagine!

Moreover, we declare imperialistically that countries surrounded by enemies who possess nuclear arsenals have no right to build nuclear weapons in order to defend themselves in the event of war, unless, of course, we give the official okay.

The hypocrisy of the West is palpable! We prop up right-wing dictators through the years like the Shah of Iran, Augusto Pinochet, the Perons, Mubarak, Pol Pot, Suharto, Mohammad Zia ul-Haq, Mobuto Sese Seko, and, yes, even Saddam Hussein, whenever we think it's in our national and international interest. We support these dictators mainly because of their vast oil reserves. Because our reliance on petroleum is virtually insatiable in the absence of any viable energy policy, "blood for oil" has become the sturdiest pillar of American foreign policy. Also, America is the biggest arms dealer in the world, we have the largest nuclear stockpile in the world, we are the only nation in the history of the world to actually drop nuclear bombs on another country, killing tens of thousands of civilians, and here we are telling the rest of the world that we, and we alone, have the moral authority to decide who has the right to develop nuclear energy and to create nuclear weapons. Who crowned us King of the World? Who made us the Divine Nuclear Monarch?

FRANK: You say *we* don't get it. Did you happen to be on campus when Dinesh D'Souza spoke to our community last year? D'Souza was practically hounded from the stage because of what you people called his "reactionary, fascist" political views. Some of your left-wing sympathizers were actually spitting at him. Others tried to drown him out with their catcalls and insults. Why, on principle, should your belief that American conservatives and neoconservatives are "screwing up the world" override D'Souza's belief that so-called progressive liberals like you are the ones screwing up the world? Why aren't you also reading D'Souza's book *What's So Great About America* [2002] in that poli-sci class of yours? Where's the balance? One of the problems with some academic departments at this university is that all the faculty seem to be political radicals who are anti-American. It's so unfair to people like me. And, as far as I'm concerned, the whole religious studies department is a cover for village atheists.

You don't seem to understand that we are in a war against terrorism. Where were you when the Twin Towers fell on 9/11? Haven't you ever heard of radical Muslim jihadists? Don't you know that even though some American Muslims might be the exception, the majority of Muslims around the world support terrorism? Our enemies are Iraq, Iran, Syria, Libya, the Sudan, and a non-Islamic country, North Korea. You've seen some of these Muslims in countries like Pakistan and Palestine, and even Iraq which we've liberated, dancing with glee in the streets when American soldiers and civilians are killed in suicide bombings. We're not the enemy. They are. They're the ones who call us "infidels," and who teach their children to hate us, and who scheme in their *Medrassahs* to kill us like dogs.

The United States of America is a beacon of light and hope throughout the world. We stand for economic justice, liberty, democracy, human rights, free markets, Judeo-Christian morality, and human decency. I'm proud to be an American patriot in the greatest country in the world. My brother, a Marine, died in Afghanistan fighting for this country. And my uncle is an on-the-ground Army captain in Iraq who has served two tours and has just volunteered for a third. They fight for freedom, for the American way of life. Sure, we're not perfect, but we're a hell of a lot better than the terrorist countries we're fighting. And you know it!

A LETTER TO OUR COLLEAGUES AND STUDENTS

The arguments for and against the political, military, religious, and moral beneficence of the United States raged on in this vein for over two hours. Many students who chose to attend the colloquium got up and left early in frustration, unable to get a word in. A few outspoken, well-prepared partisans of two extremist political positions highjacked the discussion. It wasn't long before argument replaced discussion, and insult replaced argument. Voices were raised. Tempers got hot. Colloquium facilitators lost control. What started out as a great idea—to offer a campuswide colloquium for residential life leaders and students on how to moderate the increasing conflicts between opposing political views in the residence halls—turned into just the opposite of what a genuine colloquium ought to be. The calm voice of moderation had turned into the loud shriek of extremism.

A colloquium (L. *colloquor*), at its best, is a guided conversation where people come together in order to share their views by talking *with* one another, not *at* one another. Civility, mutual respect, generosity, and intellectual curiosity are the qualities most conducive to effective colloquia conversations. Sadly absent at this colloquium, however, were all these qualities. The result was an increased polarization of political views on the campus. The campus newspaper, under the control of progressive liberal Democrats, hardened their editorial stance against the student group they called the "right-wing neocons." And the College Republicans Club proceeded to offer an invitation-only, cider-and-doughnuts get-together to discuss the "anarchistic threat of the left on our college campus."

This opening political vignette gives rise to the questions we hope to touch on in this final chapter: What is the best way to implement a cross-campus culture of conversation around controversial issues like political difference? How can we get college administrators together with faculty and other interested participants to lead these conversations? Where are the best locations for these unbounded conversational spaces? What are some innovative conversational configurations that might enhance moral conversations? What are some potential problems that might arise as students, administrators, and faculty enter into conversations that involve not just relatedness and trust but also self-criticism and mutual criticism?

What follows are several responses to these questions that we know will seem exasperatingly brief. The truth is that in the academy we are at such a primitive stage of thinking about how to build an all-university culture of conversation that we can offer only tantalizingly abbreviated suggestions for its initial formation and implementation, rather than satisfying and complete prescriptions. We formulate our recommendations in the form of a series of tersely stated propositions, listed in no special order, and framed in a personal letter to all our colleagues and students who wish to ignite the fire of conversation on their campuses. Consider these recommendations a work in progress, and we, the authors, eagerly invite your suggestions as well, perhaps in a follow-up letter to us.

Dear Colleagues and Students:

We offer you the following recommendations for thinking about, initiating, and actually implementing cross-campus conversations at your respective institutions. These will serve as a concise final summary of the main points we have been trying to make in our book. (We also urge you to read Appendix A, immediately following this letter. We use this appendix to talk about additional issues and concerns in a step-by-step format regarding the theory and practice of moral conversation that we haven't covered in this letter. Appendix D is our professional rationale for moral conversation, inspired by a report distributed by the National Association of Student Personnel Administrators [NASPA] called *Learning Reconsidered: A Campus-Wide Focus on the Student Experience* [Kneeling, 2004].)

• *Make sure that no particular individual or group has an a priori corner on what constitutes once-and-for-all "truth." In fact, what represents truth for one individual or group will, more often than not, represent something very different for another individual or group.*

We have advocated throughout our book that all of us must agree to come together at strategic teachable moments as educational allies bent on a single mission: the establishment of formal and informal cultures of conversation throughout the campus. There is no better excuse to come together than to talk about hot topics. Our major purpose in getting together, a la Diana Eck, is to give students an opportunity to experience a genuine "truth-seeking encounter" with one another. "Truth," as we use the term, has two meanings, one epistemological, one relational.

In the political polarization scenario we described earlier, one question we asked toward the end of the fireworks managed to bring to the surface some major epistemological (knowledge claims) differences between the two opposing sides. "We're curious about why you think your particular political take on the world is true and the other side's view is false. What are your criteria for truth?" Every conceivable take on truth then got aired:

If it works, it's true, said the pragmatist.

If it's logical, it's true, said the rationalist.

If it's revealed, it's true, said the religious believer.

If it's verifiable, it's true, said the scientist.

If it corresponds to reality, it's true, said the realist.

If it makes me happy, it's true, said the hedonist.

If it leads to good outcomes, it's true, said the consequentialist.

If it produces the greatest good for the greatest number of people, it's true, said the utilitarian.

If it conforms to natural law, it's true, said the Thomist.

If it fulfills a moral duty or obligation, it's true, said the Kantian.

If it advances my own enlightened self-interest, it's true, said the egoist.

If it tells a good, socially constructed story about reality, it's true, said the postmodernist.

It goes without saying, of course, that our initial question about the truth gave rise to many variations on the responses we've listed here, as well as to all the ones we haven't listed.

The reason we asked this question about truth was not because we were wishy-washy, postmodern political relativists. What we wanted to get across was the inescapable, pluralistic nature of truth understandings that people hold about a variety of topics, including, of course, the hot-button political issues. We wanted to convey the idea that it was not The Truth about one or another political position that we were interested in getting at during our campuswide moral conversation. Who, we asked, could ever possess the ultimate authority to proclaim this Truth? And what epistemological rationale would ever satisfy everyone? Rather, we wanted to get our audience talking about what represented truth for each of them. We weren't concerned about knowing whose truth was truer; what we did want to know was each person's major truth criterion. And why was this so for each of them? We took the local, rather than the global, route to asking about political truth because we wanted our audience to understand that any question of truth, especially in conversations about the hottest topics in the academy, is always complex, multilayered, contextual, and pluralistic.

Conflicts around politics, religion, social class, and other topics are unavoidably grounded in and mediated by particular worldviews and unique narratives of personal meaning. Thus the answers students are seeking will in part be determined by the types of truth questions they are asking. There will be times when the pragmatic, naturalistic, and rational questions will be necessary, and in those cases the answers will be researchable and factual. There will also be times when the less empirically testable questions will be significant, and then the answers will be nonscientific, perhaps more emotional than rational. We are convinced that most of the hot-button topics that divide college campuses today defy easily accessible, testable, factual answers. Positions on these issues are as much rooted in heated leaps of faith and passionate feelings (in *me*search) as they are in the cool waters of dispassionate reason, empirical investigation, and logic (in *re*search).

Why is this so? The various takes on political truth, for example, usually start with a series of unexamined taken-for-granteds on the part of the truth proclaimers. This includes even well-informed Republicans, Democrats, Libertarians, Independents, Socialists, anarchists, skeptics, and whomever else. Knowing that any notion of political truth is always context dependent, inconsistent, and, to some extent, hidden from the eyes of its beholder is, we believe, the precondition for examining all sides of political debates with an open mind or, at the very least, with an inclination not to "kill" the political "apostate." Most often, there are three outcomes that might issue from such an awareness: The participants agree to disagree; the participants change the subject; or the participants simply walk away. We prefer another outcome: The participants stick around in order to see if we have any overlap or common ground with others in our particular truth claims, no matter how discordant each might at first appear. We are convinced that moral conversation is more likely to produce this fourth consequence than any of the alternatives.

There is also another way to think about truth. We call this the relational approach. Etymologically, *truth* derives from the Germanic word *troth*. Troth is all about faith and trust, betrothal and engagement, affection and hospitality, generosity and love. These are all relational connotations. Thus, in this sense, truth is the cultivation of a disposition to enter into a faithful, trusting, affirming relationship in order to become a part of one another's lives. Truth is all about building relationships, trying to discover one another's common humanity and need for solidarity and support. Although, epistemologically, a truth can never be final or irrefutable, completely outside particular contexts of agreement, influence, and meaning, still there are some truths that are more likely to bind us together in our mutual search for happiness, love, and freedom from arbitrary coercion. These truths, we submit, are more likely to emanate from open-ended moral conversations than from closed-ended, fractious debates.

Imagine how the political debate that we described earlier might have taken a different turn if each of us were genuinely committed to experiencing truth as troth (building trust and relationship) rather than truth as verity (that which corresponds to somebody's preestablished, bottom-line principle, standard, rule, or fact). Moral conversation as troth conversation on political issues (and all the other red-flag issues as well) would start with the following premises: "The political language I use is merely a tool that I employ to express my deepest beliefs about power, influence, doing good, being good, and helping others. It is meant to solve human problems, including my own. I do the best I can with the language I am using, even though it is at times flawed and partial. I assume you do as well.

"I can't prove to you that my political beliefs will give you everything that you need to solve your problems. But I can respect your political beliefs and see them as your tools to make sense of the world. I will try to understand them, as best I can, from your particular vantage point. I will work hard to practice empathy when I do not understand them or when I am in total disagreement with them. In this instance, I will sensitively challenge them, and I promise not to do violence to you in any way, either passively or actively. I have faith that you will choose to do the same with me. Perhaps, if all goes well, we might even find some point of agreement in our differences, but, more important, some way to avoid inflicting pain and humiliation on one another. Maybe we will even find a way to like one another beyond the neat and tidy little labels we use to separate ourselves from each other."

- *Be prepared for conflict among individuals and among units with various vested interests.*

Conflict is the coin of the realm in higher education. Most faculty are trained, not in the arts and skills of conflict resolution or mediation, but in debate, critique, and contestation. The academic culture of higher education is rooted in a conception of teaching and learning that is primarily adversarial. Check out a thesis or dissertation defense. Most likely, committee members will be displaying their intellectual colors by poking holes and finding weaknesses in a student's scholarship. The ultimate objective in most academic rituals is to stake out one or another position and defend it with scholarly perspicacity and conviction. For most faculty, strenuous intellectual opposition and interrogation are what academic inquiry should be about. Our graduate students often remark to us that, in retrospect, their thesis and dissertation defenses seemed to be more about faculty showing off their brilliance and less about students' fledgling efforts to do creditable research and scholarship. Sadly, their doctoral defenses took on the ambience of what one of our students called an "intellectual boot camp."

So, too, with higher education administrators. All too often at meetings, administrators, both on the academic and the student affairs sides, are called on to protect their territories from those "foreign invaders" who reside in other departments and units threatening to claim a disproportionate share of scarce university resources. Administrators frequently find themselves in self-protective modes of leadership, and this can make them overly suspicious of others' motives. Thus, many administrators are prone to territorial prickliness. The administrative atmosphere on college campuses all too frequently becomes adversarial and aggressive. This is especially obvious on those campuses where faculty and staff unions see themselves as forming alliances against out-of-touch, unresponsive administrators.

Although it will be difficult to find such people on a college campus, given the presence of so much ritualized opposition between and among the various constituencies, we recommend that administrators and faculty members who are trained in conflict resolution and mediation would be an excellent addition to the educational alliance that we are advocating. We need expert mediators and conflict resolvers beause we can recall very little in our experience that ignites conflict more than an uncensored disclosure about one's own, or another's, religion, politics, social class, or personal philosophy of life, particularly when the disclosure might contain a direct or implied critique of somebody else's belief. Misunderstandings are bound to arise in moral conversations on these topics because narratives and languages are so diverse and frameworks of interpretation (what Charles Taylor [1991] calls "backgrounds of intelligibility" or "horizons") so multiple and unique. Feelings will get hurt, people will be miffed, and some students, faculty, and administrators will intentionally or unintentionally lob a sabotage bomb or two into the middle of conversation.

Perhaps the best way to deal with conflict in moral conversations about hot topics, though, is to become less preoccupied with teaching and telling, preaching and critiquing, and more concerned with listening and learning. Rachel Kessler (2000, p. 65) mentions the importance of "returning the question" to students whenever they inquire about issues that are complex and potentially contentious and that defy simple answers. In his chapter "Beyond Tolerance," Victor H. Kazanjian Jr. (2000) says it well in respect to his own institution, Wellesley College, whenever he tries to stimulate cross-campus conversations about religious difference: "Wellesley had fallen prey to the belief that in order to bring people of different traditions together, one had to find a common, neutral context in which everyone felt comfortable and in which no one was offended. The result was the stripping of all particularistic experience from community rituals and programs leaving a kind of universalistic mush in which no one's unique perspective was reflected" (pp. 216–217).

We strongly recommend "Beyond Tolerance" (in *Education as Transformation*, which Kazanjian coedited with Peter Laurence) as a source of a number of very helpful suggestions for resisting the temptation to avoid giving offense when discussing controversial, personal topics such as religion and spirituality. Genuine dialogue, built on a foundation of trust and mutual exploration, invites candor and inquiry because it conveys the message that a "neutral" approach really does not take the other's point of view very seriously.

• *Build alliances that encourage all major constituents to work together.*

For moral conversation to be effective on a college campus, all the major constituents will need to cooperate with one another. This means that faculty, staff, student affairs administrators, and, of course, students will need to stop seeing each other as adversaries and stop setting up the usual and customary authority hierarchies.

One powerful thematic focus for creating genuine "living-learning communities" (particular types of educational spaces that currently represent a high priority for many student affairs administrators) on college campuses is the problem that currently plagues the entire globe: How do we live peacefully and constructively in a pluralistic world? What do we do when worldviews collide? We've had some practice in higher education over the last decade in learning how to handle racial, ethnic, sexual orientation, and gender differences, but what about worldview differences? How can all of us on college campuses work together to build, and learn to live together in, a genuine pluralist polity? Is this even possible given the almost sacred status of identity politics on college campuses wherein groups practice a kind of multicultural endogamy rather than a pluralistic exogamy? Or when many endogamous groups think of exogamy merely as a way of compromising or selling out their deepest, most sacrosanct convictions?

In spite of the difficulties of creating authentic pluralistic polities in higher education, we still believe that there is no better way to bind together a group of students, faculty, administrators, and staff than to engage in the mutual give-and-take exploration of how to live with and profit from those who see the world differently. This robust, mutually respectful exchange of oft-colliding ideas and commitments in moral conversation would be an experiment in pluralistic living and learning that is virtually unprecedented in the academy. However, this coming together will happen only when administrators and faculty can set aside their differences and create collaborative moral conversation teams whose primary purpose is to smooth the way to pluralistic living in a cross-fertilized learning environment.

In keeping with the theme of political pluralism that introduces this chapter, a recent coteaching experiment at the University of Maryland at College Park ("Conflict Resolution," 2006) is an excellent model of a cross-fertilized learning environment. A professor and an administrator, one an Israeli and the other a Palestinian, share an office and work together on this campus with the primary aim of resolving lethal conflicts between Israelis and Palestinians. They currently coteach a course on this topic—Conflict Resolution: The Israeli-Palestinian Experiment—that is extremely popular on the Maryland campus. How has the course worked out? Listen to one of the instructors: "Some students come with a set point of view, and they'd like to see us score points, like in a Roman coliseum. We don't fall into that trap. We teach two different historical narratives but also, how they might, at some point, reach common ground." One of the students who took the course said this: "Because the two scholars were friends, they were able to create a feeling that there's lots of problems, and we're going to talk about them as best we can, and respect each other and the students."

This model of collaboration between an administrator (a former college president and ambassador) and a faculty member, both working together to engage students in a semester-long conversation about an obviously hot political topic, could well become a template for the type of cross-fertilization we would like to see on college campuses. From our experience, it is essential that, in the beginning, college administrators (both on the academic and student affairs sides) take the initiative to form these alliances. Unfortunately, due to narrowly conceived reward systems and traditional prestige factors, most faculty are encapsulated within their own disciplines. Thus interdisciplinary partnerships among faculty—both within and between academic departments—are difficult enough to establish in their own right. Often what is needed is outside instigation.

However, this will not happen simply by issuing a series of administrative dicta. Faculty are much too independent for that. The best approach will be one of experimental suasion—appealing to some faculty members' wish to try something different in order to touch their students' lives in a very special way. The key is for administrators and faculty to recognize the special talents and understandings that each brings to the venture, as in the Israeli-Palestinian coteaching experiment we have described. Contrary to most administrative opinion, not all faculty members demean the intellectual contributions of student affairs leaders. Moreover, contrary to most faculty opinion, not all student affairs administrators diminish the contributions of the professorate to student development.

Working together on a college campus to create cultures of conversation on topics of intellectual interest to both parties is an excellent way of overcoming the tired and debilitating stereotypes that many administrators and faculty tend to propagate about one another, mostly out of ignorance and fear. There is no convincing reason why student affairs administrators and college faculty can't work together to produce something as exciting and pioneering as the cotaught course dealing with the Israeli-Palestinian conflict.

Stereotypes about faculty and administrators form because of different, sometimes competing, languages and mind-sets. Student affairs administrators tend to speak the languages of cost-effectiveness, corporatization, and student development psychology. Faculty members speak the languages of scholarship, academic rigor, and disciplinary loyalty. All these languages are valuable, of course, but they too often drive a wedge between the administrative culture and the academic culture, such that the near-total estrangement of both groups is frequently the result. When administrators and faculty members can come together as educational partners in the venture we are recommending here, willing to listen to each other and learn from each other, then it is possible for suspicion and misunderstanding to give way to trust and mutual appreciation. In the end, all constituents, but especially students, stand to gain from the cross-fertilization experience.

For example, on the topic of religious and spiritual pluralism, some campus ministers will complain that "me-first spirituality is a sorry substitute for organized religion on campuses." They will argue that to remove religion from the chapels, prayer rooms, and churches on campus is to downplay the importance of institutionalized religion in favor of an ephemeral spirituality that has no specific sense of practice, place, or community. Needless to say, the importance of campus ministers might be downplayed as well. As one campus chaplain said, "What we need is not more [cross-campus] calls for spirituality, but more money for chapels and chaplains" (Schaper, 2000, p. A56).

So too, some faculty members, who inhabit different disciplinary silos, will criticize the "dumbing down" of academic topics whenever those topics leave the seminar room or travel outside the scholar's other traditional provinces—the scholarly journal, book, or conference presentation. Many faculty are more comfortable teaching about the historical intricacies, technical conflicts, and details of their specialized fields of study than they are in facilitating far-reaching process conversations outside their classrooms about an issue like improving Palestinian-Israeli relations in the Middle East. We act precisely in the way we were trained in the academy, and most faculty, for better or worse, take a worm's-eye view of knowledge, in order to dig deeper and deeper into the complexities of their respective disciplines.

When first approached by interdisciplinary enthusiasts of moral conversation, some student affairs administrators, who see themselves more as managers than educators, will raise questions about cost-effectiveness, crossing boundaries, accountability, potential student lawsuits, and the unworkability of teaching alongside professors. If they do become involved, they will comport themselves chiefly as caregivers in the conversation groups and defer to professors to do all the intellectual work. For these professionals, the type of educational alliance between administrators and professors that we are calling for is bound to be experienced as a burden.

We can only say that on the campuses where we have worked and visited, there are many wonderful exceptions to these stereotypes. The trick is to find professionals who are as student centered as they are administration and content based. It is also important to identify those professionals who are enthusiastic about new teaching-learning projects and are willing to take interdisciplinary and pedagogical risks. Sad to say, with some notable exceptions, academia does not generally reward risk taking through collaboration with those who are not members of the same professorial or professional guilds. In spite of the obstacles, however, we know from firsthand experience that potential allies are everywhere on (and off) college campuses.

One of the authors of this volume, Robert, has actively sought out campus ministers who helped him get a new religious pluralism course off the ground. At least two ministers at his campus were more than willing to cooperate and, even better, to take some specific operational initiatives. One, Sue Marie Baskette, even became a student and eventually a coinstructor for an entire semester in Robert's graduate course on religious pluralism for educators and human service professionals. Furthermore, two of the authors of this book, Robert, a full-time faculty member, and DeMethra, a full-time student affairs professional, coteach a graduate course each year covering topics related to cultural, social class, political, religious, and sexual orientation differences. They teach the course during the fall term according to the conversational principles we write about here. Together they also write articles and present throughout the country; recently, they jointly planned and organized a highly successful national conference, sponsored by the American College Personnel Association, on the topic of religious and spiritual pluralism.

In contrast to the comments we have made here about the isolation and resistance of many faculty in the disciplines, we have found a number of academicians on our campuses and elsewhere who were supportive of the cross-campus initiatives we are writing about—although most of them tend to keep a safe distance. With some cajoling and encouragement, however, many of these colleagues are eager to get involved in exciting interdisciplinary teaching projects. For example, a new honors college on one of our campuses is mainly interdisciplinary and problem centered in its curriculum and teaching. Students and faculty are flocking there. There is a fresh intellectual excitement in the air.

We have also found that those who want to play a more active role in our interdisciplinary, cross-campus conversational venture tend to come from the professional schools rather than from the arts and sciences. Thus we start with these folks before working our way to faculty in the social sciences and humanities. In time, some colleagues from all these departments and disciplines will step forward with good ideas, once we invite them to engage in the preliminary planning of cross-campus conversations on the difficult hot topics that are in the daily news. Who wouldn't? Many faculty, like professionals in all fields, need to shake things up occasionally in order to revitalize themselves. The best cure for burnout on college campuses is to start fresh fires.

We make the following a priori, general assumption about joint interdisciplinary activities in the academy. All of us—faculty, staff, students, and administrators alike—will initially be threatened by the blurring of conventional borders. There is comfort and safety in predictable norms and traditions. Some faculty members, for example, are disciplinary purists or intellectual loners; some administrators fear facing the inevitable hazards of any kind of innovation that can't be measured and defended objectively, or that might require financial resources that are already thinly distributed across campus.

Some faculty and administrators do not know how to reach out to (or be reached by) colleagues; others zero in only on what they need to do in order to win scholarly and administrative acclaim, pay raises, tenure and promotion, and institutional leadership advancement. A few from each group are just plain lazy. Interdisciplinarians and innovators on college campuses are risk-taking border dwellers and border crossers, by definition. They live at the margins of organized bodies of knowledge and top-down administrative arrangements. They are in the dangerous territory that straddles intellectual and leadership frontiers.

We fully understand that not everyone on a college campus, and this includes students, is temperamentally or intellectually comfortable with the type of teamwork and moral conversation that we are advocating. If all of us were, this book would be unnecessary. All the initiatives we are advocating in these pages would already have been well under way in every college and university in the United States.

Having said all this, however, we also need to add that we have met many enthusiastic border dwellers and border crossers in the academy, and we have worked closely with them. We have collaborated with student affairs professionals who were highly knowledgeable about academic subject matter and who adhered to high academic standards. We have also talked at length with faculty who cared greatly about their students' various quests for personal and social meaning, and who recognized the importance of moral conversations about what truly touches students' lives. This includes all the topics we have examined in this book.

We must understand that we are all rank amateurs, learning as we go along, when it comes to helping one another deal with a multiplicity of meanings and perspectives that people attach to all the difficult topics we discuss in this book. Moreover, how we might talk to one another with confidence and comfort, even if we are proverbial strangers to one another, about explosive issues that have the potential to tear apart a community and a society, remains a challenge for all of us in higher education. Sadly, we have never learned how to have free-flowing, unfinished, and unabashedly candid, personal conversations in the academy, but we have learned all too well how to start, finish, and win academic debates and arguments.

It will be difficult to shift our perspectives regarding how to facilitate fruitful conversations about the hard and troubling issues. Each conversationalist's journey is different and is to be honored. When it comes to the most complex existential questions—what the French refer to as *les profondeurs*—there are no certified experts. Consequently, the best traits for engaging in the type of conversational experiment we are describing here are patience, humility, love, faith, trust, and a natural taste for adventure. It also helps to be intensely interested in people's unique "stories of meaning" and quest narratives. Mastery of academic content and political strategies for getting what we want in higher education, though admirable, are most helpful when they go hand-in-hand with the aforementioned traits.

• *Create new configurations of teaching and learning to spread the fire of conversation throughout the academy.*

Professors have a natural fondness for the classroom. This is where they practice their craft year after year. But we are suggesting that significant learnings occur in other sites as well. Therefore, it will be necessary for all of us to emphasize the concept of intellectual diffusion in our educational efforts to promote a culture of cross-campus conversation on issues of pluralism. Diffusion means spreading out teaching and learning throughout the academy. In talking about religious pluralism, Diane Winston (1998, p. A60) makes a pertinent observation regarding the importance of diffusion: "diffusion signals the scattering of religious ideas, beliefs, and behaviors in arenas ranging from medicine (for example, medical-school courses on spirituality and health) to computing (the magazine *Christian Computing*) to cyberspace (chat rooms and Web sites devoted to religious topics)."

Winston goes on to recommend that professors encourage their students to discuss religious issues whenever they might be relevant to the topic at hand, not just in religious studies seminars, but in courses representing all the disciplines. We certainly concur, and not just with regard to religious issues, but also to all the hot-button problems that currently threaten to divide us as we make our way in our college communities, local regions, nations, and world community.

On college campuses, however, we are going one major step further than Winston. We want moral conversations about pluralism to take place outside as well as inside the officially recognized academic structure—classrooms, credit hours, research papers, semester-long courses, lectures, and exams. We encourage all campus constituents to think imaginatively about constructing new teaching-learning configurations throughout the campus—for example, in coffee houses, cafeterias, residence halls, chapels, cultural pluralism centers, and student activities rooms.

During a recent meeting one of us had with students, we brainstormed some innovative ways to encourage coming to terms with the challenges of pluralism in all the campus spaces by using creative delivery systems. The following is a list of the students' contributions, in no particular order of priority:

- All-campus town meetings with specific pluralistic themes

- Mini-retreats for students, faculty, administrators, and staff emphasizing cross-campus conversations on how to make the total educational experience better for all people at the college

- Special topics colloquia

- Comparative religion, politics, and philosophy institutes

- Leadership training institutes

- A "first-lecture" series on "what I need to learn about how to live with worldview differences"

- A "last-lecture" series on "what I think I have learned about living with worldview differences"

- Informal student-faculty get-togethers

- Off-campus ally groups

- Intellectual renewal communities

- Intellectual reflection centers

- Pluralistic journaling and personal narrative writing groups

- Distinguished controversial speakers' series

- Secular humanists' corners

- Performing artists' corners

One of the authors of this book, Robert, has had much success in working with small colloquium gatherings outside the classroom. He has held these in a variety of spaces, including campus restaurants, libraries, multicultural centers, residential life complexes, and even in students' homes. He organizes these teaching-learning groups around independent studies that students have done, as well as trips abroad they might have taken for college credit. He has also set up a series of Friday afternoon colloquia whose attendance is voluntary. Students present a formal paper or a series of short personal reflections on a special topic, one that they have rarely, if ever, discussed in public. Then they open up the session to moral conversation. The primary ground rule of the colloquium is that before formulating his or her response, the presenter must first respond to each question from the audience with a restatement of what the presenter has heard. Similarly, the questioner must frame the inquiry in terms that reflect that questioner's own interest in the topic being discussed, and it must be cleansed as much as possible of hidden agendas and built-in prejudgments and answers.

For example, the title of one recent student colloquium was "Coming Out as an Atheist to My Christian Evangelical Family." Another title was "Acknowledging My Upper Class Social Status in a College That Prides Itself on Attracting First-Generation, Blue-Collar, and Working Class Students." Still another title was "Why I Am a Proud American Patriot Who Loves Her Country, Her President, and Her God." And, finally, "I Am Not a Social Justice Advocate Because Civil Liberties Issues Are Far More Important to Me." Each of these controversial topics sparked intense and animated to-and-fro conversation.

Another ground rule for the ensuing conversations was that each of the colloquium presenters had to share with the rest of us a series of personal questions that each was still asking as a result of doing the project. The questions had to be candid, probing, and evocative, with resonance for all of us. It is rare that a Friday afternoon colloquium doesn't run beyond its two-hour time schedule, because conversations are usually so moving and intense. Most of all, however, they matter to everyone.

Recall the political polarization colloquium we described at the beginning of this chapter. If the moderators had established specific ground rules for moral conversation during this very provocative forum on political pluralism, and if participants had felt safe enough to talk about what really touched them, without the pressure of having to be politically correct or incorrect, the outcome would have been very different for all of us. For starters, we would have probed for what deeply mattered, on a personal level, to both the Republicans and the Democrats in the audience, as well as to all those who might have identified politically in other ways. Our goal would have been to move the most passionate political partisans beyond the ideological buzzwords, the moral self-righteousness, and the eventual predictable attacks on their opponents.

Other questions we could have asked, and some of which we actually did, are these: What made each of the political narratives especially desirable to their adherents? What moral needs did the particular narrative meet? How did each of the participants choose their political narratives in the first place? What was the role of their family upbringing in formulating their political beliefs? Had they ever been disappointed in their political choices? Had they undergone any minor or major changes of political mind? Why is it, did they think, that some young people are political, some are apolitical, and some are antipolitical? In what ways are their most passionate political beliefs connected to their general philosophy of life, if at all? Whom did they admire in the political world and why? Whom did they find less admirable and why?

Also, we would have encouraged all participants to be as intensely interested in what the speakers stirred in them about their own political views as they were in the exchange of clever invectives that stifled any kind of conversation among those who were turned off in the audience. We have found that unless all participants in moral conversation feel safe enough to take some risks and talk about what really matters to them, then what usually happens in public forums is that only a few people are willing to openly participate in a discussion. The others choose to go on the attack, some doodle and dawdle, but most check out by leaving early, either by actually walking away or by disappearing into their dreamy reveries.

• *Look for successful examples both inside and outside your institution.*

Take the time to research what has worked on other college campuses. Successful conversational initiatives have been present on many college campuses for years. Oftentimes, we hear the stories of where they went wrong but not the stories of where they were successful. Taking the time to seek out your peers elsewhere who have made successful attempts in the area of cross-campus conversations is a worthwhile endeavor. Their institutional mission with regard to conversations on hot topics may be different, their desired outcomes may not be parallel to your outcomes, but the key is that they have successfully incorporated and used a conversational model on their campuses.

Inviting outside consultation is an excellent way to gain immediate access to other colleges that are "doing it right." Emerson College's Campus Conversations on Race (CCOR) program, and the college's publication titled *The Other Tradition*, are excellent resources from a campus that has experienced considerable success in its initiative to promote all-campus conversation. The all-campus diversity curriculum developed by the University of Vermont's Division of Student and Campus Life is another example of how institutions are being proactive about changing culture and climate.

Investigate inside your college community as well. There may be experts in your own backyard when it comes to this type of work. Inevitably, there will be faculty members who specialize in innovative forms of communication and dialogue training. You are also likely to find other student affairs administrators who have a passion for this work and who may have even done research around it. All they are waiting for is for you to ask for their help. Be willing to make your intentions known about sustaining and improving cross-campus dialogues. Go public often. Maximize potential allies; minimize potential opponents. You just never know who on your own campus might also be an advocate for the kinds of conversational initiatives we have created in this book.

- *Spell out ground rules for civil discourse.*

The *Wingspread Declaration*, which we cited in our Introduction, says,

> The academy must preserve and enlarge its understanding of public reason by setting standards for inquiry and discourse. These standards of public reason should reflect

the principles of rational discourse that lie at the basis of all academic inquiry. It is important to distinguish the ideals of rational inquiry—which are common features of many of the world's great religious traditions as well as Western philosophy and science—from both religious and secular worldviews. Debate among worldviews is a valid, though often contentious, part of intellectual life. One of the university's most valuable contributions to democratic society lies in modeling how rational inquiry can contribute to these difficult and important kinds of public argument.

Higher education must foster a spirit of tolerance and actively champion an attitude of mutual respect and affirmation of the value of pluralism in a democracy without implicitly or explicitly privileging secularist worldviews or particular religious perspectives. . . .

Higher education must preserve the essential principles of intellectual integrity and academic freedom in the face of pressures of ideological interference, whether religious or secular, from across the political spectrum. It is particularly important to preserve the minority voice. Religious minorities have the same right to the public square as religious majorities; committed nonbelievers and passionate believers are equally entitled to academic freedom.

If we college and university trustees, administrators, faculty members, and student affairs professionals are not willing to set standards for public reason and act on them, where else in our society will these be established and modeled? If we are not willing to articulate ground rules for our own internal discourse, and learn how to abide by them, how can we hope to graduate students who are able to participate actively and responsibly in a multicultural, globally interdependent democracy?

Clarifying and agreeing on your own ground rules can create the foundation for our previous five suggestions. Ground rules can help guarantee that no individual or group has an a priori corner on the truth and that all of us—trustees, administrators, faculty members, student affairs professionals, staff, and students—are equal participants in our difficult conversations. They can help soften the inevitable conflicts that arise and improve our capacity to deal with them. They can provide an opening for crossing boundaries between our "silos" and for spreading the fire of conversation throughout our institution.

All the aforementioned stakeholders need to help identify and spell out the key ground rules. Their varied views need to be explicitly recognized and given fair hearing. In this book, we have suggested our own ground rules for moral conversations, our own approaches to discussing hot topics without getting burned. We have suggested some key principles and processes for administrative decision making and educational leadership. But no institution will simply sign on to or slavishly adopt our views or language. Nor would that be wise. Each institution will need a conceptual base and language that fits its mission, its students, and its professionals. The final result will need to be tight, parsimonious, and jargon free, using nickel words that communicate clearly to all internal and external interest groups. So the best approach is to adapt, not adopt, whatever we have said that may be useful.

Tackling this suggestion will be a time-consuming, frustrating, and challenging process. The process itself will tax the existing ability for civil conversation. It will challenge your habitual academic norms that often value winning debates and scoring points over open, sensitive, and thoughtful listening. But it can offer a major opportunity to begin practicing what you aim to preach. It will provide an opportunity to learn better how to talk with, rather than at, one another about this foundation for all your educational practices and for all your administrative decision making. So don't rush to judgment. Don't feel pressed to reach what may be premature closure. Your ground rules are not matters to be settled by majority vote. They need willing and active support from everyone. Reach for consensus. Anticipate conversations about "semantics." Expect to create multiple revisions. After all, you are trying to lay the foundation for an institutional culture quite different from that which characterizes most of our colleges and universities.

• *Support professional development activities and reward effective performance*.

Spelling out your ground rules for civil discourse will give you a basis for improving your practices. Few trustees, administrators, faculty members, or student affairs professionals have well-honed skills of the kinds we have discussed in our varied chapters. We all need to learn better how to converse with one another.

The *Wingspread Declaration* goes on to say, "Colleges and universities must support faculty development opportunities that help faculty engage in democratic dialogue that is both probative and inclusive. Higher education must develop and practice models of deliberative democracy that strengthen communities and society in general. The academy must also mediate conversations between those motivated by the desire for greater freedom of religious expression in the public square and those who believe that a more secular public square offers the best hope for religious freedom and inter-religious peace. Colleges and universities must be models for American democracy."

Divisiveness pervades our political debates and decision making. It is aggravated by varied vested interests and amplified by biased media. Educators cannot successfully encourage democratic practices in other countries and cultures if they are not able to practice these themselves. Modeling this behavior is the most important teaching that educators can do. At present educators do not do this very well. We must learn to do better. In the previous chapter, Arthur suggests some approaches that can help us achieve this learning in deliberate and incremental ways. Those, or other more institutionally appropriate approaches, need strong leadership and adequate human and financial resources.

Finally, of course, those improved behaviors will not become institutionalized if they are not rewarded. We have made good progress in learning how to recognize and reward good teaching and the scholarship of teaching, thanks largely to the leadership activities of the Carnegie Foundation for the Advancement of Teaching. And we have made good progress in strategies for recognizing and rewarding effective community service, due largely to the groundbreaking work of the New England Resource Center for Higher Education. With leadership from the Council for Adult and Experiential Learning, we have learned to adapt the Principles for Good Practice in Assessing Prior Learning from work and life experiences to be congruent with our particular institution, students, and desired outcomes. But, so far, we have no nationally recognized external agency or organization to provide leadership in recognizing and rewarding good teaching. So we will have to learn from our own internal resources and expertise.

Back in the 1980s, new communication and information technologies, with their strong potentials for improving teaching and learning, came on stream. Many teaching improvement and professional development centers created their own bootstrap programs using local expertise and resources. At George Mason University, Arthur participated in a series of weekly afternoon meetings for a full semester, learning the intricacies of word processing, e-mail, spreadsheets, and such, with about fifteen colleagues in the Graduate School of Education, led by one of their own faculty members. At the end of the semester, each successful participant was rewarded with a Texas Instruments laptop. That program went on for two years, and by then almost all the faculty members and administrators at the school were basically computer proficient. We need a similar investment in our local expertise for identifying and affirming good teaching as well as recognizing efforts to conduct research about effective teaching.

Furthermore, if this kind of competence is to become widespread throughout higher education, then it needs to be recognized by appropriate national organizations, such as the American Association of Colleges and Universities, the National Association of State Land Grant Universities and Colleges, the National Association of Student Personnel Administrators, and the American College Personnel Association. The Carnegie Foundation publicly recognizes outstanding teachers. The Council for Adult and Experiential Learning annually gives the Morris T. Keeton Award for outstanding contributions to the field of experiential learning. The New England Resource Center for Higher Education gives annual awards that recognize outstanding community service contributions. We need similar reward programs from our major national professional associations for persons demonstrating and providing leadership for moral conversations.

When we get these local and national reward systems in place, they will drive the implementation of our other six suggestions. Then we will have an impact on the larger culture of higher education, whose ability to engage in difficult conversations and whose democratic practices are so critical for our beleaguered democracy.

Sincerely Yours,
Robert J. Nash
DeMethra LaSha Bradley
Arthur W. Chickering

Appendix A

A Step-by-Step How-To Guide for Facilitators and Participants When Doing Moral Conversation

Robert J. Nash and Alissa B. Strong

Following are a series of concrete steps to think about, play with, and implement when introducing moral conversation to a community. This "how-to" guide represents the basics of engaging in moral conversation by offering useful tips for setting up, processing, and maintaining successful cross-campus conversations, either in classrooms or in a variety of alternative campus venues.

1. *Recognize when to introduce moral conversation to your community.*

Recognize the signs that faculty, staff, and students in your campus community might be ready to talk with one another collectively, without rancor, about the hot topics that threaten to divide and alienate a college campus.

- Ask student leaders, faculty, staff, and administrators to identify those controversial social, political, religious, racial topics that continue to come up in their respective spheres of influence. If there is thematic commonality between and among the various groups, then take the initiative to get people together to engage in collective conversation.

- Be on the lookout particularly for those explosive, polarized, confrontational situations and incidents

that sometimes involve a controversial guest speaker
or a campus activist group of one kind or another.
Take advantage of these opportunities to bring people
together in the spirit of civil discourse to talk about the
relevant issues.

- Locate allies across all the major campus constituencies who might welcome an opportunity to converse in
an open-ended, nonjudgmental, nonhierarchical way
about one or another potentially divisive topic. Find
participants who represent a diversity of views, perspectives, and convictions on controversial issues, but who
also tend to be nondogmatic and open minded.

- Look for speakers and group facilitators who relish
direct, face-to-face interactions around controversial issues. Be on the alert especially to find participants who might be open to new ways of engaging one
another in respectful yet robust conversation on very
difficult and controversial topics.

- Avoid creating moral conversation groups whose primary objectives are to solve specific problems or to
convey one-way information to passive audiences.
Also beware of operating under severe time constraints,
because in moral conversation the most important *product* is an unimpeded, unrushed *process*. In this regard,
patient, agenda-free, conversational leader-mediator-
facilitators are worth their weight in gold as group
processors. Fran Lebowitz once said that the "opposite of talking isn't listening; it's waiting, and waiting takes time."

2. *Create a welcoming physical space for engaging in moral conversation*.

A welcoming physical space is one that features psychological safety, encourages maximum participation, and is attentive to personal comfort.

- Small conversational circles work best for up to twenty participants.

- Large groups (fifty or more) can meet together at the beginning to discuss ground rules, purposes, and processes for the smaller groups.

- Experimentation with different types of creative group structures is always welcome.

- Small, preferably round tables with comfortable chairs work well; rows of desks and chairs are not conducive to moral conversation.

- No overheads, PowerPoints, or CDs. Moral conversation is always back-and-forth, two-way communication among facilitators and conversationalists. Sometimes the use of high technology results in one-way presentations where facilitators are active and participants are passive observers. Flip charts or blackboards are welcome, if necessary, for recording key points and summaries.

- Notebooks, pads, writing materials, or even laptops should be available at all tables for those participants who tend to be more visual than auditory.

- Stress that in the end, moral conversation is not about *I, you,* or *me* . . . it's about *we*.

- A pleasantly decorated meeting space is important: clean, well-lighted, and comfortably furnished, with food and drink available if desired.

- All cellular phones should be turned off.

3. *Establish common goals at the first meeting.*

Consensus on common goals is necessary for getting all participants on the same page in moral conversation. Common goals act as a road map in keeping participants on topic and working toward arriving at similar destinations.

Ask such questions as

- What are we here for? What are our purposes?

- What do we hope to accomplish?

- How do we hope to bring this into our work afterwards, if at all?

- How do we want the moral conversation to affect the larger institution, if at all?

- How do we bring hidden assumptions to the surface?

- What are some common assumptions that we are all making?

- How do we allow for genuine differences of opinion?

- How do we ensure that all voices, not just those of facilitators and leaders, get heard? How can we avoid status and power differentials that tend to close down, rather than open up, honest conversation?

- What are our reasonable parameters for having the conversation, in terms of time, cost, participants, location, goals, and objectives?

4. *Manage conversation starters, stoppers, and sustainers.*

The primary objective is to start and sustain a moral conversation from beginning to end and to get as many people involved in lively talk as possible. To this end, we offer the following tips for ensuring that there are conversation starters and sustainers, and avoiding conversation stoppers.

How to Introduce Conversation Starters

- Ask evocative questions that are simple, clear, open ended, agenda free, direct, and directly relevant to the topic being discussed.

- Talk about the differences between *conversation* and *contestation*, between *dialogue* and *debate*, and between *win-win*, *lose-lose*, and *win-lose* verbal exchanges.

- Talk about conversational qualities that best lend themselves to moral conversation—for example, generosity, willingness to look for common ground, humility, authenticity, and so on.

- Draw out others often by asking clarifying questions and by encouraging participants to rephrase and summarize what others have said.

- Show genuine interest both verbally and nonverbally in what others are saying.

How to Avoid Conversation Stoppers

- No name-calling.

- No repetitions of the same old, same old sharp (and dull) axes to grind. Be wary of pushing the same pet agendas over and over again, lest you become irritatingly predictable. Predictability invites resistance or, worse, tuning out and shutting down.

- No making others look bad so that you, the speaker, can shine.

- No bloviating, declaiming, denouncing, or arguing.

- No proselytizing, advertising, or evangelizing.

- No settling old (or new) scores.

- No looking for reasons why *others* in the conversation aren't working well. (Instead, ask yourself why *you're* not working well.)

- No positioning yourself on the highest moral ground.

- No relegating others to the lowest moral ground.

How to Ensure Conversation Sustainers

- Explain, clarify, question, rephrase, respect, and affirm . . . always and often.

- Evoke, don't invoke or provoke.

- Support without retort.

- Flow, glow, and let it go . . . don't fight or flee.

- Respond . . . knowing full well that you (and I) made it all up—everything.

- Be generous . . . at all times . . . without exception.

- Attribute the best motive and assume the best intentions by the one speaking.

- Look for the truth in what you oppose and the error in what you espouse.

- Speak always for yourself and not for some group.

- Come prepared, having done the background home-work.

- Help others shine, while concealing your own brilliant light under the proverbial bushel.

5. *Break down hierarchy and power dynamics.*

The hidden power dynamics often associated with formal roles and hierarchies on college campuses can stifle the free and honest flow of ideas in moral conversation. Aim instead for the authority of the "clearer idea," rather than for the authority associated with formal rank and status differences.

- Remind administrators and faculty members (early and often) to think of themselves as less the privileged "sage on the stage" and more the equalized "guide on the side." In moral conversations, a *sage* is more likely to incite group *rage;* a *guide* is more likely to instill group *pride.*

- Stress the importance of mutual vulnerability from all parties in the conversation.

- Acknowledge openly that regardless of the official job title and associated power and influence, nobody has all the answers to the difficult questions; in fact, very few of us even know how to ask these questions.

- All questions are up for grabs no matter who asks them. Good questions transcend formal rank.

- Encourage all participants to organize, structure, and take full mutual responsibility for the process and prod-uct, the means and ends, of the moral conversation.

- Everyone is in moral conversation together. Success or failure is dependent on the entire group's efforts and not on the leaders or facilitators alone.

- Mutual vulnerability and fallibility are the moral conversation equalizers.

- Vulnerability begets vulnerability; invulnerability begets defensiveness, intimidation, and ultimately sabotage or disengagement.

- Sharing personal stories and perspectives is more humanizing, and productive, than making speeches and indulging in special pleading or guilt tripping.

- Humility, openness, and a genuine spirit of free and open inquiry are the key virtues in promoting equality of participation in moral conversation.

- As a general operating rule, generosity prevents ferocity; self-righteous certainty invites it.

- Heart-to-heart conversations go hand-in-hand with head-to-head conversations. It's okay to show a little emotion and passion in moral conversation, as long as it's tempered with reason and sensitivity. Feel while you think, and think while you feel.

- The winners in the moral conversation are like coworkers in a successful barn raising. The final sign of successful moral conversation is when all the participants are working together to understand, encounter, and engage one another in a mutual understanding of hot topics. The aim is to build an edifice of increased understanding and appreciation, not necessarily to reach consensual agreement or issue a final call to action.

6. *Check in and take stock at key intervals*.

Encouraging "no-fault" group-process feedback at key intervals in the conversation can smooth the way for participants to improve the overall quality of the conversational process.

- Examples of feedback questions might be: So far, what seems to be working in our process? What can we all do together to improve the process? What would you like to do better in the time we have left?

- Leader-facilitators might inquire: Are we asking too many or too few questions? Are we giving more answers than asking questions? Are we doing more monologuing than dialoguing?

- Discuss, when necessary, the extent to which the group is engaging in a mutually reciprocal give-and-take, to-and-fro conversation. Try to move on from one-way communication or smaller conversations between the leader and a few outspoken participants.

- Sit in silence at strategic times in order to calm and center a group. Build time into the conversational process for these quiet, reflective intervals.

- Decide beforehand on the importance of hand raising as opposed to spontaneous responding. Also, agree on a practical strategy for allowing everyone the desired airtime when necessary.

- Talk during the start of the conversation about how to give constructive, not destructive, feedback. Here are some examples of constructive conversational feedback:

    "Let me try saying what I think you are saying, and you tell me where I might be off."

    "Would you say that one more time, using some different words?"

    "I think I've got it, but let me check it out with you, just to be sure."

"If I were to return your question to you, how would you answer?"

"Could you respond to what I said by perhaps using different words?"

"What assumptions do you think I might be making in order for me to take the position I did?"

"Here are some assumptions I think you might be making about the position you are taking. Please tell me if I'm hearing you accurately."

"What might I do in the future to make you less defensive?"

"What hot buttons might I be inadvertently pushing that tend to upset you? Help me learn how to draw you out instead of shutting you down."

"Is there a way we can talk with one another about what's important with 'cool passion' instead of with 'red-hot fire'?"

7. *Deal openly with common conversational potholes.*
Unless anticipated beforehand, potholes can make the road to moral conversation a bumpy one. Knowing beforehand how to deal with conversational potholes can improve the entire process and prevent unwitting acts of sabotage.

- Experiment with how to give constructive feedback to those who intentionally or unintentionally shut down or marginalize others in discussion.

- Point out when factioning, politicizing, monopolizing, debating, and special-interest pleading are occurring in the conversation without silencing those who are consciously or unconsciously engaging in these activities.

- Know the group well enough to empower the quieter participants to converse without embarrassing or forcing them to do so.

- Know how to deal with either-or, dualistic thinkers without further fueling their zeal or discouraging them from participating in the conversation.

8. *Affirm others in conversation.*

Affirmation acts as positive reinforcement in continuing and sustaining the process of moral conversation. Disaffirmation stops moral conversation cold in its tracks.

- Affirmation leads to individual participation and celebration. Resist the academic urge to criticize, debunk, or critique.

- Keep all responses to one another respectful, generous, kind, and thoughtful.

- Circle back frequently by referring to what someone has said earlier that might relate to what is being said in the present.

- The best response is the one that promotes further thinking and reflection. For example, "Could you develop that a little more for me? Your point is fascinating."

- Affirmation begins with respect for the other. Here are a few examples of self- and other-respecting, affirming responses:

    "Your words made me think about . . ."

    "I respect that you . . ."

    "I relate to what you just said in that . . ."

"I'm sure you must have considered this . . . so what do you think?"

"Let me tell you where I'm coming from, and I'd love to hear your response."

"Please tell me why you feel so strongly about that point."

"I like very much what you are saying, but I'm going to need time to think it through. . . . Is this okay with you?"

"Could you put what you just said into a story format? I react really well to stories about people's beliefs."

"Thank you very much for what you've just said. I can see places where I resonate and places where I don't. I'd like to talk with you further about this."

"Here's what you've added to my thinking, and I appreciate it greatly."

"Do you know how important your voice has been in our conversation? Thank you for joining us in this space."

9. *Conclude the conversation.*

Some type of formal conclusion, summary, or review gives all participants a sense that the conversation was worthwhile, that it led to some important conclusions, and that it resulted, at the very least, in a vigorous and respectful meeting or departing of the minds on controversial issues heretofore ignored or overlooked.

- In one sense, moral conversation never truly ends; it simply stops . . . for the time being. The conversation stops when people agree that it is time to take a breather and to let things settle down and settle in . . . until the next time.

- The facilitator could ask such questions as these: "Does it seem to anyone else that perhaps we might be reaching an end point?" "If so, where do we go from here?" "What might we do with what we've talked about?" "Is anyone willing to identify a few themes that kept coming up in our conversation?"

- Do a one-minute closing round. Ask the group to think for a minute about responding in one sentence to a prompt. Then do a one-minute whip-around of individual responses without commenting on what you've heard. Here's a prompt to think about: "One new insight I had as a result of our conversation today was . . ." Here's another: "One question that keeps nagging me after our conversation is . . ."

Appendix B

Additional Text References and Internet Resources

Text References

Brookfield, S. D., and Preskill, S. *Discussion as a Way of Teaching: Tools and Techniques for Democratic Classrooms*. (2nd ed.) San Francisco: Jossey-Bass, 2005.

Burbules, N. C. *Dialogue in Teaching: Theory and Practice*. New York: Teachers College Press, 1993.

Colby, A., Ehrlich, T., Beaumont, E., and Stephens, J. *Educating Citizens: Preparing America's Undergraduates for Lives of Moral and Civic Responsibility*. San Francisco: Jossey-Bass, 2003.

Goleman, D. *Emotional Intelligence*. New York: Bantam Books, 1995.

Innovation Associates. *Systems Thinking: A Language for Learning and Acting: The Innovation Associates Systems Thinking Course Workbook*. Framingham, Mass.: Innovation Associates, 1992.

Parini, J. *The Art of Teaching*. New York: Oxford University Press, 2005.

Senge, P., and others. *The Fifth Discipline Fieldbook: Strategies and Tools for Building a Learning Organization*. New York: Doubleday, 1994.

Internet Resources

The Wingspread Declaration on Religion and Public Life: Engaging Higher Education is a statement on the key issues facing higher education regarding the intersection of religion and public life. It is downloadable free of charge through the Society for Values in Higher Education (www.svhe.org). Hard copies are available for a nominal fee through the main office of SVHE.

The Public Conversations Project   (www.publicconversations.org)   provides trainings, presentations, and workshops on the power of dialogue, inquiry as intervention, and the architecture of dialogue. PCP's Web site offers a variety of tools and downloadable resources for organizing and facilitating a dialogue.

The Study Circles Resource Center and the Paul J. Aicher Foundation (www. studycircles.org) promote and support study circles (small-group, democratic, peer-led dialogues on community and public policy issues). Study Circles will provide facilitator training and technical support for communities and organizations interested in convening community or organizational dialogues. The Web site provides downloadable dialogue guides, guides for community organizing, facilitation tips, training materials, and other resources.

The National Issues Forums (www.nifi.org) is a national network of education and community organizations that convene forums on national issues of public interest. NIF publishes discussion guides, guides for framing issues for public discussion, and a guide for moderators. Issue Forums include a survey component that is then used to inform policymakers and organizations interested in public policy development and change.

The Interaction Institute for Social Change (www.interactionassociates) offers public workshops in Facilitative Leadership®, coaching, diversity management, and advanced facilitation skills. The workshops help participants build skills both in facilitation and in organizing programs and activities for social change.

The National Association of Student Personnel Administrators (NASPA) published a report called *Learning Reconsidered: A Campus-Wide Focus on the Student Experience* in January 2004. This report has been an important resource for our book, and it can be accessed in its entirety at www.naspa.org/membership/leader _ex_pdf/lr_long.pdf.

The Ford Foundation promotes campus environments where sensitive subjects can be discussed in a spirit of open scholarly inquiry and academic freedom, and with respect for different viewpoints. Their *Difficult Dialogues* project was created in response to reports of growing intolerance and efforts to curb academic freedom at colleges and universities. The goal is to help institutions address this challenge through academic and campus programs that enrich learning, encourage new scholarship, and engage students and faculty in constructive dialogue about contentious political, religious, racial, and cultural issues. *Difficult Dialogues* has also been an important resource for our book, and the report can be accessed in its entirety at www.fordfound.org/news/more/dialogues/index.cfm.

Appendix C

Western Stereotypes About Islam from Both the Left and the Right

Robert J. Nash

1. *The Western misconception, fueled by the media and special-interest, right-wing politics, that Islam is a violent, fanatical religion that resorts to acts of terror, such as suicide bombings, in order to impose a particular religious ideology on the world.*

This stereotype continues to put all Muslims in the West on the defensive and, in some cases, even endangers their lives. The suicide bombers of 9/11, like the majority of terrorists throughout the world today, were not Muslims in the most traditional sense. They were members of a Wahhabi-Saudi group (founded by Abd al-Wahhab during the eighteenth century) of extremists who are often referred to by moderate Muslims as a death cult. This is the same group that claims Osama bin Laden as one of its leaders. These extremists are dedicated to policies of separatism, supremacism, and aggression.

Thus Wahhabi-Saudi extremists are to Islam what members of the radical, militant Christian identity movements are to Christianity. Think of Timothy McVeigh, the Oklahoma City bomber who destroyed a federal building, killing 168 civilians, in order to bring down a "Zionist-occupied" government and replace it with a Christian one. In other words, Muslim and Christian extremists are dangerous, heretical, fringe members of two world religions that actually teach peace, mercy, compassion, hope, and love, and not their opposites.

Also, there is not a single passage in the Qur'an that equates the term *jihad* with "holy war" or "terrorism." These are gross distortions of the word. Jihad actually means "effort, excellence, and exertion" in behalf of an individual's becoming stronger in Islamic spirituality and moral behavior. Muslims are urged by their sacred scriptures to wage jihad with the Qur'an, not with weapons of destruction, mass or otherwise (except in self-defense and fighting against oppression, much like just war theory in Christianity). A genuine Muslim jihadist works on himself or herself first and foremost.

Moreover, a growing number of scholars are conducting empirical studies of every single act of terrorism occurring in the last twenty-five years. The results of these studies show that upwards of 90 percent of all terrorist acts in the Middle East, including suicide bombings, have little or nothing to do with the religion of Islam. In actuality, the world's leading terrorists today are not Muslims. They are the Tamil Tigers in Sri Lanka, a secular, Marxist-Leninist group with Hindu roots. Also, savage acts of terrorism have occurred in Northern Ireland for decades, committed by Catholic and Protestant Christians against one another. And it was Serbian Christians who initiated and participated in the terrible ethnic cleansing of Muslims in Bosnia and Kosovo. Ironically, very few paramilitary, non-Islamic terrorist groups throughout the world are readily identified by their religious affiliations the way that Muslims are.

These same scholars also make the case that acts of terrorism did not originate with Muslims. Rather, they have a long history dating back to the Christian Crusades. In fact, at one time or another, all the world's major religions resorted to acts of terrorism whenever their leaders felt called by God to convert nonbelievers, to protect their special religio-political interests, and to advance their "divinely inspired," imperialistic agendas. For example, during the Second World War, more than three thousand Japanese kamikaze pilots flew their planes into fully loaded aircraft carriers in complete dedication to the Emperor Hirohito, whom they considered to be divine. They were later lionized as holy martyrs by the Japanese people. And Baruch Goldstein, a Zionist Jew who wanted to expel Muslims from Israel, embarked on a deadly suicide mission in 1994, resulting in the massacre of innocent Arab worshippers in the al Ibrahimi Mosque in Hebron.

Moreover, acts of terrorism originating in Muslim territories have a secular and political, not a religious, objective: to remove U.S. military troops from Arabic homelands. Even al-Qaeda, led by Osama bin Laden, is driven, first, by nationalism. Al-Qaeda's primary objective is to expel U.S. troops from the Persian Gulf region; and, only second, to restore Islamic rule to Arabic countries.

Obviously, when it is in the interests of terrorists, they will justify their aggression by appealing to specific religious passages in their holy scriptures. Most of these passages are taken completely out of context and interpreted in such a way that God is on the side of terrorists, who then become "holy warriors" or even religious "freedom fighters." In reality, however, it is governments, not religions, that fund and sanction terrorism throughout the world. Whether innocent victims die in New York City, Washington DC, Saudi Arabia, Jerusalem, Palestine, Lebanon, Kurdistan, Afghanistan, or Chechnya, it is legally constituted governments that sanction and support these barbaric horrors. Distorted, self-serving, and highly selective scriptural passages are merely frosting on the cake.

2. *The general Western misperception that Islam is an Arabic religion and that therefore only Arabs are Muslims. Moreover, Islam has little or no place in Judeo-Christian countries because its way of life and value system are thought to be totally antithetical to democracy and human rights.*

The fact is that not all Muslims are Arabs or people living in the Middle East. Currently, there are approximately ten million Muslims living peacefully and productively in the United States, who think of themselves as proud and loyal American citizens. In this country alone, there are more than fourteen hundred mosques. (A little known fact is that although approximately 40 percent of all Muslims in the United States are African American, contrary to media-generated sensationalism only a tiny percentage of these follow Louis Farrakhan's Nation of Islam.) Clearly, Islam is here in America to stay, as are millions of Muslims of all colors and backgrounds.

So, too, there is a growth explosion of Muslims throughout the United Kingdom, France, Canada, and Western Europe, in addition to Africa, India, the Middle East, and even South America. Also, sometime between 2025 and 2050 (depending on the particular projections), if current conversion trends in the West and escalating population growth in the Islamic world continue, then Islam could very well become the largest religious community in the world, easily surpassing two billion committed and practicing (not nominal) believers. This is roughly one-third of the world's population.

The coming Islamic global community will be pluralistic, not monistic, just as it is today. It will feature a number of Islamic subgroups distinguished as much by their particular ethnicities, cultures, nationalities, politics, traditions, and histories as by their common religious beliefs and practices.

Contrary to popular opinion in this country, throughout the Qur'an and throughout Muhammad's hadiths (the Prophet's sayings), there is a palpable and strong defense of human rights. Among the many human rights championed by the Qur'an and by Muhammad in his hadiths are the following: the right to die; the right to equality; the right to freedom; the right to justice; the right to equality before the law; the right to the basic necessities of life; the right to marriage; the right to privacy; and the right to education. One important example regarding Islam's advocacy of the right to religious freedom is the oft-quoted Surah 2:256 in the Qur'an: "Let there be no compulsion in religion."

3. *The stereotype that Islam subjugates and oppresses women*.

One misconception that continues to plague Muslims in the United States and elsewhere has to do with women's rights. Many people in the Western nations believe that Muslim women are completely subjugated and subordinated in the name of a "misogynistic" religion that confers all power on men. For example, some anti-Islamic Western commentators claim that Islam encourages the mutilation of a woman's clitoris. In actuality, excision, infibulation, and female genital mutilation have nothing whatever to do with Islam. (Clitoridectomy is a practice common in some African tribes, especially in Somalia.) The Qur'an neither sanctions nor encourages any of these practices. In fact, it frowns on them.

Progressive Muslims are the first to admit that greater improvement in the area of women's rights is always desirable in Islamic countries, as it is in the United States, where women only in recent history won the right to vote, but still have not yet won an Equal Rights Amendment or been elected to the presidency. Some Muslim scholars actually argue that, in many ways, women's rights are respected more in the Muslim world than in parts of the Christian world.

For example, Islamic doctrine teaches that men and women were created equal, from the same, single "soul" (Surah 4:1). Thus women's rights and responsibilities are equal to men's. Both men and women can initiate divorce proceedings in most Islamic countries. Furthermore, women, even female orphans, are granted strong financial rights in divorce and inheritance settlements everywhere. Muslim women are able to own property, accumulate financial wealth, and be fully self-supporting, if they so choose. Muhammad's first wife, Khadijah, was a successful and wealthy businesswoman, who was actually Muhammad's employer before they married.

In fact, there is almost no exploitation of women in the workforce in Islamic countries because of the clear injunction throughout the Qur'an to respect the rights and integrity of women.

Because the Qur'an speaks so highly and respectfully of women in a number of Surahs, as does Muhammad in his hadiths, sexual harassment is virtually nonexistent in the Arabic workplace, unlike in the United States. On those very rare occasions when it does occur in Islamic countries, the abuser is quickly called to account. Usually his employment is immediately terminated.

Moreover, women are paid fairly, and they have a right to decent working conditions at all times. Although there are undoubtedly male chauvinists in Arabic countries who mistreat women, so too there are male chauvinists, regardless of their religious beliefs, in all countries throughout the world. Mistreatment of women is a global problem sometimes inspired and justified by religion, sometimes not.

Contrary to Western opinion, Muslim women in most countries are rarely forced to seclude themselves (purdah), unlike Persians, Byzantines, ultraorthodox Jews, upper-class Hindus and even some women who belong to conservative Christian sects. Neither, in most Arabic countries, are they forced to wear clothes that cover every part of their bodies (burqa), including the customary veil (hijab). It is important to understand that in the vast majority of Muslim countries, how a woman dresses, behaves, and interacts with others, including men, is entirely the woman's choice. And this is becoming even more widespread in the more conservative Islamic countries, due to better education and employment opportunities.

On those occasions when some Muslim women do choose to wear more conservative clothing, they make the choice without apology. Why, they question, should women who are Muslims be forced to adopt the modernist dress styles of the West? Why should they be coerced to separate their religious beliefs from their secular lives? For many Muslim women, Islam is everything, and it touches all of life, not just a portion of it.

Moreover, in those rare circumstances in Arabic countries where polygamy is practiced (one study says that less than 0.02

percent of Muslim men are polygamous), those women who freely choose polygamy over monogamy do it, in part, as a protest against Western forms of women's liberation. Why, they challenge, should a Judeo-Christian, Anglo-Saxon ideal of marriage—one man, one woman—be imposed on every man and woman on the face of the earth? Is this not just another example of Western imperialism at its worst? Some Muslim women believe that with the soaring divorce rate in the Western secular democracies, in reality it is serial monogamy and assorted extramarital affairs that have become the actual templates for Christian marriages. Why, they ask, is this better, on its face, than polygamy? (Three narrative perspectives different from my own on Islam's treatment of women are Ayaan Hirsi Ali, 2006; Geraldine Brooks, 1995; and Irshad Manji, 2003.)

4.   *The overall misperception that Islam is a cruel, unforgiving religion, with a concept of criminal justice that seems barbaric, and a theological mission hell-bent on worldwide "coerced conversions."*

It is true that graphic images of beheadings, cutting off of hands, public beatings, and stonings in Islamic countries are becoming more common in the Western media. The stereotype that Islamic punishment of criminals is severe and barbaric hangs in the Western air. The Qur'an does indeed make a strong case for corporal punishment regarding the most reprehensible crimes committed against human beings. In those few states (Saudi Arabia is one of the most publicized by Western media) where such heinous punishments do occur, theft, burglary, mugging, rape, and murder are rare to nonexistent.

Most important, however, is that these types of corporal punishments are rarely practiced in the majority of Muslim countries, and never in South Asia. The Qur'an teaches that compassion, mercy, and kindness must always be the first, and last, resort in dealing with criminals. In fact, in most cases, a bereaved family of the victim can forgive a murderer, and this will be taken into account in sentencing by the courts.

It is also important to note that, on their part, Muslims are shocked at the cruelty of gassing, electrocuting, and lethally injecting human beings—punishments that they see as America's only solution to capital crimes. Many Muslims are quick to note that with the number of violent and deadly crimes on the rise in the West, capital punishment hardly acts as a deterrent.

Finally, contrary to popular opinion in the West, Islam does not advocate hunting down unbelievers and then torturing and killing them unless they either recant or convert. The passage usually taken out of its full historical context (and mistranslated) in the Qur'an (9:5) and often used to justify this stereotype reads, "Slay the unbelievers wherever you find them, and take them captives and besiege them and lie in wait for them in every ambush."

The Arabic word for "unbelievers" is more accurately translated as "idolaters." Thus the entire passage (9:1–6) goes on to explain that the idolaters are actually a group of pagan warriors who violated a peace treaty with the Muslims. It is a specific instruction for Muslims, subject to all the rules for just war, who find themselves unfairly attacked by an enemy. The passage commands that a four-month warning period be given to the enemy before war commences. And it allows the military opponent to renounce the fight and seek help, with no precondition requiring a conversion to Islam.

(Background information for the claims I make in this essay comes from the following sources: Akbar S. Ahmed, *Islam Today;* Karen Armstrong, *A History of God;* Mia Bloom, *Dying to Kill;* Anatol Lieven, *America Right or Wrong;* Robert A. Pape, *Dying to Win;* Imam Feisal Abdul Rauf, *What's Right with Islam Is What's Right with America;* Malise Ruthven, *Islam in the World,* 2nd edition; Stephen Schwartz, *The Two Faces of Islam;* Jessica Stern, *Terror in the Name of God;* and *The Glorious Qur'an Translation,* trans. Mohammed Marmaduke Pickthall.)

Appendix D

A Whole-Campus Teaching and Learning Rationale for Moral Conversation

Inspired by the 2004 NASPA Report Learning Reconsidered: A Campus-Wide Focus on the Student Experience

Robert J. Nash

Everything that we say in this book regarding the educational value of cross-campus conversations on difficult topics finds its overall rationale in the observations and recommendations of the NASPA report *Learning Reconsidered: A Campus-Wide Focus on the Student Experience*, issued January 2004. Among the report's specific observations and recommendations are the following italicized sentences along with our with our recommendations for faculty, student affairs leaders, and academic administrators. administrative implications following each:

- *"Learning is a complex, holistic, multi-centric activity that occurs throughout and across the college experience. Student development, and the adaptation of learning to students' lives and needs, are fundamental parts of engaged learning and liberal education. True liberal education requires the engagement of the whole student—and the deployment of every resource in higher education. Experiences with out-of-classroom learning can, however, be as centrifugal as any general education sequence. . . . The idea of transformative learning reinforces the root meaning of liberal education itself—freeing oneself from the constraints of a lack of knowledge and an excess of simplicity."*

What is liberal education? According to the authors of *Learning Reconsidered*, a genuine liberal education engages the "whole student," body, mind, spirit, feelings, and character. In fact, "transformative learning" is liberal in the etymological sense of "belonging to the people," "freeing," and conducive to "growing." Furthermore, a liberal education implies tolerance for opposing views, as well as an open-mindedness to ideas that challenge the conventional wisdom. A broad, liberal education, according to the NASPA report, is one that is "complex, holistic, and multi-centric." It frees students "from the constraints of a lack of knowledge and an excess of simplicity."

From another angle, listen to Dr. Lewis Thomas, former president of the Memorial Sloan-Kettering Cancer Center: "These are not the best of times for the human mind. All sorts of things seem to be turning out wrong. . . . We do not know enough about ourselves. We are ignorant about how we work, about where we fit in, and most of all about the enormous, imponderable system of life in which we are embedded as working parts. . . . We are *dumb*" (cited in Oakley, 1992, p. 17). We believe that Thomas is right and, therefore, that the NASPA report's pivotal proposal to transform education throughout the college campus is on the mark.

An education grounded in moral conversation seems best equipped to help students, and all the rest of us, to know about ourselves; about making important distinctions among labor, work, job, career, and vocation; and about where each of us fits into the smaller and larger schemes of our daily lives. Most of all, however, moral conversation is built on the premise that multiple opportunities to talk about the inescapable and imponderable mysteries of life are what a good liberal education should be about. Pondering the imponderable mysteries, after all, is why all the "great books" have been written, why the great poems, paintings, and plays have been created, and why, through the centuries, the great music has possessed those unique charms to soothe the savage beast.

Thus we go one concrete step further than both Thomas and the NASPA report. We maintain that all types of transformative education must begin, progress, and end with some attention to moral conversation. It is mainly through the process of moral conversation, as we have elaborated it throughout this book, that students can best create and re-create meaning. They can think more deeply about the differences between what they believe truly matters and what ought to matter, both personally and interpersonally. They can reflect together with others on the importance, at all levels, of their studies, and how they will fit this newfound knowledge into the larger social scheme when they graduate. Most important, and we believe that Thomas is right on this point, moral conversation has the unlimited potential of helping students ponder those nagging existential questions that each of us must inescapably confront every single day of our lives.

We have alluded throughout this book to the importance of building what we will call "conversational capital" on college campuses. Conversational capital is the fruit of liberal education at its best. It is through genuine moral conversation that students learn how to talk about what is truly important to them and to others. It also encourages them to think deeply and compassionately together about many of the critical issues and problems facing their unique communities of belonging. It brings them face-to-face, or better voice-to-voice, with serious differences in beliefs, attitudes, and practices. It enriches the process of meaning making, both at the individual and the communal levels. In this sense, there is no false dichotomy between talk and action. In fact, it is only through conversation that all of us are able to create new worlds of meaning, whether these be in educational institutions or in other social systems, such as governments, families, and businesses.

We believe that everything human beings do, they do in conversation with one another. Every day of our lives, we actually live in communities of conversation making. Why? "We enjoy it, we caress each other in language. We can also hurt each other in language. We can open spaces or restrict them in conversations. This is central to us. And we shape our own path, as do all living systems" (Maturana and Bunnell, cited in Brown, 2005, p. 19). Thus, the very essence of liberal education ought to be about creating an ethos of conversational inquiry on college campuses. This ethos begins with one of the golden rules of moral conversation: converse as you would have others converse with you. Listen as you would have others listen to you. Search for your truths as you would have your truths search for you—if they were able to do this.

The NASPA report also speaks of the "centrifugal force" of out-of-classroom learning. Engaging in planned cross-campus conversation about timely controversial issues takes learning far beyond the conventional classroom for all campus constituencies, including students, administrators, and faculty. Moral conversation is noted for its power to involve the whole student in what we might call whole-campus teaching and learning. Cross-campus conversations, planned and directed by all the appropriate teaching-learning constituents, do in fact "deploy" an assortment of resources in the academy. For starters, there is almost unlimited learning potential for everyone exposed to an assortment of guest speakers, alternative campus locations, and a diverse array of controversial topics. Similarly, there is an unprecedented opportunity to create a variety of innovative assessment techniques.

In this sense, learning is truly transformed. Learning is not only "centrifugal," moving from the center of conventional classroom learning to the outside campus, but also "recursive," shifting back and forth, again and again, to the point from which it originates. In this way, the center gets renewed, as the outside gets integrated into the teaching-learning process. Classroom learning informs and leads to the outside world for validation and experimentation. Outside-world learning moves back to the classroom for reflection and analysis. Sometimes this is called *praxis*—the cross-pollination of theory and practice. This is what moral conversation accomplishes when it is going well. In this way, therefore, centrifugal and recursive teaching and learning hold the promise to enrich the entire process and content of liberal education as we know it today.

- *"The degree of [disconnection in the classroom, personal development, and society on college campuses today] is profound and has serious implications for both teaching processes and the structures institutions use to help students learn. Today's growing emphasis on integrated learning structures, such as cluster courses and living-learning communities, may in some cases be an acknowledgement of the need to restore the missing holism."*

How often have we heard college students at all levels complain bitterly about all the classroom and out-of-classroom disconnects in their education? The observation that a number of students today think of their education in purely instrumental terms has become almost a cliché, a settled premise in the conventional wisdom of the academy. Diplomas, for these students, become nothing more than hard-won passports to employment markets or to professional graduate schools. "Doing" college is tantamount to "surviving" college as a painful prerequisite for going out to the "real world" where life really counts (see Karabell, 1999).

It is no surprise, therefore, that many students experience all the formal academic rituals (courses, lectures, reading assignments, exams, grades, and so forth) as nothing more than a series of worrisome and exhausting obstacles on the way to winning the real prizes at the end of the college endurance contest. How sad! This is a dramatic example of how the total dissociation of means and ends in college learning can turn students into frantic grade-grubbers and opportunistic résumé builders. Why, after decades of a plethora of such real-life data, haven't we educators learned to repair the damage of part-whole, inside-outside, thinking-doing, teaching-learning disconnection?

One of the advantages of engaging students, professors, and administrators in cross-campus conversational settings is the possibility of actually modeling and practicing a genuine "integrative, holistic" educational experience. We can restore means-ends continuity to the educational process, if we extend learning to the entire campus and beyond. Listening to a controversial speaker or a series of speakers discourse about such provocative topics as those covered in this book can be life changing for many of us. For one, learning how to actively and respectfully engage these speakers, as well as one another, in moral conversation challenges each of us to make connections among all those complex, interrelated "meaning narratives" within which we live.

The fact is that in addition to living our lives in such campus community settings as classrooms, residence halls, faculty offices, and a variety of cocurricular campus sites, each of us also lives in our own evolving stories of personal meaning. Each of us must, at various times during our life cycle, remake our selves and our relationships. This is the meaning of holistic and integrative learning. We believe that participating in moral conversation, both inside and outside the conventional academic structures, will effectively teach all of us how to integrate site, self, selves, and subject matter into a holistic learning experience.

Learning how to participate actively in moral conversations by listening carefully and respectfully to the diverse ideas of others; engaging these others in compassionate yet robust back-and-forth dialogue; and eventually struggling to integrate all these learnings into some kind of unified, personal story of meaning are the irreducible elements of holistic education. At the very least, this kind of learning prepares all of us for life in the real, pluralistic world. This is a world that is not completely religious *or* nonreligious, upper *or* middle *or* lower class, politically conservative *or* moderate *or* radical. Life in the real world is at once all of these, some of these, or even, at times, none of these. It is something far more complex and mysterious. Or, as William James once said about life: it is full of "blooming, buzzing confusion . . . always and everywhere . . . without exception."

- *"[B]rain based learning [is an] important new [methodology] that serve[s] as a foundation for the mapping approach to student learning. [Learning] has a neurobiological framework—the activation of neural processes that contribute to the deep transformation of cognition and patterning, or meaning making. For such transformative learning to occur, students must 1) enter a state of relaxed alertness, 2) participate in an orchestrated immersion in a complex experience that in some way illustrates phenomena that are connected to the subject and 3) engage in active processing or reflection on the experience. . . . This kind of transformative learning is what student affairs professionals understand as student development education."*

The NASPA report goes on to say that the most important factor in student development is learning within "the active context of students' lives." Real-life contexts happen when students learn how to resolve conflicts, actively encounter others, and take leadership responsibility in a group. According to the latest research on brain-based learning (Edelman, 2006; Gazzaniga, 2005), students are almost always in a state of "relaxed alertness" whenever they realize that the threat level in a classroom is low, no matter how challenging and controversial the subject matter might be. During this time, their neurons are at optimal firing capacity, and their cognitive patternings are rich and complex. Also, according to this brain-based research, although students highly appreciate some type of evaluative feedback from educators, nearly always the imposition of grades acts as a serious deterrent to their relaxed alertness and complex cognitive processing.

Some recent, fascinating research by Ken Bain (2004) on effective teachers confirms the latest findings of the brain-based learning sciences. According to Bain's extensive research, the "best" teachers know their subject matter well and have created a variety of hands-on, as well as heads-on, techniques to transmit their knowledge to students. The best teachers always recognize, however, that the ultimate purpose of any education is to help students construct and apply new knowledge, rather than simply build storehouses of information. This is called the *constructivist* approach to education, and it is predicated on an epistemology that defines knowledge as conditional, developmental, socially and culturally constructed, and nonfoundational (Brooks and Brooks, 1993).

Moreover, the best teachers always mix up their pedagogical techniques. They are as apt to engage their students in lively, field-based, collaborative, problem-solving activities as they are to give lectures, lead seminar discussions, and sponsor clerkships. They want to teach students how to think and act in real life instead of preparing them simply to pass tests. Finally, the best teachers trust that their students want to learn, and that, given time and care on the teacher's part, students will eventually accept a sense of control over their own learning.

All these findings are consistent with the outcomes of successful moral conversation. We have witnessed these successes firsthand in our work with students throughout the country. When moral conversation is working well, the following learning patterns are clearly evident: (1) students engage actively in their learning with a vibrant sense of expectancy and excitement; (2) open-ended, evocative, problem-based questions in conversation are far more prominent than closed-ended, test-based answers; (3) learning is interdisciplinary, unbounded, and wide ranging; (4) teaching and learning are frequently story based, vulnerable, and honest; (5) a variety of pedagogical techniques fill the learning space, including lecture, small and large group conversations, online learning, service learning, and field-based assignments, among others (see Light, 2001).

Teachers who want to use some form of conversation-based learning report that they are most successful when they are able to (1) get students' attention and keep it; (2) start with the interests of their students rather than with the interests and demands of their disciplines; (3) convince students to make commitments to the entire learning community as well as to the mastery of subject matter; (4) encourage and assist students to learn outside of formal class and academic structures; (5) create a diversity of teaching-learning experiences that focus on getting students to talk things out, to interact with each other, and, when necessary, to reflect independently of the group in order to make personal sense of the new learnings gained in face-to-face conversation (Bain, 2004).

- *"Assessment tools should include—but not be limited to—formal written inventories, questionnaires and web surveys; faculty, staff, and mentors' observations of student behavior; peer assessments; information gained from individual interviews, presentations, journals, and portfolios; and data gathered from group work, focus groups, and case studies. . . . As part of the assessment process, faculty and student affairs educators should also work together to complete conceptual mapping of student learning, collaboratively identifying activities inside and outside the classroom that focus upon and contribute to specifically defined learning objectives."*

Finally, what types of evaluation best lend themselves to an accurate assessment of learning by moral conversation? Once again, according to Bain's research on effective teaching (2004), the best evaluation stresses learning rather than performance. Performance means living up to others' expectations and requirements. Learning means that students take full responsibility for their own intellectual, emotional, kinesthetic, and personal development. Performance is mainly about acquiring and storing information and taking tests. Learning is developmental and an end in itself. Moral conversation educators are as interested in knowing *who* the student is as *what* the student knows.

A moral conversation approach to learning teaches to the *person* rather than to the *test*. It recognizes that any kind of evaluation process is flawed at best, because, in some sense, it always represents the personal judgment and intellectual biases of the evaluator. Furthermore, as most of us know intuitively, no judgment ever originates from an "immaculate perception" of what constitutes "objective" failure or success. Robert, one of the authors of this book, often says to his teacher education students: "Tell me how *you* were judged in school, and I'll tell you how you will judge *others*. Better still, tell me how you *felt* about being judged throughout your education, and I'll tell you what you purposely *include*, and *exclude*, in your assessment of students."

Some of Bain's best teachers asked their students to evaluate themselves, while still requiring them to provide various types of hands-on evidence that learning did indeed occur. Often these students presented this evidence in face-to-face conversation with their teachers, in addition to writing extensive narrative self-evaluations, complete with such "evidence" as learning portfolios, time logs, daily or weekly written reports, and a variety of independently designed work projects. The upshot for the successful assessment of learning in moral conversation is to encourage students to set their own goals and to take full responsibility for determining whether or not they were able to meet those goals.

To conclude this appendix, I leave you with a powerful statement by Anne W. Dosher, founder of the World Café, an organization that shapes futures that matter through conversation, as well as a cofounder of the Institute for Relational Development. This quotation sums up why moral conversation is so important to the three of us at these particular stages in our professional lives. It is the fuel that stokes our fire! Dosher asks,

> *How can we talk it through?* The question that has informed all of my life choices, now lies, I believe, at the heart of our capacity to survive as a species and to ensure that our home, this beautiful planet, survives. For me, it is the core question that informs all of our other

questions. If we could converse and talk things out, we would find new ways of being together in the world. But, instead, we separate, conflicts begin, and when worse comes to worse, we go to war. Then death comes in as a walking partner, instead of life [quoted in Brown, 2005, p. 214].

Appendix E

Naturalistic and Narrativistic Paradigms in Academia
Implications for Moral Conversation

Robert J. Nash

I believe that there are significant differences in the background beliefs, perspectives, and practices of two opposing academic paradigms in the American university. I call these the *naturalistic* and the *narrativistic* approaches to scholarship and teaching. In academia today, however, the naturalistic paradigm is dominant. The norms for maintaining the naturalistic status quo in the academy are unyielding. Entire reward and status systems are built on them. Many faculty members who inhabit different disciplinary silos will criticize the "anecdotal quality," the "dumbing down," the "subjectivity," and the "softness" of research and teaching that push the traditional boundaries—particularly narrativistic, more personal, less empirical forms of scholarship and pedagogy.

Many faculty prefer to concentrate their scholarship and their classroom lectures and discussions on the intricacies, technical conflicts, and details of their specialized fields of study. Although there is nothing inherently wrong with this concentration on micro-investigation (in fact, much good has come of it in the natural and social sciences), it is in their training that graduate students and junior faculty are conditioned to privilege some research and pedagogical methodologies over others under the threat of excommunication from their scholarly guilds.

This socialization experience all too often results in a "do-as-I did-or-else" imperative. Thus naturalistic inquiry gets certified as the only "rigorous" approach to researching, creating, and communicating knowledge. Only a few faculty will dare to become genuine interdisciplinarians and innovators, capable of creating their own intellectual revolutions. And if they do become revolutionaries, they are likely to be castigated as heretics and iconoclasts who dare to challenge the intellectual totems and taboos of the academy. As a consequence, they will be ostracized as mere border dwellers who are doomed to live on the margins of organized bodies of knowledge, but who will never really fit in anywhere.

Such is the fate of most academic norm breakers in the academy. Unfortunately, too, the fate of scholarship and teaching in higher education is destined to be nothing more than what Keyes (1995) calls "neotribal bafflegab . . . filled with inflated language, [busy charts and graphs, oceans of statistics], obscure references, and needlessly complex sentences . . . all of which leads to passivity, vagueness, and abstraction on the part of both researchers and potential consumers of that research" (p. 100).

NATURALISTIC AND NARRATIVISTIC NOTIONS OF TRUTH

Conflicts around truth questions are unavoidably grounded in and mediated by particular worldviews, socialization, enculturation, academic and professional training, and unique narratives of personal meaning. Thus the answers scholars are seeking will in part be determined by the types of truth questions they are asking. There will be times when the pragmatic, naturalistic, and analytical questions will be necessary, in which case the answers will be empirically researchable, evidentially based, and factual. I call this approach to knowledge and truth *academic objectivism*. There will also be times when the less empirically testable questions that are value laden, existential, and even metaphysical will be significant; then the answers will be nonscientific, perhaps more emotional than rational, more philosophical than data based, more theological than logical, or more autobiographical than veridical. I call this approach *academic constructivism*.

Naturalism (Academic Objectivism)

What counts as true knowledge in the naturalistic paradigm is knowledge that proceeds from testable, verifiable hypotheses and premises; that allows for continual reexamination and questioning of these hypotheses and findings, leading to the possible falsification or validation of evidence; and that emerges as most empirically and rationally persuasive (as well as useful) for the largest number of researchers in any specific scientific community. Examples of true knowledge from within the naturalistic disciplinary matrix are the laws of gravity, quantum mechanics, combustion, natural selection, planetary motion, general relativity, and chemical composition. In the social sciences, examples of "true" knowledge (those candidates seeking the status of scientific truth but without the predictive accuracy of the natural sciences) are the law of supply and demand, rational-choice theory, multiple intelligences, and sociobiology—the latter being knowledge that crisscrosses the social sciences and the natural sciences. For many naturalistic scientists, "objective" knowledge is the ultimate goal—knowledge that is fact independent rather than mind dependent.

In actuality, however, many natural scientists, social scientists, and humanities scholars recognize that a perfect separation of domains, though in theory desirable, is virtually impossible to achieve. As but one example, researcher bias is inevitable, indeed unavoidable, and for those naturalistic scholars who believe that an attitude of immaculate perception is possible, there are any number of scientists who will challenge the research results in such a way as to uncover even a modicum of researcher bias. Some researchers create elaborate methodologies, such as double-blind studies, control, randomization, repeatability, openness, statistics, and complete reporting—all calculated to factor out any hint of subjective bias. But whether bias is systematically bracketed, accepted as a given, reduced in influence, neutralized, or marginalized, alas, the bias is there, always there, always waiting to compromise or contaminate the research findings of immaculate perceivers, and receivers, of "objective" data.

This is where Popper's principle of falsifiability (1968) can help everyone on college campuses, as it is an excellent check on the arrogance of those objectivist academicians who believe they have arrived at a once-and-for-all, indisputable, bias-free, scientific truth. For Popper, knowledge can never be absolute or certain. Scientists guess, conjecture, and interpret, just as all human beings do whenever they observe the so-called factual world. Corroboration of data is, at its best, imperfect and, in theory, always capable of being falsified. New frameworks of understanding and interpretation relativize even the most basic, agreed-on facts. For this reason, Popper advocates a continuing, systematic practice of scientific self-criticism. No scientific finding is immune to further testing, refinement, or interpretation. In fact, for Popper, falsification is the royal road to scientific truth. Or as Alfred Lord Tennyson once said about religion, "There is more truth in honest doubt than in all the creeds of the world."

In general, however, and despite the inevitability of perceptual bias, with few exceptions objectivist academicians believe that there is a tangible world "out there" for scholars and researchers to explore and possibly even discover. There are lawful regularities that control and predict this world. This is a representational take on reality. Truth is that which can be measured, weighed, tested, interviewed, and arrived at by the discipline's standard empirical research methods. In this model, the mind of the researcher is like a camera that, when working according to the strict standards of the scientific method, takes representative pictures of what exists outside the mind. Although the scientific mood is one of intellectual agnosticism, buttressed by an open-minded skepticism toward any "final" claims of bias-free Truth, evidence that is representational is the ultimate indicator of what counts as naturalistic truth and what doesn't. Disciplined adherence to the scientific method is the best guarantee of whether or not one is able to arrive at this truth. The natural sciences and to some extent the social sciences are the best domains of knowledge for discovering naturalistic truths.

Narrativism (Academic Constructivism)

Although I greatly respect naturalistic approaches to intellectual inquiry, I also believe that some notions of truth are more personally rooted, context dependent, ever changing, and, to a large extent, hidden from the eyes of a beholder. In this sense, the scholar constructs (narrativizes, tells stories about) truth instead of "objectively" representing or mirroring it. Freedman (2001) goes so far as to hold that "It is inevitable that much if not *all* scholarship, student work, and real-world writing and talking is personal. Joining the personal and professional, analysis and emotion, 'self and other,' connects readers to texts, to their own writing, to our own critical process, and to one another. . . . The making of such connections between one's life and one's work is 'vulnerable writing.'" She adds quickly, however, that "vulnerability doesn't mean anything personal goes. The exposure of the self who is also a spectator has to take us somewhere we couldn't otherwise get to. It has to be essential to the argument, not a decorative flourish, not self-exposure for its own sake" (p. 206).

What Freedman (2001) calls vulnerable writing, I call narrativistic scholarship. Whether scholars call it personal research, radical introspective inquiry, or self-inclusive, self-disclosing, or self-creating scholarship, narrativistic scholarship starts with the author's personal take on the world of ideas and experience. The narrativist understands that all authors (whether they be scientists, social scientists, or humanities scholars) live in stories about reality and not in a neo-Platonic world called "reality in itself." Thus empirical truth cannot exist out there as "objective" or "situation independent," because stories about truth, constructed in context-dependent language, cannot exist out there. They exist in human beings and in the cultures they construct and share. Without the stories, and the language and discourse to promulgate these stories, there can be no unfiltered, unnarrativized reality, or truth, out there. Only the stories and the language can be examined for truth or falsity, validity or nonvalidity.

First-person, narrativistic scholarship encourages scholars to see themselves as the pivotal variables in their research and teaching, without whom there would be no research or teaching at all. Why? Narrativistic inquiry locates the author's life and experiences as central to a scholarly analysis or a research study. Behar (1996), the MacArthur Fellows Award–winning anthropologist, calls this kind of writing and speaking "an act of personal witness." Bérubé (1994) goes so far as to say that "In fields like history, anthropology, sociology . . . the interests of the observer are an integral element of research, so much that to ignore those interests is to run the risk of pretending that the human sciences might aspire to the accuracy of the physical sciences if only humanists would conduct human sciences without hermeneutics" (p. 106).

In the last few decades, narrativistic scholarship has found a home in such disciplines as multicultural studies, women's studies, religious studies, postmodern philosophy and literature, and certain types of composition and rhetoric studies. Many feminists, social justice activists, and postmodern authors "re-vision" their scholarly inquiries to emphasize the lived life of the writer-teacher-scholar as the major source of questions, perspectives, and methods. For oppressed people of color throughout the world, narrativistic scholarship has given them long overdue permission to insert their own authentic voices into their writing. Whatever the academic or professional discipline, however, I believe that narrativistic inquiry is a scholarly methodology that effectively blends stories, interpretation, theory, and universalizable themes.

Nietzsche was one of the first thinkers to develop an idea he called *perspectivism*. Nietzsche believed that there was a provisional character to all knowledge. No knowledge, scientific or otherwise, transcends individual or social perspectives. To think otherwise, according to Nietzsche, is to indulge in a fantasy. Thus what counts as truth has very little to do with finding some unfiltered representation of an absolute reality, a representation that results in a one-to-one correspondence with an outside world.

Although Nietzsche never negated the importance of naturalistic ways of knowing, he did warn us that our comprehension of truth is very much dependent on our unique personal and cultural perspectives. Consequently, his statement that "all truth is fiction" was far less relativistic and nihilistic than it might at first sound. What Nietzsche was getting at was that in order for us to comprehend the full meaning of truth for the truth proclaimer, it is important that we understand the narrative perspective out of which the truth claim emerges. Nietzsche would be very comfortable in reversing the words of the seventeenth-century English philosopher, John Locke: *Nihil est in mundi quod not prius fuerit in narratio.* (Nothing is in the world that is not first in a story about that world).

SO WHAT? NOW WHAT? IMPLICATIONS FOR MORAL CONVERSATION

So, what does all of this have to do with moral conversation? In a word, *everything*! On the one hand, academic objectivists will be more likely to challenge the legitimacy of moral conversation on college campuses because, for them, it is not the best way to conduct rigorous, testable inquiry on the hot topics. Most objectivist critics of moral conversation will dismiss it as being too subjective, touchy-feely, and intellectually suspect. On the other hand, academic constructivists will be more likely to give moral conversation a chance, because it is a way to explore the relational, as well as the rational, complexities of hot topics.

For constructivists like Bruner (1990), truth is judged according to such narrativist criteria as "external and internal coherence, livability, creativity, utility, plausibility, and adequacy" (p. 112). Thus moral conversation, with its extremely high tolerance for personal vulnerability, ambiguity, uncertainty, risk taking, and imaginative forays into dangerous, unknown intellectual territory, appears to be the most compatible strategy for arriving at constructivist notions of truth and meaning and, ipso facto, for talking about hot topics across campus, where final solutions and answers to the most difficult social, religious, and political problems are at best tenuous and always in process.

Another way to look at the potential fit between academic constructivism and moral conversation is to remember that, in the ideal, talking with one another about hot topics across campus and beyond the traditional disciplinary enclaves is as much about making personal connections as it is about coming up with final solutions. The university is full of expert analysts, problem solvers, and policymakers. However, what it desperately needs at this time are people who know how to make personal connections with one another, people who are willing to view the world from the other sides of their own perspectives. The university also needs experts who recognize that the ways they approach and attempt to solve problems are largely a function of their own self-interests. To ignore the impact of individual self-interests, as well as particular worldviews, in any cross-campus conversation on the hot topics is to pretend that one, and only one, perspective contains the whole truth because it transcends particular times, places, people, and self-interests.

In order for us to get both constructivists *and* objectivists on board as supporters of moral conversation, we in the academy need to find ways to reconcile our paradigm differences rather than polarize them any further. Why can't we think of truth as being both naturalistic *and* narrativistic, objectivist *and* constructivist, and, at times, one more or less than the other? The possibility of finding areas of intellectual overlap in scholarly interchanges begins in a commitment to academic pluralism. This commitment gets expressed in the following way: "The academic language and techniques I employ to analyze and solve problems are merely useful tools to declare my deepest beliefs about all the hot topics we are examining. I promise to do the best I can with the language I am using, even though at times it might seem to you to be flawed and partial. I assume you will do your best as well. There will be times when I will choose to use both the naturalistic *and* narrativistic languages in order to inch closer to some kind of defensible (even inspiring) truths about the hot topics we are trying to understand.

"I can't prove to you that *my* particular choice of truth finding and problem solving will give you everything that *you* need to solve *your* problems regarding these controversial issues. But I can respect your truth-finding style, and see it as your best tool to make sense of the world. I will try to understand it, as best I can, from your particular vantage point. I will work hard to practice empathy when I do not understand it or when I am in total disagreement with it. In this instance, I will respectfully challenge you, and I promise not to do violence, either passively or actively, to your cherished way of finding and creating knowledge. I have faith that you will choose to treat me the same way. Perhaps, if all goes well, we might even reach some point of agreement in our moral conversations but, more important, also discover some way to avoid inflicting pain and humiliation on one another because we might think of the other as doing 'soft' or 'hard,' naïve or realistic scholarly analysis and problem solving. Maybe, if it all works out, we will even find a way to respect one another beyond the neat and tidy little labels we use to separate ourselves from each other."

In summary, I am convinced that some academic questions require scholarly methodologies that result in accessible, testable, factual answers. I am also convinced that some academic investigations are, de facto, rooted in personal leaps of faith, intuition, what Michael Polyani called "tacit knowledge," and passionate feelings. I call this *mesearch*. Other inquiries reside in the cool waters of dispassionate reason, empirical investigation, and logic. I call this *research*. Mesearch is more likely to find a methodological home in the humanities, where narrative reigns. Research is more likely to locate its place in the natural sciences and social sciences, where naturalism reigns. The ideal blending of the two results in what I think of as a more universalizable *wesearch*, an attitude that realizes we are all in the human adventure together . . . seeking to understand it and doing our best to solve its most vexing mysteries and dilemmas. The best moral conversation features equal amounts of research, mesearch, and wesearch.

Finally, I believe that when done well, moral conversation has the potential of producing wonderful results in building cross-campus alliances, collegiality, and solidarity among all its constituencies. Why? Because its major aim is to get together as many participants as possible to talk with mutual respect and generosity about the hot topics—in their own languages, out of their own worldviews, and in their own best ways. Moral conversation will help us understand the indisputable wisdom in Nietzsche's words, "The general imprecise way of observing sees everywhere in nature opposites where there are, not opposites, but differences of degree. . . . An unspeakable amount of painfulness, arrogance, harshness, estrangement, frigidity has entered into human feelings because we think we see opposites instead of transitions" (Hollingdale, 1977).

Whether participants are naturalistic or narrativistic, objectivist or constructivist in their perspectives, I believe that moral conversation will help us find the "transitions" and narrative overlaps in our differing perspectives on even the hottest of hot topics . . . rather than dwell mainly on their "opposites."

References

Ahmed, A. S. *Islam Today: A Short Introduction to the Muslim World*. New York: Tauris, 2001.

Ali, A. H. *The Caged Virgin: An Emancipation Proclamation for Women and Islam*. New York: Free Press, 2006.

Allison, D. *Skin: Talking About Sex, Class, and Literature*. Ithaca, N.Y.: Firebrand Books, 1994.

Alper, L., and Leistyna, P. *Class Dismissed: How TV Frames the Working Class* [film]. Northampton, Mass.: Media Education Foundation, 2005.

Anyon, J. "Social Class and the Hidden Curriculum of Work." In J. Ballantine (ed.), *School and Society*. Mountain View, Calif.: Mayfield, 1980.

Appiah, K. A. *The Ethics of Identity*. Princeton, N.J.: Princeton University Press, 2005.

Appiah, K. A. *Cosmopolitanism: Ethics in a World of Strangers*. New York: Norton, 2006.

Argyris, C., and Schön, D. *Theory in Practice*. San Francisco: Jossey-Bass, 1974.

Armstrong, K. *A History of God: The 4000-Year Quest of Judaism, Christianity, and Islam*. New York: Knopf, 1993.

Bain, K. *What the Best College Teachers Do.* Cambridge, Mass.: Harvard University Press, 2004.

Behar, R. *The Vulnerable Observer: Anthropology That Breaks Your Heart.* Boston: Beacon Press, 1996.

Berlin, I. *Four Essays on Liberty.* New York: Oxford University Press, 1969.

Berube, M. *Public Access: Literary Theory and American Cultural Politics.* London: Verso, 1994.

Bloom, M. *Dying to Kill: The Allure of Suicide Terror.* New York: Columbia University Press, 2005.

Blumberg, P. *Inequality in the Age of Decline.* New York: Oxford University Press, 1980.

Brezeale, D. (ed.). *Philosophy and Truth: Selections from Nietzsche's Notebooks of the Early 1870s.* Buffalo, N.Y.: Prometheus, 1990.

Bromwich, D. *Politics by Other Means: Higher Education and Group Thinking.* New Haven, Conn.: Yale University Press, 1992.

Brooks, G. *Nine Parts of Desire: The Hidden World of Islamic Women.* New York: Random House, 1995.

Brooks, J., and Brooks, G. *The Case for Constructivist Classrooms.* Alexandria, Virg.: Association for Supervision and Curriculum Development, 1993.

Brown, J. *The World Café: Shaping Our Futures Through Conversations That Matter.* San Francisco: Berrett-Koehler, 2005.

Bruner, J. *Acts of Meaning.* Cambridge, Mass.: Harvard University Press, 1990.

Callahan, D. "Universalism and Particularism: Fighting to a Draw." *Hastings Center Report,* 2000, pp. 37–44.

Carter, S. *The Culture of Disbelief: How American Law and Politics Trivialize Religious Devotion.* New York: Basic Books, 1993.

Carter, S. *Civility: Manners, Morals, and the Etiquette of Democracy.* New York: Basic Books, 1998.

Chickering, A. W., Dalton, J. C., and Stamm, L. *Encouraging Authenticity and Spirituality in Higher Education.* San Francisco: Jossey-Bass, 2005.

Churchill, W. "Some People Push Back: On the Justice of Roosting Chickens." www.kersplebedeb.com/mystuff/s11/churchill.html. Dec. 2005.

"Conflict Resolution: The Israeli-Palestinian Experiment." *Chronicle of Higher Education,* Sept. 22, 2006, p. A2.

Correspondents of the *New York Times. Class Matters.* New York: Times Books, 2005.

Cupitt, D. *The Great Questions of Life.* Santa Rosa, Calif. Polebridge Press, 2005.

"Dangerous Ideas." *Chronicle Review,* Oct. 1, 2004, p. B2.

D'Souza, D. *What's So Great About America.* Washington, D.C.: Regnery, 2002.

Eck, D. *Encountering God: A Spiritual Journey from Bozeman to Banaras.* Boston: Beacon, 1993.

Eck, D. *A New Religious America: How a "Christian Country" Has Become the World's Most Religiously Diverse Nation.* San Francisco: HarperCollins, 2001.

Edelman, G. *Second Nature: Brain Science and Human Knowledge.* New Haven, Conn.: Yale University Press, 2006.

Fish, S. *The Trouble with Principle.* Cambridge, Mass.: Harvard University Press, 1999.

Flick, D. L. *From Debate to Dialogue.* Boulder, Colo.: Orchid, 1998.

Freedman, D. P. "Life Work Through Teaching and Scholarship." In D. H. Holdstein and D. Bleich (eds.), *Personal Effects: The Social Character of Scholarly Writing.* Logan: Utah State University Press, 2001.

Gallagher, W. *Spiritual Genius: The Mastery of Life's Meaning.* New York: Random House, 2001.

Gazzaniga, M. S. *The Ethical Brain.* New York: Dana Press, 2005.

The Glorious Qur'an Translation. (M. M. Pickthall, trans.). Elmhurst, N.Y.: Tahrike Tarsile Qur'an, 2000.

Goleman, D. (1995). *Emotional Intelligence: Why It Can Matter More Than IQ.* New York: Bantam Books.

Gravois, J. "The Making of a Political 'Circus.'" *Chronicle of Higher Education,* Oct. 23, 2004, p. A48.

Harris, S. *The End of Faith: Religion, Terror, and the Future of Reason.* New York: Norton, 2004.

Heyneman, S. P. "Student Background and Student Achievement: What Is the Right Question?" *American Journal of Education,* 2005, *112,* 1–9.

Hollingdale, R. J. (trans.). *A Nietzsche Reader.* New York: Penguin, 1977.

Holstein, M., and Ellingson, W. "Voices from Left Field: Civil Discourse from the Edges." *Park Ridge Center Bulletin,* May/June 1999, pp. 13–14.

hooks, b. *Where We Stand: Class Matters.* New York: Routledge, 2000.

Hunter, J. D. *Before the Shooting Begins: Searching for Democracy in America's Culture War.* New York: Free Press, 1994.

Isaacs, W. *Dialogue and the Art of Thinking Together.* New York: Doubleday, 1999.

Jenkins, P. *The Next Christendom: The Coming of Global Christianity.* New York: Oxford University Press, 2002.

Kallen, H. *Cultural Pluralism and the American Idea.* Philadelphia: University of Pennsylvania Press, 1956.

Karabell, Z. *What's College For? The Struggle to Define American Higher Education.* New York: Basic Books, 1998.

Kazanjian, V. H. "Beyond Tolerance: From Mono-Religious to Multi-Religious Life at Wellesley College." In V. H. Kazanjian and P. L. Laurence (eds.), *Education as Transformation: Religious Pluralism, Spirituality, and a New Vision for Higher Education in America*. New York: Lang, 2000.

Kazanjian, V. H., and Laurence, P. L. (eds.). *Education as Transformation: Religious Pluralism, Spirituality, and a New Vision for Higher Education in America*. New York: Lang, 2000.

Kessler, R. *The Soul of Education: Helping Students Find Connection, Compassion, and Character at School*. Alexandria, Virg.: Association for Supervision and Curriculum Development, 2000.

Keyes, R. *The Courage to Write: How Writers Transcend Fear*. New York: Holt, 1995.

Kimball, C. *When Religion Becomes Evil*. San Francisco: Harper, 2002.

Kneeling, R. (ed.). *Learning Reconsidered: A Campus-Wide Focus on the Student Experience*. Washington, D.C.: NASPA/ACPA, 2004.

Lee, J-S., and Bowen, N. K. "Parent Involvement, Cultural Capital, and the Achievement Gap Among Elementary School Children." *American Educational Research Journal*, 2006, 43(2), 193–218.

Lieven, A. *America Right or Wrong: An Anatomy of American Nationalism*. New York: Oxford University Press, 2004.

Light, R. J. *Making the Most of College: Students Speak Their Minds*. Cambridge, Mass.: Harvard University Press, 2001.

Lubrano, A. *Limbo*. Hoboken, N.J.: Wiley, 2004.

MacLeod, J. *Ain't No Makin' It: Aspirations and Attainment in a Low-Income Neighborhood*. Boulder, Colo.: Westview Press, 1995.

Manji, I. *The Trouble with Islam: A Muslim's Call for Reform in Her Faith*. New York: St. Martin's Press, 2003.

Marty, M. E. *The One and the Many: America's Struggle for the Common Good.* Cambridge, Mass.: Harvard University Press, 1997.

Marty, M. E. *When Faiths Collide.* Malden, Mass.: Blackwell, 2005.

Mill, J. S. *On Liberty.* New York: Penguin, 1982. (Originally published 1859.)

Nash, R. J. "Fostering Moral Conversations in the College Classroom." *Journal on Excellence in College Teaching,* 1996, 7(1), 83–106.

Nash, R. J. *Answering the Virtuecrats: A Moral Conversation on Character Education.* New York: Teachers College Press, 1997.

Nash, R. J. "Constructing a Spirituality of Teaching." *Religion & Education,* Spring 2001a, 28(1), 1–20.

Nash, R. J. *Religious Pluralism in the Academy: Opening the Dialogue.* New York: Peter Lang, 2001b.

Nash, R. J. "A Letter to Secondary Teachers: Teaching About Religious Pluralism in the Public Schools." In N. Noddings (ed.), *Educating Citizens for Global Awareness.* New York: Teachers College Press, 2005.

Nash, R. J. "Understanding and Promoting Religious Pluralism on College Campuses." *Spirituality in Higher Education Newsletter,* August 2007, 3(4), 1–9.

Nash, R. J., and Bradley, D. L. "A Theoretical Framework for Talking About Spirituality on College Campuses." In S. L. Hoppe and B. W. Speck (eds.), *Searching for Spirituality in Higher Education.* New York: Lang, 2006.

Nash, R. J., and Bradley, D. L. "The Different Spiritualities of the Students We Teach." In D. Jacobsen and R. H. Jacobsen (eds.), *The American University in a Postsecular Age: Religion and the Academy.* New York: Oxford University Press, 2007.

Natoli, J. *A Primer to Postmodernity.* Malden, Mass.: Blackwell, 1997.

Nord, W. A. *Religion and American Education: Rethinking a National Dilemma.* Chapel Hill: University of North Carolina Press, 1995.

Oakley, F. *Community of Learning: The American College and the Liberal Arts Tradition.* New York: Oxford University Press, 1992.

Oakeshott, M. "The Idea of a University." *Listener*, 1950, *43*, 424.

Pape, R. A. *Dying to Win: The Strategic Logic of Suicide Terrorism.* New York: Random House, 2005.

Popper, K. R. *Conjectures and Refutations: The Growth of Scientific Knowledge.* New York: Harper, 1968.

Rauf, I.F.A. *What's Right with Islam Is What's Right with America.* New York: HarperCollins, 2004.

Rodriguez, R. *Hunger of Memory: The Education of Richard Rodriguez.* New York, Bantam, 1982.

Rorty, R. *Contingency, Irony, and Solidarity.* New York: Cambridge University Press, 1989.

Rorty, R. *Objectivity, Relativism, and Truth: Philosophical Papers.* Vol. 1. New York: Cambridge University Press, 1991.

Rorty, R. *Philosophy and Social Hope.* New York: Penguin, 1999.

Ruthven, M. *Islam in the World.* (2nd ed.) New York: Oxford University Press, 2000.

Sacks, J. *The Dignity of Difference: How to Avoid the Clash of Civilizations.* New York: Continuum, 2003.

Schaper, D. "Me-First Spirituality Is a Sorry Substitute for Organized Religion on Campuses." *Chronicle of Higher Education*, Aug. 18, 2000, p. A36.

Schwartz, S. *The Two Faces of Islam: The House of Sa'ud from Tradition to Terror.* New York: Doubleday, 2002.

Schwen, M. *Exiles from Eden: Religion and the Academic Vocation in America.* New York: Oxford University Press, 1993.

Senge, P. M., Kleiner, A., Roberts, C., Ross, R. B., and Smith, B. J. *The Fifth Discipline Yearbook: Strategies and Tools for Building a Learning Organization.* New York: Doubleday, 1994.

Sennett, R., and Cobb, J. *The Hidden Injuries of Class.* New York: Norton, 1993.

Smart, N. *Worldviews: Crosscultural Explorations of Human Beliefs.* (3rd ed.) Upper Saddle River, N.J.: Prentice Hall, 2000.

Smith, B. H. *Belief and Resistance: Dynamics of Contemporary Intellectual Controversy.* Cambridge, Mass: Harvard University Press, 1997.

Smoch, D. R. (ed.). *Interfaith Dialogue and Peacebuilding.* Washington, D.C.: United States Institute of Peace Press, 2002.

"Sociology at Hewett." www.hewett.norfolk.sch.uk/curric/soc/class/class.htm. Sept. 2006.

Stern, J. *Terror in the Name of God: Why Religious Militants Kill.* New York: HarperCollins, 2003.

Taylor, C. *The Ethics of Authenticity.* Cambridge, Mass.: Harvard University Press, 1991.

Tirman, J. *100 Ways America Is Screwing Up the World.* New York: HarperCollins, 2006.

Tivnan, E. *The Moral Imagination: Confronting the Ethical Issues of Our Day.* New York: Simon & Schuster, 1995.

Tracy, D. *Plurality and Ambiguity: Hermeneutics, Religion, Hope.* San Francisco: HarperCollins, 1987.

Washington, J. *Dialoging Across Difference.* Presentation at the University of Vermont, May 2006.

Welch, S. D. *Sweet Dreams in America: Making Ethics and Spirituality Work.* New York: Routledge, 1999.

Wilson, J. "Thou Shalt Not Take Cheap Shots." *Books & Culture*, Sept./Oct. 1999, p. 3.

Winston, D. "Campuses Are a Bellwether for Society's Religious Revival." *Chronicle of Higher Education*, Jan. 16, 1998, p. A60.

Yankelovich, D. *The Magic of Dialogue: Transforming Conflict into Cooperation.* New York: Touchstone, 1999.

Zohar, D. D., and Marshall, I. *The Quantum Society.* New York: Morrow, 1994.

Zuniga, X., Nagda, B. A., Chesler, M., and Cytron-Walker, A. *Intergroup Dialogue in Higher Education: Meaningful Learning About Social Justice.* San Francisco: Jossey-Bass, 2007.

Index

Liberal democracy, 6
Liberals, postmodern, 30
Lieven, A., 228
Light, R. J., 236
Limbaugh, Rush, 54
Lippman, Walter, 51–52
"Little Eichmanns," 16
Living-learning communities, 187
Locke, John, 247
Lubrano, A., 105, 116, 117

M

MacLoed, J., 106
Mainline believers, 84
Malhorta, Ruth, 46
Manji, I., 227
Marshall, I., 91, 122
Marty, Martin E., 7–8, 39
Massachusetts Institute of Technology (MIT), 163
Maturana, H., 232
McVeigh, Timothy, 221
Meaning making–action cycle, 153
Meaning, narrative construction of, 40
Memorial Sloan-Kettering Cancer Center, 230
Mental models, 152–155
Meritocracy myth, 113, 169
Merriam-Webster Online, 112–113
Mesearch, 249–250
Metathought, 154
Middle East, 222–224
Mill, J. S., 6, 24
Mind, 11
Moore, Michael, 16
Moral, 7
Moral conversation: cultivating classroom climate for, 91–97; cultivating classroom climate for, in cocurricular setting, 119–126; culture of, 5; and culture of conversation *versus* culture of contestation, 4–5; examination of, 6–11; faculty member's view on, from the classroom, 65–97; igniting fire of, 3–33; and internal contradictions, 29–33; introducing, in cocurricular settings, 124–126; overview of, 3–4; and politics, 15–18; preparing a division of student affairs for, 129–131; and religion, 14–15; and selective list of hot topics on college campuses, 11–29; and

social class, 18–19; underlying assumptions about, 19–29; whole-campus teaching and learning rationale for, 229–239
Moral conversation, facilitation of: and balance of inquiry and advocacy, 155–156; and calls for action, 135–138; and encouraging improvisation, 162; and hot topics, 146–148; how-to guide for, 205–217; and institutional culture, 148–152; and meaning making and action, 152–155; overview, 133–134; and pacing, 159–160; perspective on, 169–170; and policy statement of ground rules, 157–158; and principles for good practice, 158–159; and recognizing and rewarding professional competence and improvement, 168–169; suggestions for, 156–169; and use of process observers, 159; and use of three-column exercise, 161
Moral police, 24
Morality, God and, 15
Moyers, Bill, 140
MSN-Encarta online dictionary, 120
Muhammad, 224–226
Multiclass lingual students, 117–118
Multiculturalism, 10, 17, 35, 42
Muslims, 73, 74–75, 221–228
Myers-Briggs Type Indicator (MBTI), 170
Mystics, 85

N

Nagda, B. A., xi
Narrative overlap, 8, 25
Narratives, sharing personal, 149
Narrativism, 245–247
Narrativistic paradigms, 241–250
Nash, Robert J., 27, 31, 46, 65, 72, 73, 75, 83, 88, 89, 114, 122, 125, 158, 161, 162, 191, 196, 205, 229, 241
NASPA. *See* National Association of Student Personnel Administrators
National Association of Land Grant Universities and Colleges, 204
National Association of Student Personnel Administrators (NASPA), 104, 179, 204, 220, 229–232, 235
National Conference for Community and Justice, 163